Study Guide
for Jurmain, Kilgore, Trevathan, and Nelson's

Introduction to Physical Anthropology
Ninth Edition

Andrew Kramer
University of Tennessee, Knoxville

THOMSON

WADSWORTH

Australia • Canada • Mexico • Singapore • Spain • United Kingdom • United States

For more information about our products,
contact us at:
Thomson Learning Academic Resource Center
1-800-423-0563

For permission to use material from this text,
contact us by:
Phone: 1-800-730-2214
Fax: 1-800-731-2215
Web: www.thomsonrights.com

Asia
Thomson Learning
5 Shenton Way #01-01
UIC Building
Singapore 068808

Australia
Nelson Thomson Learning
102 Dodds Street
South Street
South Melbourne, Victoria 3205
Australia

Canada
Nelson Thomson Learning
1120 Birchmount Road
Toronto, Ontario M1K 5G4
Canada

Europe/Middle East/South Africa
Thomson Learning
High Holborn House
50-51 Bedford Row
London WC1R 4LR
United Kingdom

Latin America
Thomson Learning
Seneca, 53
Colonia Polanco
11560 Mexico D.F.
Mexico

Spain
Paraninfo Thomson Learning
Calle/Magallanes, 25
28015 Madrid, Spain

TABLE OF CONTENTS

PREFACE

This Study Guide is designed to accompany and complement the textbook *Introduction to Physical Anthropology, 9th Edition*, by Jurmain, Kilgore, Trevathan, and Nelson. It is intended to aid you in your learning, understanding and test preparation of the material in your introductory physical anthropology course. In addition, it is hoped that this Study Guide will stimulate you to explore this fascinating subject beyond the limits of your text and classroom by exploiting the opportunities for anthropological learning afforded by the Internet.

The following paragraphs will describe the structure of this Study Guide and suggest to you how to use it to your best advantage. The sixteen chapters in this book correspond to the same chapters in your textbook. Each Study Guide chapter opens with a list of **LEARNING OBJECTIVES** that you should try to attain after completing each chapter. To aid you in this goal, you should review the next section in your Study Guide, the **CHAPTER OUTLINE**, before reading the corresponding text chapter. These outlines emphasize the major concepts and many of the minor points discussed in your text and are written in order to prepare you to understand the text as well as possible. Finally, before reading your text chapter, review the **KEY TERMS** following the outline to familiarize yourself with the most important words, concepts and processes of that chapter.

After reading your text return to the Study Guide to examine how well you have assimilated the knowledge. There are a series of "test questions" in various formats including **TRUE/FALSE, MULTIPLE CHOICE** and **SHORT ANSWER**. Following completion of the tests correct them with the answers and textbook page references at the end of each Study Guide chapter. Note the areas in which you are strong and weak to guide you in your studying. Finally, answer the sample **ESSAY QUESTIONS** (page references to the text are provided with those as well).

Many chapters in the Study Guide have a section called the **CONCEPT APPLICATION** that challenges you to examine major issues, or to apply concepts or processes introduced in that text chapter. This section precedes the sample test questions and will hopefully provoke you to think more critically about physical anthropology. Finally, each chapter has an **INTERNET EXERCISES AND *INFOTRAC COLLEGE EDITION* EXERCISES** section immediately after the key terms. In these you will find the internet addresses of many useful and content-rich websites relevant to physical anthropology. You will be asked to do some guided exploration through these sites to gain a greater understanding of, and perhaps attain some new perspectives about, the information you have learned in class. *InfoTrac College Edition* is an internet site produced and maintained by the publisher of your text and Study Guide that provides an online repository of over 11 million articles that is updated daily. Each chapter in your Study Guide will point you to these *InfoTrac* resources to broaden your understanding of the field.

ACKNOWLEDGEMENTS

I would first like to express my heart-felt gratitude to the authors of the 8th Edition of this Study Guide, Drs. Denise Cucurny and Marcus Young Owl of the Department of Anthropology of California State University, Long Beach. Their work provided the foundation upon which the current edition of this Study Guide was built. My sincere thanks to Analie Barnett, assistant editor for anthropology at Wadsworth Publishing, who invited me to undertake this project, supplied expert editorial assistance when requested, and provided enthusiastic encouragement throughout. Many thanks to my doctoral student and friend, Arthur Durband, whose undergraduate training in English proved invaluable in his role as proofreader for this book. Finally, thanks to my wife Dina and my children Miriam and Zachary for putting up with their stressed-out husband and grumpy dad while I feverishly tried to meet my deadline(s).

Andrew Kramer
Department of Anthropology
University of Tennessee

CHAPTER 1
INTRODUCTION TO PHYSICAL ANTHROPOLOGY

LEARNING OBJECTIVES
After reading this chapter you should be able to:
- define the word hominid (p. 2)
- define biocultural evolution (pp. 5-6)
- discuss the subject matter of anthropology (p. 6)
- identify the four main subfields of anthropology (pp. 6-14)
- identify the main research areas within physical anthropology (pp. 10-14)
- understand the steps involved in analyzing a situation scientifically (pp. 15)
- describe how anthropologists attempt to understand the world (pp. 15-16)

CHAPTER OUTLINE
Anthropology is the scientific discipline that has the human species as its subject matter.
Anthropologists study all aspects of the human species including our biology (from an
evolutionary perspective).

I   INTRODUCTION
   A. Humans belong to the taxonomic family Hominidae.
      1. A critical feature of hominids is that they are bipedal, which means that we walk on
         two legs.
      2. Humans are also members of the Order Primates, the group of mammals that includes
         prosimians, monkeys and apes, as well as humans.
   B. Physical anthropologists, also known as biological anthropologists, focus largely on the
      study of human evolution, variation and adaptation.
      1. Physical anthropologists study human biology from an evolutionary perspective.
      2. Most human biologists approach the study of humans from a clinical perspective.
   C. Human evolution must consider the influence of culture on the development of our
      species.
      1. Culture is the strategy by which humans adapt to the natural environment.
         a. It includes technologies ranging from simple stone tools to computers.
         b. It also includes subsistence patterns ranging from hunting and gathering to
            agribusiness.
      2. Other aspects of culture include religion, social values, social organization, language,
         kinship, marriage rules, and gender roles, among others.
      3. An important property of culture is that it is learned, not biologically inherited.
   D. Humans, as biological organisms, are subject to the same evolutionary forces as all other
      species.
      1. Evolution is a change in genetic makeup of a population from one generation to the
         next.
      2. Evolution can be defined and studied at two different levels.
         a. At the population level (microevolution), there are genetic changes within the
            population from generation to generation.
         b. At the species level (macroevolution), the result is the appearance of a new species.

E. Biocultural Evolution
1. Over the vast time of human evolution, the role of culture has increasingly assumed greater importance.
2. Over time, biology and culture have interacted in such a way that we say that humans are the result of biocultural evolution.

II WHAT IS ANTHROPOLOGY?
A. Anthropology is the scientific study of humankind.
B. Anthropology is a multidisciplinary field in that it integrates the findings of many disciplines, including sociology, economics, history, psychology, and biology.
C. In the United States anthropology consists of three main subfields:
   <u>1.</u> cultural
   <u>2.</u> archeology
   <u>3.</u> physical
      a. Some universities include linguistics as a fourth area of anthropology.

III CULTURAL ANTHROPOLOGY
A. Cultural anthropology is the study of all aspects of human behavior.
B. The recorded description of traditional lifestyles is called an ethnography.
C. Ethnographic accounts formed the basis for cross-cultural studies which broadened the context within which cultural anthropologists studied human behavior and enabled them to formulate theories about the fundamental aspects of human behavior.
D. The focus of cultural anthropology has shifted over the twentieth century. Some of the new subfields of cultural anthropology include:
   1. Urban anthropology which deals with issues of inner cities.
   2. Medical anthropology explores the relationship between various cultural attributes and health and disease.
   3. Economic anthropology is concerned with factors that influence the distribution of goods and resources within and between cultures.
E. Many of the subfields of anthropology have a practical application, this type of anthropology is called applied anthropology.

IV ARCHEOLOGY
A. Archeology is the discipline that studies and interprets material remains recovered from earlier cultures.
B. Archeologists are concerned with culture, but obtain their information from artifacts and other material culture, rather than from living people.
C. Archeology is aimed at answering specific questions.
   1. Excavation is conducted for the purpose of gaining information about human behavior, not simply for the artifacts present at a site.
   2. By identifying human behavior patterns on a larger scale, archeologists attempt to recognize behaviors shared by all human groups, or commonalities.

V LINGUISTIC ANTHROPOLOGY
A. The field that studies the origin of language, as well as specific languages, is linguistic anthropology.
B. Linguistic anthropologists also examine the relationship between culture and language. These include:
   1. how members of a society perceive phenomena.
   2. how the use of language shapes perceptions in different cultures.

2

C. The spontaneous acquisition and use of language is a unique human characteristic. Research in this area may have implications for the evolution of language skills in humans, making this area of research of interest for physical anthropologists.

VI PHYSICAL ANTHROPOLOGY

A. Physical anthropology is the study of human biology within the framework of evolution. Many physical anthropologists emphasize the interaction between biology and culture.

B. Physical anthropology is divided into a number of subfields. Some of these are:

1. Paleoanthropology, which is the study of human evolution, focuses particularly on the fossil record.

   a. The goals of paleoanthropology are to identify early hominid species, establish their chronology and ultimately reconstruct their evolutionary relationships.

2. Human variation is a field which looks at observable physical variation in humans.

   a. This field was prominent in the nineteenth century.

   b. Techniques used to measure human physical variation are still used today and are called anthropometry.

3. Genetics is the field which studies gene structure and action as well as the patterns of inheritance.

   a. Genetics is crucial to the study of evolutionary processes.

   b. Genetics can help anthropologists investigate the evolutionary distance between living primate species.

4. Primatology is the discipline that studies nonhuman primates.

   a. Because primates are humanity's closest living relatives, anthropologists feel that the study of these animals can shed light on our own behavior and other aspects of our biology.

   b. The declining number of primates species in their natural environments has placed a greater urgency on the study of these animals.

5. Primate paleontology is the study of the primate fossil record.

6. The field which studies skeletal biology and is central to physical anthropology is osteology.

   a. The subdiscipline of osteology that studies disease and trauma in archeologically derived populations is paleopathology.

   b. Forensic anthropology is a field directly related to osteology and paleopathology. It applies the techniques of anthropology to law.

7. Many physical anthropologists specialize in anatomy, the study of structure.

VII PHYSICAL ANTHROPOLOGY AND THE SCIENTIFIC METHOD

A. Science is a process of understanding phenomena through observation, generalization and verification.

1. Scientists rely on experimentation and/or observation. This is referred to as an empirical approach, which is part of the scientific method.

2. As scientists, physical anthropologists must adhere to the scientific method, whereby a research problem is identified, and information is subsequently gathered in order to solve it.

B. The gathering of information is referred to as data collection.

1. An approach should be used in which the investigator can precisely describe their techniques and results in a manner that facilitates comparison with the work of others.

2. In physical anthropology, data is usually expressed numerically, or quantitatively.

C. Once facts have been established, scientists attempt to explain them.
1. A hypothesis, a provisional explanation of phenomena, is developed.
   a. Before a hypothesis can be accepted, it must be tested by means of data collection and analysis.
   b. The testing of hypotheses with the possibility of demonstrating them false is the very basis of the scientific method.
2. If a hypothesis cannot be demonstrated to be false, it is accepted as a theory.
   a. A theory is a statement of relationships that has a firm basis as demonstrated through testing and through the accumulation of evidence.
   b. A theory should also predict how new facts may fit into the established pattern.
D. Bias
1. Scientific method permits various types of biases to be addressed and controlled.
2. Bias occurs in all studies due to many different factors.
3. Science is an approach used to control bias.
VIII THE ANTHROPOLOGICAL PERSPECTIVE
A. All branches of anthropology seek to broaden our viewpoint through the anthropological perspective.
1. This perspective views humanity over time and space.
B. From this viewpoint we can grasp the contemporary diversity of the human experience and more fully understand our potentialities and constraints.
1. The anthropological perspective can teach us to avoid ethnocentrism, a biased viewpoint in which other cultures are seen as inferior to one's own.

KEY TERMS

adaptation: functional response of organisms or populations to the environment.
anthropology: the scientific discipline that studies all aspects of the human species.
anthropometry: the measurement of the human body.
archeology: the discipline of anthropology that interprets past cultures through their material remains which are recovered through excavation.
artifacts: objects that have been modified or, in some other way, used by ancient humans.
biocultural evolution: the interaction between biology and culture in human evolution.
bipedal: walking habitually on two legs as in humans and ground birds.
cultural anthropology: the area within anthropology that focuses on the study of human behavior.
culture: the behavior aspects of humans, including their technology and institutions, which is learned and transmitted between generations.
ethnocentrism: viewing other cultures from the inherently biased perspective of one's own culture.
ethnography: the study of human societies.
forensic anthropology: the field that applies the techniques of anthropology to the law. This usually refers to the techniques used by osteologists and sometimes archeologists.
genetics: the study of gene structure and action, and the patterns of inheritance of traits.
Hominidae: the taxonomic family that humans belong to.
hominid: a member of the family Hominidae.
linguistic anthropology: the area within anthropology that studies the origins and cultural

perceptions and uses of language.

material culture: the physical remains of human cultural activity.

osteology: the study of skeletal biology. Human osteology focuses on the interpretation of the skeletal remains of past populations.

paleoanthropology: the subdiscipline within physical anthropology which studies human evolution.

paleopathology: the branch of osteology that studies the evidence of disease and injury in human skeletal remains.

primate: a member of the mammalian Order Primates. Primates include lemurs, lorises, tarsiers, monkeys, apes, and humans.

primatology: the study of the mammalian Order Primates. Humans are members of this order.

species: a group of interbreeding organisms that produce fertile offspring and are reproductively isolated from other such groups.

INTERNET & *INFOTRAC COLLEGE EDITION* EXERCISES

Are you interested in becoming a physical anthropologist someday? If so, then check-out the official site of the "American Association of Physical Anthropologists" (http://physanth.org/). What kind of graduate programs and career opportunities are there for undergrads aspiring to a career in physical anthropology?

Why is evolution such a controversial topic in America today? Browse the "Talk Origins Archive" (http://www.talkorigins.org/) for answers to frequently asked questions ("FAQs") such as:

1. Isn't evolution just a theory?
2. Don't you have to be an atheist to accept evolution?
3. If evolution is true, then why are there so many gaps in the fossil record? Shouldn't there be more transitional fossils?
4. Where can I find more material on the Creation/Evolution debate?

Find some specific examples of current research conducted by physical anthropologists in the various subdisciplines. Use an internet search engine (such as Google http://www.google.com/) to locate researchers' web sites. Be specific in your search criteria, e.g. "primatology, chimpanzees, communication".

In *InfoTrac*, do a Keyword search on "ethnocentrism" and read some articles demonstrating how the lack of an anthropological perspective can have important social and political ramifications for our public policy and policy makers.

In *InfoTrac*, do a Subject search on "paleoanthropology" and see how many different topics this rather small subset of physical anthropologists can actively engage in research.

CONCEPT APPLICATIONS

1. Fill in the "Anthropology Flow Chart" below with the appropriate labels provided in the accompanying list. One correct answer for each level has been provided for your assistance.

Choices:
1. Primatology
2. human identification
3. biology & culture
4. Archeology
5. human evolution
6. Linguistic Anthropology
7. cross cultural studies
8. Anthropological genetics
9. Physical Anthropology
10. Paleopathology
11. language & culture
12. Forensic Anthropology
13. Paleoanthropology
14. Anthropological genetics

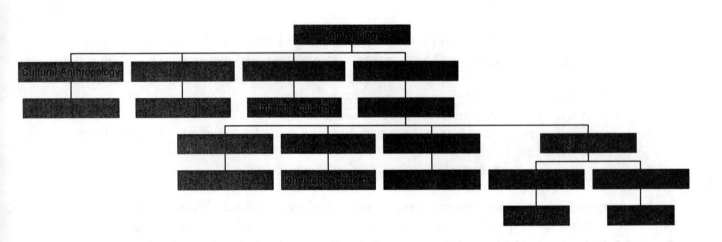

2. Fill in the "Scientific Method Concept Map" on the following page using the choices below:

1. Analyze data
2. New data inconsistent with hypothesis
3. Reject hypothesis
4. Develop theory
5. Collect data
6. Identify problem
7. Collect and analyze more data
8. Form hypothesis
9. Verify hypothesis
10. New data consistent with hypothesis
11. Reject hypothesis

Scientific Method

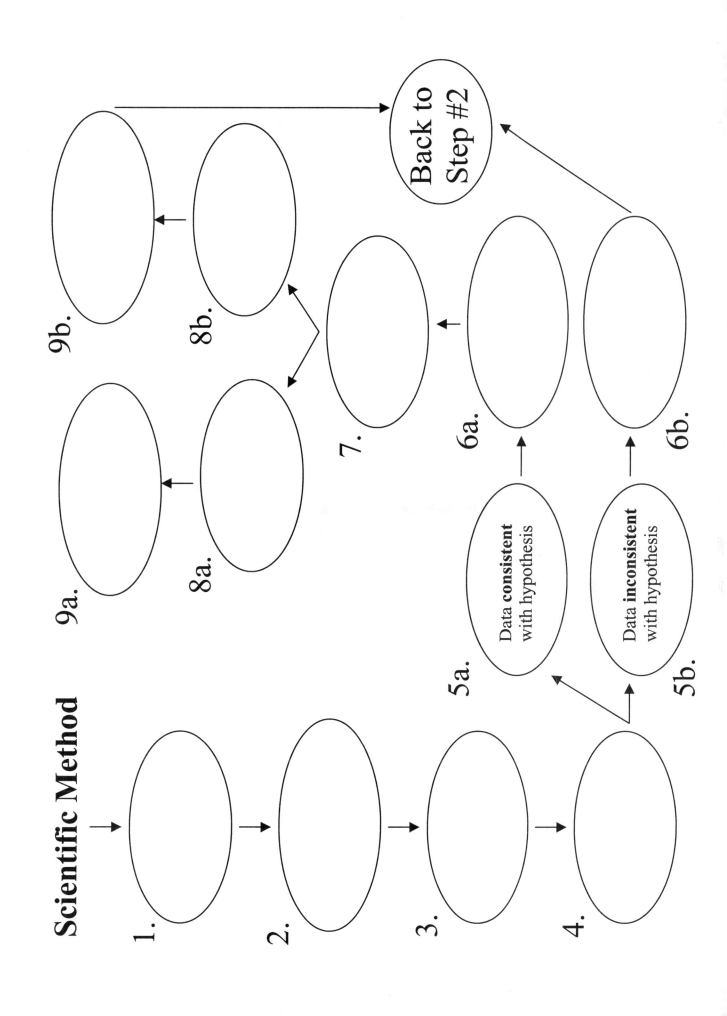

Back to Step #2

5a. Data **consistent** with hypothesis

5b. Data **inconsistent** with hypothesis

1.

2.

3.

4.

6a.

6b.

7.

8a.

8b.

9a.

9b.

Now answer the Multiple Choice, True/False and Short Answer sample test questions. Following completion of the tests correct them with the answers and textbook page references at the end of this Study Guide chapter. Note the areas in which you are strong and weak to guide you in your studying. Finally, answer the sample Essay Questions.

TRUE/FALSE QUESTIONS

1. Anthropology is the scientific study of humankind.
    TRUE   FALSE

2. Over the vast time period of human evolution, the role of culture becomes less and less important as we approach the present.
    TRUE   FALSE

3. Paleoanthropology is a subfield of cultural anthropology.
    TRUE   FALSE

4. Evolution is a change in genetic makeup of a population from one generation to the next.
    TRUE   FALSE

5. Physical anthropology is the study of human biology within the framework of evolution.
    TRUE   FALSE

6. Because primates are humanity's closest living relatives, anthropologists feel that the study of these animals can shed light on our own behavior and other aspects of our biology.
    TRUE   FALSE

7. Primate paleontology is the field which studies gene structure and action as well as the patterns of inheritance.
    TRUE   FALSE

8. Physical anthropology is the discipline of anthropology that interprets past cultures through their material remains which are recovered through excavation.
    TRUE   FALSE

9. As scientists, physical anthropologists must adhere to the scientific method, whereby a research problem is identified, and information is subsequently gathered in order to solve it.
    TRUE   FALSE

10. The anthropological perspective can teach us to embrace ethnocentrism, a valid viewpoint in which other cultures are seen as inferior to one's own.
    TRUE   FALSE

MULTIPLE CHOICE QUESTIONS

1. Walking on two legs, as humans and chickens do, is referred to as
   - A. bipedalism.
   - B. quadrupedalism.
   - C. cursorial.
   - D. brachiation.

2. The mammalian group to which humans belong is the Order
   - A. Carnivora.
   - B. Rodentia.
   - C. Primates.
   - D. Chiroptera.

3. Culture is
   - A. inherited by a simple genetic transmission.
   - B. a biological trait of our species.
   - C. learned.
   - D. the strategy by which many mammals adapt to their environments.

4. The biological characteristics of humans enabled culture to develop and culture, in turn, influenced human biological development. This is called
   - A. biocultural evolution.
   - B. microevolution.
   - C. quantum evolution.
   - D. convergent evolution.

5. Anthropology differs from other disciplines which study humans in that anthropology
   - A. studies humans exclusively.
   - B. allows no biases from other disciplines to interfere in anthropological studies.
   - C. never uses an evolutionary perspective.
   - D. is integrative and interdisciplinary.

6. An anthropologist who is studying the subsistence strategy of the Mbuti pygmies in Zaire belongs to the anthropological subfield of
   - A. archeology.
   - B. cultural anthropology.
   - C. linguistic anthropology.
   - D. physical anthropology.

7. Anthropologists who conduct excavations in order to recover artifacts, and other aspects of material culture, are
    A. archeologists.
    B. cultural anthropologists.
    C. linguistic anthropologists.
    D. medical anthropologists.

8. The applied approach in archeology that has expanded greatly in recent years is
    A. magnetometry.
    B. climatic reconstruction.
    C. cultural resource management.
    D. dendrochronology.

9. Physical anthropology has its origins in
    A. physics.
    B. natural history.
    C. anatomical observation of human physical variation.
    D. both B and C are correct.

10. Physical anthropologists became interested in human change over time (i.e. evolution) with the publication of
    A. Blumenbach's *On the Natural Varieties of Humankind*.
    B. Malthus' *An Essay on the Principle of Population*.
    C. Darwin's *Origin of Species*.
    D. Wood Jones' *Man's Place Among the Mammals*.

11. Anthropologists who specialize in the fossil remains and the physical evidence of early human behavior are called
    A. cultural anthropologists.
    B. linguists.
    C. paleoanthropologists.
    D. geneticists.

12. Contemporary physical anthropologists, whose main interest is in modern human variation, approach their subject matter from the perspective of
    A. racial typologies.
    B. adaptive significance.
    C. behavioral genetics.
    D. constitutional typology.

13. Physical anthropologists developed techniques for measuring the human body, but they are not the only ones who employ these methods. Such measurements are used at health clubs and include techniques for measuring body fat. These types of measurements are called
    A. calibration.
    B. dermatoglyphics.
    C. genetics.
    D. anthropometrics.

14. A researcher is studying the nutritional ecology of howler monkeys in Panama. Her area of expertise is
    A. primatology.
    B. paleoanthropology.
    C. osteology.
    D. genetics.

15. A family reports to the police that their dog has brought home a leg bone that appears to be human. The police also believe this bone is human. To find out whether or not this bone is indeed human the police will consult a(n)
    A. forensic anthropologist.
    B. primatologist.
    C. paleoanthropologist.
    D. evolutionary geneticist.

16. A physical anthropologist who studies bones exclusively is called a(n)
    A. primatologist.
    B. paleoanthropologist.
    C. mammalogist.
    D. osteologist.

17. An important and basic discipline, for osteology, paleopathology, and paleoanthropology is
    A. ecology.
    B. anatomy.
    C. ethology.
    D. genetics.

18. A scientific hypothesis
    A. must always be a correct statement.
    B. is not a necessary part of the scientific method.
    C. is the same thing as a law.
    D. must be falsifiable.

19. If a researcher measures some biological variable and then uses the numbers obtained to arrive at conclusions we would say that this study is
    A. quantitative.
    B. qualitative.
    C. descriptive .
    D. natural history.

20. Viewing other cultures from the inherently biased perspective of one's own culture is known as
    A. linguistics.
    B. ethnocentrism.
    C. ethnography.
    D. paleopathology.

SHORT ANSWER QUESTIONS (& PAGE REFERENCES)

1. What is biocultural evolution? (p. 6)

2. Why is archeology relevant to human evolutionary reconstructions? (p. 9)

3. Why is primatology considered a subfield of physical anthropology and not zoology? (p. 12)

4. What do forensic anthropologists do? (p. 13)

5. How do the colloquial and scientific definitions of the term "theory" differ? (p. 15)

ESSAY QUESTIONS (& PAGE REFERENCES)

1. How does anthropology differ from other social and natural sciences? How do the subfields of anthropology reflect these differences? (pp. 6-9)

2. What can physical anthropologists tell us of the human condition? (pp. 9-14)

3. What is the scientific method and how do physical anthropologists put it into practice? (pp. 9-15)

ANSWERS, *CORRECTED STATEMENT* IF FALSE & REFERENCES TO TRUE/FALSE QUESTIONS

1. TRUE, p. 6

2. FALSE, p. 5, Over the vast time period of human evolution, the role of culture becomes *more* important as we approach the present.

3. FALSE, p. 10, Paleoanthropology is a subfield of *physical* anthropology.

4. TRUE, p. 4

5. TRUE, p. 9

6. TRUE, p. 12

7. FALSE, p. 11, *Genetics* is the field which studies gene structure and action as well as the patterns of inheritance.

8. FALSE, p. 8, *Archeology* is the discipline of anthropology that interprets past cultures through their material remains which are recovered through excavation.

9. TRUE, p. 15

10. FALSE, p. 16, The anthropological perspective can teach us to *avoid* ethnocentrism, a *biased* viewpoint in which other cultures are seen as inferior to one's own.

ANSWERS & REFERENCES TO MULTIPLE CHOICE QUESTIONS

1. A, p. 2
2. C, p. 3
3. C, p. 4
4. A, pp. 5-6
5. D, p. 6
6. B, pp. 6-7
7. A, pp. 8-9
8. C, p. 9
9. D, pp. 10-11

11. C, p. 10
12. B, p. 11
13. D, p. 11
14. A, pp. 11-12
15. A, pp. 13-14
16. D, p. 12
17. B, p. 14
18. D, p. 15
19. A, p. 15

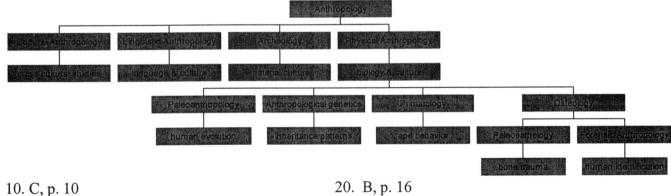

10. C, p. 10

20. B, p. 16

CONCEPT APPLICATIONS SOLUTIONS

"Anthropology flow chart":

Scientific Method

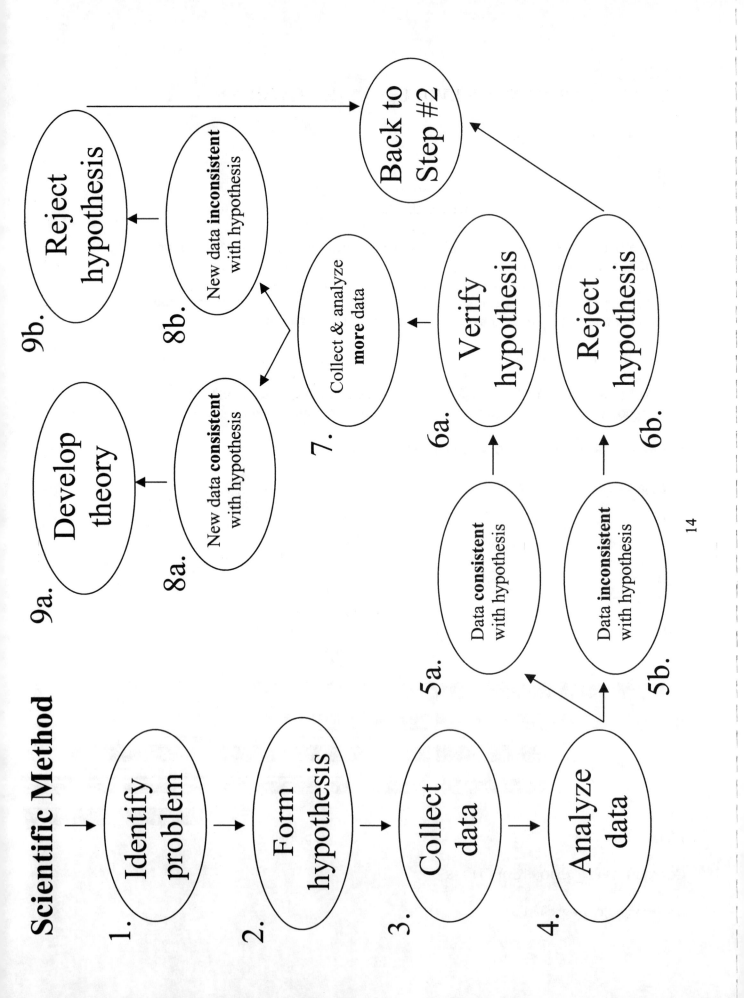

1. Identify problem

2. Form hypothesis

3. Collect data

4. Analyze data

5a. Data **consistent** with hypothesis

5b. Data **inconsistent** with hypothesis

6a. Verify hypothesis

6b. Reject hypothesis

7. Collect & analyze **more** data

8a. New data **consistent** with hypothesis

8b. New data **inconsistent** with hypothesis

9a. Develop theory

9b. Reject hypothesis

Back to Step #2

14

CHAPTER 2
THE DEVELOPMENT OF EVOLUTIONARY THEORY

LEARNING OBJECTIVES
After reading this chapter you should be able to
- trace the development of evolutionary thought (pp. 22-33)
- identify the major influences on the thought of Charles Darwin (pp. 24-32)
- describe the processes of natural selection (pp. 32-36)
- describe a case of natural selection (pp. 33-36)
- understand the shortcomings of Nineteenth-Century evolutionary thought (p. 36)
- understand historical and current opposition to evolution. (pp. 37-38)

CHAPTER OUTLINE
Introduction

Evolution is a theory that has been increasingly supported by a large body of evidence. Evolution is the single-most fundamental unifying force in biology. Evolution is particularly crucial to the discipline of physical anthropology because its subject matter deals with human evolution and the physiological adaptations we have made to our environment. This chapter presents the development of evolutionary thought as well as the social and political context in which it developed.

I   A BRIEF HISTORY OF EVOLUTIONARY THOUGHT
  A. The pre-scientific view:
    1. The European world view throughout the middle ages was one of stasis, the idea that the world was fixed and unchanging.
      a. Part of this world view was the Great Chain of Being. This was a hierarchy in which life was arranged from the simplest to the most complex (i.e., humans).
      b. It was believed that the world was "full" of species and there could not be any other species added, nor had any species disappeared.
      c. The world was seen as the result of the "Grand Design," in which anatomical structures were viewed as planned to meet the purpose for which they were required - an argument from design.
    2. The creation of the world was believed to be recent, the earth being only about 5500 years old; this was a major obstacle to the idea of evolution, which requires immense time.
  B. The scientific revolution:
    1. The discovery of the New World challenged the traditional ideas of Europe. The world could not be perceived as flat. Exposures to new plants and animals increased the awareness of the biological diversity on the planet.
    2. Copernicus challenged the old idea that the earth was the center of the universe.
    3. Galileo's work further pushed the notion that the universe was a place of motion rather than of fixity.
    4. By the 16th and 17th centuries scholars began searching for natural laws rather than supernatural explanations. This approach viewed nature as a mechanism.

15

C. The Path to Natural Selection
  1. John Ray, living in the 16th century, distinguished groups of plants and animals from other such groups.
     a. Organisms capable of reproducing and producing offspring were classified by Ray as species.
     b. Ray also recognized that species shared similarities with other species. He grouped similar species together in a genus.
  2. Carolus Linnaeus developed a system of classification and laid the basis for taxonomy.
     a. Linnaeus standardized the use of the genus and the species to identify each organism, a procedure called binomial nomenclature.
     b. Linnaeus' most controversial act was to include humans among the animals in his taxonomy.
  3. Comte de Buffon
     a. Buffon stressed the important of change in nature.
     b. Buffon recognized that the environment was an important agent of change.
  4. Jean-Baptiste Lamarck
     a. Lamarck was the first scientist to produce a systematic explanation for the evolutionary process.
     b. Lamarck postulated that the environment played a crucial role in the physical change an organism would go through.
        i) As the environment changed, the organism would adjust to the environment by changing also.
     c. Lamarck believed that as an organism used certain body parts, or did not use those regions, the structures would change in response to the environment.
        i) Future offspring would inherit the modified condition.
        ii) This idea of Lamarck was called the Inheritance of Acquired Characteristics. It is also called use-disuse theory.
  5. Georges Cuvier was the archenemy of Lamarck.
     a. Despite founding vertebrate paleontology (as well as comparative anatomy and zoology), Cuvier believed strongly in the fixity of species.
     b. Cuvier is strongly associated with the idea that animal and plant species disappeared because of local disasters.
        i) This theory was called catastrophism.
        ii) Following a set of extinctions, new life forms migrated in from unaffected neighboring areas.
  6. Charles Lyell is considered the founder of modern geology.
     a. Lyell emphasized that the earth had been molded by the same geological forces observable today. This theory is called uniformitarianism.
     b. In order for uniformitarianism to be explanatory, the earth would have to be immensely old.
  7. Thomas Malthus was a political economist.
     a. Malthus wrote about the relationship between food supplies and population increase.
     b. He stated that population size increases geometrically while food supplies remained relatively stable.

      c. Malthus' ideas contributed to the thinking of both Darwin and Wallace, namely the idea of competition for food and other resources.

D. Charles Darwin
1. Many of Darwin's ideas were formed from his observations while serving as a naturalist on *H. M. S. Beagle*'s surveying voyage around the world.
2. In the late 1830's a number of ideas coalesced for Darwin.
    a. Darwin saw that biological variation within a species was critically important.
    b. Darwin also recognized the importance of sexual reproduction in increasing variation.
    c. Malthus' essay was a watershed event for Darwin. From Malthus, Darwin realized:
        i) that animals' population size is continuously checked by limits of food supply,
        ii) and that there is a constant "struggle for existence."
3. By the year 1844 Darwin essentially had completed the work that he would publish fifteen years later.
4. Alfred Russell Wallace
    a. Wallace was a naturalist who worked in South America and Southeast Asia.
    b. Wallace's observations led him to conclusions similar to Darwin's, namely that
        i) species are descended from other species
        ii) and that the emergence of new species was influenced by the environment.
    c. The coincidental development of evolution by natural selection by both Darwin and Wallace was resolved by the joint presentation of their papers to the Linnaean Society of London.

E. The processes of natural selection
1. All species can produce offspring at a faster rate than food supplies increase.
2. There is biological variation within all species.
3. Over-reproduction leads to competition for limited resources.
4. Those individuals within a species that possess favorable traits are more likely to survive than other individuals and to produce more offspring.
5. The environmental context determines whether a trait is favorable or not.
6. Traits are inherited.
    a. Individuals with traits favored by the environment contribute more offspring to the next generation.
    b. Over time such traits will become more common in the population.
7. Over long periods of geological time, successful variations accumulate in a population, so that later generations may become distinct from their ancestors; thus, in time, a new species may appear.
8. Geographical isolation may also lead to the formation of new species.
    a. When populations of a species inhabit different ecological zones they begin to adapt to the different environments.
    b. Over time each population responds to the different selective pressures and the end result, given sufficient time, may be two distinct species.

F. Natural selection operates on individuals, but it is the population that evolves.
1. The unit of natural selection is the individual.
2. The unit of evolution is the population.

II   NATURAL SELECTION IN ACTION
   A. Industrial melanism is one of the best documented cases of natural selection.
      1. Two forms of peppered moth exist: a light gray mottled form and a dark form.
         a. Prior to the industrial revolution the light morph predominated.
            i)   When resting on lichen covered tree trunks the mottled moth was camouflaged from birds.
            ii) In contrast, the dark forms stood out on light, lichen covered trees.
            iii) Birds served as selective agents which resulted in few dark moths surviving to produce offspring.
         b. By the end of the nineteenth century the dark form was the more common.
            i)   As the industrial revolution progressed coal dust settled on trees.
            ii) The light moths stood out on the dark tree trunks and were preyed upon by birds; this resulted in dark forms leaving more offspring in the next generation and subsequently becoming the more common variety.
   B. The example of industrial melanism emphasizes several of the mechanisms of evolutionary change through natural selection.
      1. A trait must be inherited to have importance in natural selection.
      2. Natural selection cannot occur without variation in inherited characteristics.
      3. Selection can work only with variation that already exists.
         a. Fitness is a relative measure that changes as the environment changes.
         b. Fitness is simply reproductive success.
   C. Differential Net Reproductive Success refers to the number of offspring produced by an individual that survive to reproductive age.

III   CONSTRAINTS ON NINETEENTH-CENTURY EVOLUTIONARY THEORY
   A. Variation
      1. The source of variation was a major gap in 19th century evolutionary theory.
      2. Darwin suggested that use-disuse might cause variation.
   B. Transmission
      1. Darwin did not understand the mechanisms by which parents transmitted traits to offspring.
      2. The most popular contemporary idea was blending inheritance; the idea that offspring expressed traits intermediate between the traits of their parents.

IV   OPPOSITION TO EVOLUTION
   A. When Darwin proposed evolution it was controversial mainly because it denied humanity its unique and exalted place in the universe; to many it denied the existence of God.
   B. Nearly a century and a half later, debates still center around evolution.
      1. For the vast majority of biological scientists evolution is an accepted scientific theory.
      2. Nevertheless, almost half of all Americans believe that evolution has not occurred.
   C. Why evolution is not easily accepted.
      1. Evolutionary mechanisms are complex and cannot be explained simply.
      2. Most people want definitive answers to complex questions, rather than the tentative and uncertain answers that scientists work with.
      3. While religions and belief systems deal with some natural phenomena, none propose biological change over time.
   D. The relationship between science and religion has never been easy.
      1. Scientific explanations are based on analysis and interpretation; they are testable and capable of being falsified.

2. Religious beliefs are not falsifiable and are based on faith.
E. Various Judeo-Christian denominations deal with evolution differently.
  1. Catholics, mainstream Protestants and Jews generally do not see a conflict between evolution and religion.
     a. Pope John Paul II issued a statement in 1996 re-affirming the Catholic Church's acceptance of evolution as a sound scientific theory.
     b. In contrast, Fundamentalist Protestant groups do not accept evolution in any form.
  2. Anti-evolutionists are opposed to the teaching of evolution in public schools.
     a. In the 1970s and '80s "creation science" movements attempted to legislate evolution out of public school curricula and replace it with thinly-veiled, Genesis-based accounts of creation.
        i) These efforts were deemed unconstitutional by the courts because they clearly violated the separation of Church and State.
     b. Within the last decade the "theory of intelligent design" has become the most popular with anti-evolutionists.
        i) However, both "creation science" and the "theory of intelligent design" are not considered science because both invoke a supernatural deity as the basis of creation.
     c. Therefore these ideas are religious, not scientific, because it is impossible to test for the existence, or attempt to falsify, God or an "intelligent designer."

KEY TERMS

binomial nomenclature: identifying each organism by two names, the genus and the species.

biology: the study of life.

catastrophism: a view that the earth's geology is the result of a series of cataclysmic events.

"creation science": a view that explains the existence of the universe as a result of a sudden creation. "Creation science" asserts its views to be absolute and infallible and therefore is religious and not scientific.

differential net reproductive success: the number of offspring that are produced, survive, and reproduce themselves.

evolution: changes in the genetic structure of a population from generation to generation.

fitness: a measure of the relative reproductive success of individuals and, hence their genetic contribution to the next generation.

fixity of species: the idea that species do not change, i.e., they do not evolve.

genus: the taxon (category) in biological classification that consists of similar and related species.

natural selection: the mechanism of evolutionary change in which certain traits from among existing variation are favored resulting in an increase in those traits in the next generation.

reproductive success: the number of offspring that an individual produces and the genetic contribution to the next generation that this implies.

selective pressures: forces in the environment that influence reproductive success in individuals.

species: a group of organisms capable of interbreeding under natural conditions and producing fertile and viable offspring; the second name in a binomen.

stasis: in biology, this was the view that nature and all of its organisms were unchanging.

taxonomy: the biological discipline that names and classifies organisms.

transmutation: the word that meant change in species that predated the word evolution.

uniformitarianism: the theory that the earth's geology is the result of long-term processes, still at work today, that requires immense geological time.

world view: general cultural orientation or perspective shared by members of a society.

INTERNET & *INFOTRAC COLLEGE EDITION* EXERCISES

Take a virtual tour through the University of California's Museum of Paleontology. In the "Evolution Wing" (http://www.ucmp.berkeley.edu/history/evolution.html) click on the "History of evolutionary thought" link and scroll down through the list of "key players ... over the last 300 years." Choose one thinker that was not profiled in your text and compare his ideas/accomplishments to one that was. Finally, read the biography of one of the figures that was discussed in the text and discover something new that you had not learned from your book.

The current anti-evolutionary approach of "intelligent design" can be traced back, at least in part, to the publication of Lehigh University biochemist Michael Behe's 1996 publication of *Darwin's Black Box: The Biochemical Challenge to Evolution*. In this book Behe presents his idea of "irreducible complexity" which he characterizes as absolutely incompatible with Darwinian natural selection. Read about Behe and his ideas online in TalkOrigins.org (http://www.talkorigins.org/faqs/behe.html). What is irreducible complexity and does it stand up to mainstream scientific scrutiny?

In *InfoTrac*, do a Keyword search on "uniformitarianism" and read the article by Richard Monastersy that shows how this two-century-old concept still resonates in today's geology. Does this article support Cuvier's "catastrophism"? (Follow-up with a keyword search on "catastrophism" to see how this concept is interpreted today.)

CONCEPT APPLICATION

Match the historical figures and events to the time-lines on the next page.

A. Carolus Linnaeus publishes the first edition of *Systema Naturae*

B. Charles Darwin publishes *On the Origin of Species*

C. Archbishop Ussher determines Earth was created in 4004 B.C.

D. Comte de Buffon and Linnaeus are born

E. Georges Cuvier is born

F. Great Chain of Being proposed

G. Charles Darwin reads Malthus' essay

H. Charles Darwin is born

I. Erasmus Darwin dies

J. Charles Darwin dies

K. Copernicus proposes heliocentric solar system

L. Lamarck is born

M. John Ray publishes *The Wisdom of God Manifested in the Works of Creation*

N. First volume of Lyell's *Principles of Geology* published

O. Alfred Russell Wallace dies

P. Malthus writes his "Essay on the Principle of Population"

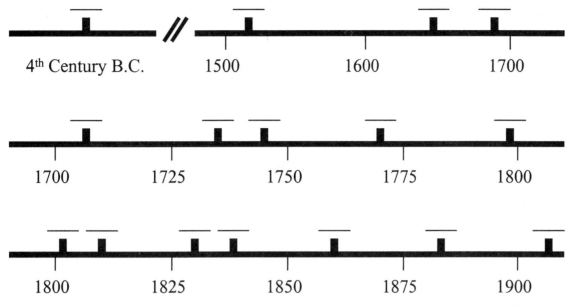

4th Century B.C.   1500   1600   1700

1700   1725   1750   1775   1800

1800   1825   1850   1875   1900

Now answer the True/False, Multiple Choice and Short Answer sample test questions. Following completion of the tests correct them with the answers and textbook page references at the end of this Study Guide chapter. Note the areas in which you are strong and weak to guide you in your studying. Finally, answer the sample Essay Questions.

TRUE/FALSE QUESTIONS

1. The belief that life forms could not change came to be known in European intellectual circles as the fixity of species.
   TRUE   FALSE

2. The Comte de Buffon developed the system of classification that became the basis for taxonomy we still use today.
   TRUE   FALSE

3. The inheritance of acquired characteristics was an early mechanism of evolution proposed by Georges Cuvier.
   TRUE   FALSE

4. Charles Lyell's geological research supported the theory of uniformitarianism, an idea that states that processes observed in the present are the same as those that occurred in the past.
   TRUE   FALSE

5. Erasmus Darwin's "Essay on the Principle of Population" greatly influenced his grandson Charles Darwin's view of the importance of competition in nature.
   TRUE   FALSE

6. Charles Darwin and John Ray independently devised the idea of natural selection in the mid-17th century.
   TRUE   FALSE

7. A basic premise of natural selection is that variation is the normal state of affairs in species.
   TRUE   FALSE

8. Fitness, a measure of relative physical strength, can be measured by an individual's contribution to the protection of their social group.
   TRUE   FALSE

9. Darwin's greatest strengths were his ability to explain the origins of variation and his complete understanding of the mechanism by which parents transmitted traits to their offspring.
   TRUE   FALSE

10. The 1990s anti-evolutionary idea of "intelligent design" has its intellectual roots in the early 19th century "argument from design."
    TRUE   FALSE

MULTIPLE CHOICE QUESTIONS

1. The idea that organisms never change is called
   A. catastrophism.
   B. fixity of species.
   C. transmutation of species.
   D. evolution.

2. Which of the following is a **correct** statement?
   A. Scientific knowledge is usually gained through a series of small steps rather than giant leaps.
   B. Wallace developed the idea of natural selection a decade before Darwin.
   C. The predominant world view of the Middle Ages was that there was constant change in life forms with the exception of humans.
   D. The Great Chain of Being is an evolutionary scheme in which the organisms are arranged beginning with those whose ancestors first appeared in the fossil record and ending with those forms whose ancestors are the most recent.

3. The naturalist who first developed the concepts of the genus and species was
   A. Charles Darwin.
   B. John Ray.
   C. Carolus Linnaeus.
   D. Jean-Baptiste Lamarck.

4. The discipline within biology that is concerned with the rules of classifying organisms on the basis of evolutionary relationships is
   A. anatomy.
   B. genetics.
   C. taxonomy.
   D. ethology.

5. Which of the following is an example of binomial nomenclature?
   A. vole.
   B. chimpanzee.
   C. human.
   D. *Homo sapiens* .

6. The formal science of classifying animals and plants is called _____ and was invented by _____.
   A. natural selection; Wallace
   B. taxonomy; Linnaeus
   C. genetics; Mendel
   D. bioeconomics; Malthus

7. The first person to class humans with another animal group, the primates, was
   A. Linnaeus.
   B. Aristotle.
   C. John Ray.
   D. Archbishop James Ussher.

8. The naturalist who believed that species could change by adapting to new environmental conditions, yet rejected the notion of one species evolving out of another, was
   A. Linnaeus.
   B. Buffon.
   C. Lamarck.
   D. Cuvier.

9. Lamarck believed that
   A. organisms do not change.
   B. only genetically determined traits are passed from parent to offspring.
   C. the environment plays a major role in evolution.
   D. only populations evolve.

10. The first natural historian to codify evolutionary ideas in a comprehensive system that attempted to explain the evolutionary process was
    A. Linnaeus.
    B. Buffon.
    C. Lamarck.
    D. Erasmus Darwin.

11. The opposite of Fixity of Species is
    A. evolution.
    B. typology.
    C. stasis.
    D. immutability of species.

12. A body builder works hard to build large muscles. He marries a beauty queen/life guard. The body builder expects his male offspring to be born muscle bound. His beliefs resemble those of
    A. catastrophism.
    B. uniformitarianism.
    C. the inheritance of acquired characteristics.
    D. evolution by natural selection.

13. The idea that species were fixed, but became extinct due to sudden, violent events and were replaced by neighboring new species is called
    A. evolution.
    B. phyletic gradualism.
    C. catastrophism .
    D. uniformitarianism.

14. Which scientist was most associated with the concept of catastrophism?
    A. Lamarck.
    B. Cuvier.
    C. Buffon.
    D. Lyell.

15. The idea presented by Lyell that the geological forces active today are no different from those acting in the past is known as
    A. Catastrophism.
    B. Uniformitarianism.
    C. Creationism.
    D. Conservatism.

16. Uniformitarianism implies which of the following
    A. new species are created by natural disasters.
    B. the earth is very old.
    C. the earth has a living history, short as it may be.
    D. biological species evolve.

17. Which of the following ideas of Charles Lyell contributed to Darwin's thinking?
    A. there is variation within any population of organisms.
    B. there is a "struggle for existence" between individuals.
    C. a trait must be inherited to have any importance in evolution.
    D. there is an immense geological time scale.

18. The concept of the "struggle for existence," the constant competition for food and other resources, was the idea of
    A. Charles Darwin.
    B. Charles Lyell.
    C. Thomas Malthus.
    D. A. R. Wallace.

19. Which of the following developed a theory of evolution by natural selection?
    A. Lamarck.
    B. A. R. Wallace.
    C. Erasmus Darwin.
    D. Lyell.

20. Which of the following is **not** a statement that Darwin would have made?
    A. There is biological variation within all species.
    B. The environment selects which traits are beneficial.
    C. Geographical isolation may lead to a new species.
    D. Traits acquired during an individual's lifetime are passed to the next generation.

21. Those individuals that produce more offspring, relative to other individuals in the population, are said to have greater
    A. fitness.
    B. selective pressure.
    C. variation.
    D. survival potential.

22. Forces in the environment which influence reproductive success are called
    A. k-selection.
    B. selective pressures.
    C. phyletic gradualism.
    D. differential reproduction.

23. Which of the following did **not** believe in the Fixity of Species?
    A. Lamarck.
    B. Linnaeus.
    C. Cuvier.
    D. Buffon.

24. One of the best documented case of natural selection acting on non-human populations is
    A. starfish as keystone predators of mussels in the Pacific Northwest.
    B. mutualism involving sharks and remoras.
    C. industrial melanism involving peppered moths near Manchester, England.
    D. the symbiosis formed by cork sponges and hermit crabs.

25. What happened to the peppered moth population in England?
    A. There was a change in wing length due to the stability of the environment.
    B. There was a loss of functional wings due to a change in the environment.
    C. They became extinct because these moths could not adapt to the environment.
    D. There was a shift in body color from light to dark in this population.

26. Industrial melanism refers to
    A. a case of natural selection in Britain.
    B. Lamarck's example for the inheritance of acquired characters.
    C. Darwin's example for evolution by natural selection.
    D. A and C.

27. Differential net reproductive success refers to
    A. an individual leaving more offspring than another.
    B. the number of offspring that survive to reproduce relative to other individuals.
    C. an evolutionary shift in a trait.
    D. the development of new traits.

28. Darwin's explanation for evolution suffered from his inability to explain
    A. the role of variation in natural selection.
    B. the origins of variation.
    C. the effects of the environment.
    D. the immense time span that would be required.

29. The unit of natural selection is the _____ while the unit of evolution is the
    _____.
    A. species; gene
    B. genus; family
    C. chromosome; cell
    D. individual; population

30. Which of the following did **not** influence Charles Darwin?
    A. Lamarck.
    B. Malthus.
    C. Mendel.
    D. Lyell.

31. Which of the following statements is **true**?
    A. "Creation Science" is falsifiable.
    B. "Creation Science" and "Intelligent Design Theory" both invoke a supernatural creator.
    C. Evolutionary science asserts that its theories are absolute and infallible.
    D. "Creation Science" is amenable to modification based on hypothesis testing.

32. "Creation Science"
    A. asserts that its ideas are absolute and infallible.
    B. is not amenable to scientific testing and falsification.
    C. is religion, not science.
    D. All of the above.

SHORT ANSWER QUESTIONS (& PAGE REFERENCES)

1. What is the fixity of species? (pp. 22-23)

2. Why was Lamarck important is the development of evolutionary thought? (p. 25-26)

3. Why was the voyage of the *H.M.S. Beagle* so important for the development of Darwin's ideas? (p. 29-30)

4. Why must a trait be inherited to have importance in natural selection? (p. 35)

5. What were Darwin's weaknesses in understanding evolution? (p. 36)

ESSAY QUESTIONS (& PAGE REFERENCES)

1. Who were the most important pre-Darwinian figures and how did they contribute to the development of Darwin's evolutionary synthesis? (pp. 24-27)

2. Compare and contrast Darwin's natural selection to Lamarck's inheritance of acquired characteristics as competing mechanisms for explaining evolutionary change? (pp. 25-27, 32-33)

3. Why is "creation science" not really science? (pp. 37-38)

ANSWERS, *CORRECTED STATEMENT* IF FALSE & REFERENCES TO TRUE/FALSE QUESTIONS

1. TRUE, p. 23

2. FALSE, p. 25, *Carolus Linnaeus* developed the system of classification that became the basis for taxonomy we still use today.

3. FALSE, p. 26, The inheritance of acquired characteristics was an early mechanism of evolution proposed by *Lamarck*.

4. TRUE, p. 27

5. FALSE, p. 28, *Thomas Malthus'* "Essay on the Principle of Population" greatly influenced Charles Darwin's view of the importance of competition in nature.

6. FALSE, pp. 28-32, Charles Darwin and *Alfred Wallace* independently devised the idea of natural selection in the *mid-19th* century.

7. TRUE, pp. 31-32.

8. FALSE, p. 35, Fitness, a measure of relative *reproductive success*, can be measured by an individual's *genetic* contribution to the *next generation*.

9. FALSE, p. 36, Darwin's *weaknesses* were his *inability* to explain the origins of variation and his *incomplete* understanding of the mechanism by which parents transmitted traits to their offspring.

10. TRUE, pp. 23 & 38

ANSWERS & REFERENCES TO MULTIPLE CHOICE QUESTIONS

1. B, pp. 22-23	17. D, pp. 27-28
2. A, p. 22	18. C, p. 28
3. B, p. 24	19. B, p. 32
4. C, pp. 24-25	20. D, pp. 25-26
5. D, p. 25	21. A, p. 35
6. B, pp. 24-25	22. B, p. 33
7. A, p. 25	23. A, pp. 25-26
8. B, p. 25	24. C, pp. 33-34
9. C, pp. 25-26	25. D, pp. 33-34
10. C, p. 25	26. A, pp. 33-34
11. A, p. 23	27. B, p. 35
12. C, p. 26	28. B, p. 36
13. C, p. 27	29. D, p. 33
14. B, p. 27	30. C, p. 36
15. B, p. 27	31. B, pp. 37-38
16. B, p. 27	32. D, pp. 37-38

CONCEPT APPLICATION SOLUTION

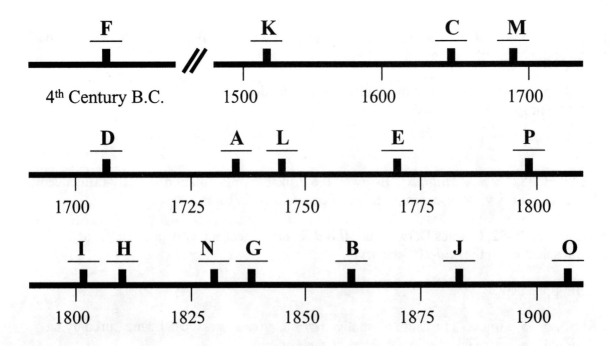

28

CHAPTER 3
THE BIOLOGICAL BASIS OF LIFE

LEARNING OBJECTIVES

After reading this chapter you should be able to
- to describe the structure of a generalized cell (pp. 42-43).
- to describe the structure and function of DNA (pp. 43-46).
- understand the process of protein synthesis (pp. 46-48).
- to define a gene and what it does (pp. 49-52).
- understand how a mutation occurs (pp. 52-53).
- understand the importance of mitosis and meiosis and what their differences are (pp. 57-60).
- understand why genetics is important to the study of evolution (pp. 60-61).
- understand the basics of the new genetic technologies (pp. 62-64).

CHAPTER OUTLINE

Introduction

    Human evolution and adaptation are intimately linked to life processes stemming from the genetic functions of cells. This occurs in cell replication, in the translation of genetic information into products usable by the organism and finally into the transmission of this information to future generations.

I   THE CELL
  A. The cell is the basic unit of life in all living organisms.
    1. Complex multicellular life forms, such as plants and animals, are made up of billions of cells.
    2. Prokaryote cells are single-celled organisms.
      a. The earliest life on earth, appearing by at least 3.7 billion years ago, were such life forms.
      b. Prokaryote cells lack a nucleus.
    3. More complex cells with a nucleus first appeared around 1.2 billion years ago.
      a. These cells are called eukaryote cells.
      b. Multicellular organisms, which include humans, are composed of eukaryotic cells.
  B. General structure of a eukaryotic cell
    1. The type of cell studied in textbooks is a generalized or composite cell.
      a. A generalized cell contains structures known to exist in cells.
      b. On the other hand, no single cell has all the structures seen in a general cell.
    2. The cell membrane is the outermost and functional boundary of the cell.
    3. Organelles are functional structures found within the cytoplasm.
    4. The third major region of the eukaryotic cell is the nucleus which is surrounded by the cytoplasm and contains chromosomes.
    5. This section of the textbook discusses organelles important for the discussion of genetics (and ultimately variation and evolution).

    a. Mitochondria
      i) These organelles produce energy for the cell.
      ii) Mitochondria also contain their own DNA which directs mitochondrial activities.
    b. Ribosomes are structures that are essential for the production of protein.
  C. There are two types of cells found in the animal body.
    1. Somatic cells are the cells of the body with the exception of the sex cells.
    2. Gametes are sex cells involved with reproduction.
      a. Ova are egg cells produced in female ovaries.
      b. Sperm are sex cells produced in male testes.
      c. A zygote is the union between a sperm and an ovum.

II DNA STRUCTURE

  A. Cellular function and an organism's inheritance depends on the structure and function of DNA.
  B. DNA is composed of two chains of nucleotides.
    1. A nucleotide consists of a sugar, a phosphate, and one of four nitrogenous bases.
    2. Nucleotides form long chains and the two chains are held together by bonds formed by the bases with their complements on the other chain. This complementary phenomenon is what enables DNA to fulfill its functions. (This is sometimes called the "base pairing principle").
      a. Adenine (A) is the complement of thymine (T).
      b. Guanine (G) is the complement of cytosine (C).
      c. The complementary property of the DNA bases is what enables DNA to make exact copies of itself.

III DNA REPLICATION

  A. The most important property of DNA is that it can replicate itself.
  B. The replication process:
    1. Specific enzymes break the bonds between the DNA molecule.
    2. The two nucleotide chains serve as templates for the formation of a new strand of nucleotides.
    3. Unattached nucleotides pair with the appropriate complementary nucleotide.
    4. The end result is two newly formed strands of DNA. Each new strand is joined to one of the original strands of DNA.
  C. See figure 3-3 (p. 45).

IV PROTEIN SYNTHESIS

  A. One of the most important functions of DNA is that directs protein synthesis within the cell.
  B. Structure and function of proteins:
    1. Proteins are the major structural components of the body.
    2. Many proteins serve as catalysts, i.e. they initiate and enhance chemical reactions.
    3. The building blocks of proteins are smaller molecules called amino acids.
      a. There are 20 biologically important amino acids.
      b. What makes proteins different from one another is the number of amino acids involved and the sequence in which they are arranged.

C. The agents of protein synthesis:
   1. Ribosomes are cytoplasmic organelles which help convert the genetic message from the DNA into protein.
   2. Messenger RNA (mRNA) carries the genetic message from the cell nucleus to the ribosome.
      a. RNA differs from DNA in that it is single-stranded, has a different type of sugar and substitutes the base uracil (U) for thymine (T).
      b. mRNA has triplets (a series of three bases) called codons which specify a particular amino acid.
   3. Transfer RNA (tRNA) is another type of RNA that is usually found in the cytoplasm
      a. tRNA binds to one specific amino acid.
      b. Each tRNA has a triplet (an anti-codon) which matches up with a codon on the mRNA strand.
D. The process of protein synthesis:
   1. Transcription
      a. A portion of the DNA unwinds and serves as a template for the formation of a mRNA strand.
      b. The process of coding a genetic message for proteins by formation of mRNA is called transcription.
   2. Translation
      a. The mRNA leaves the nucleus, enters the cytoplasm, and attaches to a ribosome.
      b. tRNAs arrive at the ribosome carrying their cargoes of specific amino acids.
      c. The base triplets on the tRNA match up with the codons on the mRNA.
      d. As each tRNA line up according to the sequence of mRNA codons, their amino acids link together to form a protein.
      e. The process in which the genetic message on the mRNA is "decoded" and implemented is called translation.

V WHAT IS A GENE?
A. The entire sequence of DNA bases that code for a particular polypeptide chain is a gene.
   1. Those proteins composed of only a single polypeptide chain are produced through the actions of a single gene.
   2. Other proteins are made up of two or more polypeptide chains and require the action of two or more genes.
B. If the sequence of bases in a gene are altered a mutation has occurred.
   1. This may interfere with the organisms ability to produce vital proteins.
   2. It may also lead to a new variety within the species and, hence, evolution.
C. The gene consists of exons and introns.
   1. DNA segments transcribed into mRNA that code for specific amino acids are called exons.
   2. DNA sequences not expressed during protein synthesis are called introns.
D. Not all genes produce structural proteins.
   1. Some genes are regulatory and produce enzymes and other proteins which switch on or turn off other segments of DNA.
   2. All cells contain the same genetic information, but only a small fraction of the DNA is used for the specialized functions of any particular cell.
      a. Some genes are only active during particular periods of the life cycle.

  b. Alterations in the behavior of regulatory genes may be responsible for some of the physical differences between closely related species.

 E. The universality of the genetic code:

  1. The genetic code is universal; this means that the DNA of all life forms on earth is composed of the same molecules and carries on similar functions.

  2. The universality of the genetic code implies a common ancestry for all of this planet's life forms; what makes organisms different is the arrangement of their DNA.

VI MUTATION: WHEN A GENE CHANGES

 A. A change in genetic material is called mutation.

 B. An example of a mutation: sickle-cell hemoglobin.

  1. Hemoglobin consists of four polypeptide chains, two alpha chains and two beta chains.

   a. A defect in the beta chain leads to a condition called sickle-cell anemia.

 C. Sickle-cell anemia is a genetic condition in which the affected individual inherits a variant of the gene from both parents.

  1. Sickle hemoglobin is caused by the substitution of one amino acid (valine) for another (the normally occurring glutamic acid) on the beta chain.

  2. This substitution impairs the ability of the blood to distribute oxygen.

  3. Such a substitution is called a point mutation.

   a. In evolution point mutations are probably the most common and most important source of new variation.

   b. However, a new mutation will only have evolutionary significance if it is passed on to offspring and is selected by other evolutionary forces.

VII CHROMOSOMES

 A. Much of a cell's existence is spent in interphase.

  1. During this period the cell is involved with normal cellular and metabolic processes.

  2. During interphase the cell's DNA exists as a substance called chromatin.

 B. Cell division is the process that results in the production of new cells. It is during cell division that DNA becomes visible under a light microscope as chromosomes.

 C. Chromosome structure:

  1. A chromosome is composed of a DNA molecule and associated proteins.

  2. During interphase chromosomes exist as single-stranded structures.

  3. During early cell replication chromosomes consists of two strands of DNA.

   a. These two strands are joined together at a constricted region called the centromere.

   b. The reason there are two strands of DNA is because replication has occurred and one strand is an exact copy of the other.

 D. Each species is characterized by a specific number of chromosomes.

  1. Humans have 46 chromosomes.

  2. Chromosomes occur in pairs, therefore humans have 23. The members of chromosomal pairs are called homologous.

   a. Homologous chromosomes carry genetic information influencing the same traits.

   b. However, homologous chromosomes are not genetically identical.

    i) The position a gene occupies on a chromosome is called the locus.

    ii) There can be alternative versions of a gene on the homologous loci. These different forms are called alleles.

E. Types of Chromosomes
   1. Autosomes carry genetic information that governs all physical characteristics except primary sex determination.
   2. The two sex chromosomes are the X and Y chromosomes.
      a. Genetically normal mammalian females have two X chromosomes.
      b. Genetically normal mammalian males have one X chromosome and one Y chromosome.
   3. In order to function properly a human cell must have both members of each chromosome pair.
F. Karyotyping chromosomes
   1. A photomicrograph that displays an individual's chromosomes is called a karyotype.
   2. Karyotypes are constructed from photographs taken through a microscope of chemically treated chromosomes.
      a. Homologous chromosomes are matched up.
      b. Chromosomes are arranged by size, and centromere position.
   3. Technological advances now allow us to identify every chromosome on the basis of banding patterns.
      a. Karyotypes and banding patterns enable researchers to deduce relationships between different species.
      b. The chromosome patterns of humans, chimpanzees, and gorillas indicate a very close relationship between these three species.
   4. Karyotypes have numerous practical applications.
      a. They can be used in diagnosis of chromosomal disorders.
      b. They can also be employed in prenatal diagnosis of developing fetuses.
VIII CELL DIVISION
   A. Mitosis
      1. Cell division in somatic cells is called mitosis.
      2. Mitosis occurs during growth and repair/replacement of tissues.
      3. Steps in mitosis:
         a. By the time that chromosomes can be seen they have already duplicated - hence, what we see represents two DNA molecules.
         b. The 46 chromosomes line up in the center of the cell (see fig. 3-10c).
         c. The chromosomes are then pulled apart at the centromere.
         d. The separated chromosomes are pulled towards opposite ends of the cell; each separated chromosome is composed of one DNA molecule.
         e. The cell membrane pinches in and two new cells now exist.
      4. The result of mitosis is two identical daughter cells that are genetically identical to the original cell.
   B. Meiosis
      1. Meiosis is the production of sex cells, or gametes.
         a. Male sex cells are sperm, produced in the testes.
         b. Female sex cells are eggs (ova) produced in the ovaries.
      2. Meiosis is a reduction division.
         a. Initially the sex cells have the diploid number, or full complement, of chromosomes.
         b. After meiosis has taken place, the gametes are haploid, i.e. they have half the normal complement of chromosomes.

    c.   Meiosis is characterized by 2 divisions resulting in 4 haploid daughter cells.
    3.   Recombination, or crossing over:
        a.   The homologous chromosomes form into pairs on the cell's equator.
        b.   While the homologous chromosomes are together they exchange pieces of genetic material.
    4.   Reduction division is critical in meiosis because the fusion of two haploid gametes results in the restoration of the diploid number of chromosomes.

C. The evolutionary significance of meiosis
    1.   Meiosis and sexual reproduction are highly important evolutionary innovations.
        a.   Meiosis increases genetic variation at a faster rate than mutation alone could.
        b.   Offspring in sexually reproducing species represent the combination of genetic information from two parents.
        c.   Darwin emphasized that natural selection acted on hereditary variation in all populations.
        d.   Mutation is the only source of *new* genetic variation.
            i)   However, in sexually reproducing species recombination (sexual reproduction, crossing-over) produces new combinations of genetic information, providing additional material for natural selection to act on.

D. Problems with meiosis
    1.   Meiosis must be an exact process that produces a viable gamete that has exactly 23 chromosomes, having only one member of each homologous pair present.
        a.   Errors in meiosis may lead to spontaneous abortions, or miscarriages.
        b.   Chromosomes may fail to separate during meiosis. This is called nondisjunction.
        c.   Nondisjunction may lead to an affected gamete fusing with a normal gamete.
            i)   An affected gamete that contains one less chromosome and fuses with a normal gamete will produce a monosomy, i.e. the zygote will contain 45 chromosomes with one chromosome pair only represented by a single chromosome.
            ii)   An affected gamete that contains an extra chromosome and fuses with a normal gamete will produce a trisomy, i.e. the zygote will contain 47 chromosomes, with one chromosome pair represented by three chromosomes.
    2.   Examples of abnormal numbers of chromosomes:
        a.   Down syndrome, or trisomy 21, occurs because of three copies of chromosome #21.
            i)   Congenital problems associated with Down Syndrome include mental retardation, heart defects, and increased susceptibility to respiratory infections.
            ii)   Trisomy 21 is associated with advanced maternal age (over 35 years of age).
    3.   Nondisjunction may also occur in the sex chromosomes resulting in impaired mental function, sterility, or death.

IX   NEW FRONTIERS
A. The field of genetics has revolutionized biological science.
B. The polymerase chain reaction (PCR - developed in 1986), makes it possible to produce and amplify multiple copies of tiny bits of DNA.
    1.   This allows researchers to analyze and identify very small segments of DNA that otherwise would have been impossible without this new technology.
    2.   For example, PCR has been used to isolate and amplify DNA from Neandertal fossils!

C. Recombinant DNA technology allows genes from one species to be transferred into another.
   1. One use of this technology is to enable bacteria to produce medically valuable human gene products.
D. Cloning research has generated the most recent controversy.
   1. A clone is an individual that is genetically identical to another individual.
E. The single most important advance in genetics has been the progress made on the Human Genome Project.
   1. The goal is to sequence the entire human genome, in other words to produce a "road-map" of the human genetic sequence.
   2. In July 2000, scientists announced the completion of the "rough draft" of the sequence.

KEY TERMS

alleles: alternate forms of a gene. Alleles occur at the same locus on homologous chromosomes and thus govern the same trait. However, because they are different, their action may result in different expressions of that trait. Synonym: gene.

amino acids: small molecules that are the basic building blocks of proteins.

autosomes: one of the pairs of chromosomes that determines traits other than sex.

cell (plasma) membrane: the living boundary of an animal cell.

centromere: the constricted portion of a chromosome. After replication, the two strands of a double-stranded chromosome are joined at the centromere.

chromatin: the loose, diffuse form of DNA seen during interphase. When condensed, chromatinforms into chromosomes.

chromosome: structures that are composed of DNA and protein, found in the nucleus of the cell, and are only visible during cell replication.

clone: an organism that is genetically identical to another organism.

codon: three nitrogeneous bases (i.e., a triplet) found on the mRNA which complements three bases on a tRNA carrying a specific amino acid.

complementarity (,principle of): the rule that certain bases in DNA and RNA always bind together. Cytosine always pairs with guanine and, in DNA, Adenine always pairs with Thymine. In RNA Uracil replaces Thymine and pairs with Adenine. Sometimes referred to as the "base-pairing principle."

cytoplasm: the region of a cell that is contained within the cell membrane, excluding the nucleus.

diploid: the full complement of chromosomes of a species.

DNA (deoxyribonucleic acid): a double-stranded molecule that contains the genetic information.

enzyme: specialized proteins that initiate and direct chemical reactions in the body.

eukaryotic cell: cells of organisms in which the DNA is enclosed by a nucleus.

gametes: sex cells, viz. ova (eggs) and sperm.

gene: a seqeuence of DNA nucleotides that code for a particular polypeptide chain.

generalized cell: a eukaryotic cell that has all of the structures known to exist in cells; also referred to as a composite cell. The generalized cell is a teaching device. Most cells are specialized and may not have some of the structures of a generalized cell. For example, mature red blood cells do not have a nucleus.

genetics: the discipline within biology that studies the inheritance of biological characteristics.

genome: the complete genetic makeup of an individual or a species.

haploid: half the normal complement of chromosomes of a species. The haploid condition is characteristic of animal sex cells.

hemoglobin: a protein molecule that occurs in red blood cells and binds to oxygen molecules.

homologous: the pair of chromosomes that carry genes for the same traits.

hormones: substances that are produced by specialized cells and that travel to other parts of the body, where they influence chemical reactions and regulate various cellular functions.

Human Genome Project: an international effort aimed at sequencing and mapping the entire human genome.

interphase: the portion of a cell's cycle during which metabolic processes and other cellular activities occur. DNA replication occurs during interphase.

karyotype: the chromosomal complement of an individual or that typical for a species. Usually displayed as a photomicrograph, often using special stains to highlight the bands or centromeres.

locus: position on a chromosome where a given gene occurs.

meiosis: specialized cell division in the reproductive organs which produce gametes. The gametes are haploid and are not identical.

messenger RNA (mRNA): a form of RNA, formed on one strand of the DNA, that carries the DNA code from the nucleus to the cytoplasm where protein synthesis takes place.

mitochondria: organelles found in the cytoplasm which produce cellular energy.

mitosis: cell division in somatic cells.

mutation: a change in the sequence of bases coding for the production of a protein.

nondisjunction: the failure of homologous chromosomes to separate during meiosis.

nucleotide: the basic unit of DNA. A nucleotide consists of one of four nitrogeneous bases, plus a sugar and a phosphate.

nucleus: a structure found in eukaryotic cells which contains chromosomal DNA.

organelle: a structure found in the cytoplasm that performs some physiological function.

point mutation: a mutation that results from the substitution of one nitrogenous base by another.

polar body: small nonviable cell that is a product of meiosis in females.

polymerase chain reaction (PCR): a method of producing thousands of copies of a DNA segment using the enzyme DNA polymerase.

polypeptide chain: a sequence of amino acids that may act alone or in combination as a functional protein.

prokaryote cell: a single-celled organism that lacks a nucleus.

proteins: three-dimensional molecules composed of amino acids that serve as structural components of animal bodies and as catalysts for biochemical reactions.

protein synthesis: the process by which proteins are produced from amino acids.

random assortment: the random distribution of chromosomes to daughter cells during meiosis; along with recombination, the source of variation resulting from meiosis.

recombination (crossing over): the exchange of genetic material between homologous chromosomes during meiosis.

ribosome: a cytoplasmic organelle, made up of RNA and protein, where protein synthesis takes place.

RNA (ribonucleic acid): a single-stranded molecule, similar in structure to DNA. The three types of RNA are essential to protein synthesis.

sex chromosomes: in animals, those chromosomes involved with primary sex determination. The X and Y chromosomes.

sickle-cell anemia: a severe inherited disease that results from a double dose of a mutant allele, which in turn results from a single base substitution at the DNA level.

somatic cells: the cells of the body, excluding the cells involved with primary reproduction.

transcription: the formation of a messenger RNA molecule from a DNA template.

transfer RNA (tRNA): the form of RNA that binds to a specific amino acid and, during translation, transports them to the ribosome in sequence.

translation: the process of sequencing amino acids from a messenger RNA template into a functional protein or a portion of a protein.

triplet: a set of three nitrogenous bases on the DNA molecule.

zygote: a cell resulting from the fusion of a sperm and an egg (ovum).

INTERNET & *INFOTRAC COLLEGE EDITION* EXERCISES

Explore the official Human Genome Project suite of web sites sponsored by the U.S. Department of Energy (http://www.ornl.gov/hgmis/). What are some new medical applications that are being projected to grow out of this massive research effort? In this context, what are the ethical, legal and social issues involved with the HGE?

Take an online visit to "The Human Cloning Foundation" and explore its content (http://www.humancloning.org/). This site describes itself as "The Official Site in Support of Human Cloning". Review its arguments and commentaries. Do you agree with their Mission Statement that cloning technology should be used to cure human diseases and prolong our lives? Why or why not?

In *InfoTrac* do a keyword search on "Recombinant DNA or cloning" and then click the "Limit Search" button and add "ethics or debate" in the "by **entering a word** (or words)" box. Read a few of the articles that are listed on rDNA and/or cloning. What are the ethical challenges posed by these new technologies? Do you think that these obstacles can be overcome? Should they be?

CONCEPT APPLICATION

First, convert the following string of DNA bases into its complementary mRNA molecule. Next, translate the mRNA into a polypeptide chain of amino acids using the Table 3-1 on p. 47. (Remember that mRNA is read in three-base words called codons).

> 1. CAATATGGAAGCCGACTCACCCTAATT

Now we will introduce a substitution point mutation into this genetic sequence. The third base mutates into a "T" instead of an "A". What is the ultimate effect of this genetic change on the resultant polypeptide chain? How does this illustrate the concepts of "redundancy" and "neutral mutations"?

> 2. CA**T**TATGGAAGCCGACTCACCCTAATT

Now answer the True/False, Multiple Choice and Short Answer sample test questions. Following completion of the tests correct them with the answers and textbook page references at the end of this Study Guide chapter. Note the areas in which you are strong and weak to guide you in your studying. Finally, answer the sample Essay Questions.

TRUE/FALSE QUESTIONS

1. Mitochondria and ribosomes are found within the nucleus of the cell.
   TRUE   FALSE

2. Enzymes are specialized proteins that initiate and direct chemical reactions in the body.
   TRUE   FALSE

3. The mRNA message transcribed from the DNA is read in 4-letter words called quadrates at the site of protein synthesis, the mitochondria.
   TRUE   FALSE

4. Genes include both exons, DNA that codes for particular amino acids, and introns, non-coding DNA.
   TRUE   FALSE

5. Sickle-cell anemia results from a chromosomal mutation causing a trisomy at the 15th chromosomal pair.
   TRUE   FALSE

6. Humans have 48 chromosomes while chimps and gorillas only have 46.
   TRUE   FALSE

7. A zygote is the chromosomal complement of an individual or that which is typical for a species.
   TRUE   FALSE

8. Somatic cells are diploid while gametes are haploid.
   TRUE   FALSE

9. The exchange of genetic material between homologous chromosomes during meiosis is known as crossing over.
   TRUE   FALSE

10. Recombinant DNA technology is a method for producing thousands of copies of a DNA segment using the enzyme DNA polymerase.
    TRUE   FALSE

MULTIPLE CHOICE QUESTIONS

1. The discipline that links or influences the various subdisciplines of physical (biological) anthropology is
   A. genetics.
   B. cell biology.
   C. paleontology.
   D. primatology.

2. A cell that has its DNA enclosed by a nucleus is called a
   A. karyote cell.
   B. prokaryote cell.
   C. eukaryote cell.
   D. prion.

3. The two nucleic acids that contain the genetic information that controls the cell's functions are
   A. ribosomes and Golgi apparati.
   B. mitochondria and desmosomes.
   C. the endoplasmic reticulum and ribosomes.
   D. DNA and RNA.

4. Organelles found in the cytoplasm that contains their own DNA are the
   A. ribosomes.
   B. mitochondria.
   C. lysosomes.
   D. vacuoles.

5. Which of the following is **not** a sex cell?
   A. gamete.
   B. ovum.
   C. sperm.
   D. skin cell.

6. A cell formed by the union of an egg and a sperm is called a
   A. gamete.
   B. zygote.
   C. neuron.
   D. ovum.

7. The smallest unit of DNA consists of one sugar, one phosphate, and one of four bases. This unit is called a
   A. sperm.
   B. nucleotide.
   C. nucleus.
   D. ribosome.

8. Researchers found that certain bases of the DNA macromolecule always pair. These bases are referred to as
    A. independently assorted.
    B. segregated.
    C. in equilibrium .
    D. complementary.

9. A parental chain of DNA provides the following template: AAT CGA CGT. Which of the following sequences of free nucleotides would pair with the parental template?
    A. TTA GCT GCA.
    B. AAT CGA CGT.
    C. GGC TAG TAC.
    D. UUA GCU GCA.

10. The end result of DNA replication is
    A. two new strands of DNA.
    B. the fusion of the mother's DNA with the father's DNA.
    C. the formation of a mRNA molecule.
    D. the production of an amino acid molecule.

11. A type of protein which helps to enhance chemical reactions in the body is a(n)
    A. bone.
    B. muscle.
    C. enzyme.
    D. hemoglobin.

12. Proteins consists of chains of
    A. carbohydrates.
    B. lipids.
    C. amino acids.
    D. fatty acids.

13. Which of the following is **not** true about RNA?
    A. It is single stranded.
    B. Some forms of RNA are involved with protein synthesis.
    C. It has a different type of sugar than DNA has.
    D. It contains the base thymine.

14. The formation of a mRNA molecule from DNA is called
    A. transcription.
    B. translation.
    C. translocation.
    D. transformation.

15. The reading of mRNA by a ribosomes to produce protein is called
    A. transcription.
    B. translation.
    C. translocation.
    D. transforamation.

16. A portion of a mRNA molecule that determines one amino acid in a polypeptide chain is called a
    A. nucleotide.
    B. gene.
    C. codon.
    D. polymerase.

17. In protein synthesis all of the following occur **except**
    A. amino acids are initially bonded to specific tRNA molecules.
    B. animo acids are transported to the nucleus to bond with DNA molecules.
    C. the sequence of amino acids is determined by the codon sequence in mRNA.
    D. amino acids are bonded together to form a polypeptide chain.

18. What is the name of the molecule that amino acids bind to?
    A. messenger RNA (mRNA).
    B. ribosomal RNA (rRNA).
    C. transfer RNA (tRNA).
    D. mitochondral DNA (mtDNA).

19. The following segment of mRNA contains the bases UUA CGC UGA. Which triplets on three different tRNAs will line up in order during translation?
    A. UUA CGC UGA.
    B. AAT GCG ACT.
    C. AGU CGC AUU.
    D. AAU GCG ACU.

20. The entire sequence of DNA bases on the chromosome that code for a particular polypeptide chain is a(n)
    A. ribosome.
    B. amino acid.
    C. gene.
    D. polypeptide chain.

21. Which of the following is **not** true regarding the DNA code?
    A. The code is universal.
    B. The code is continuous.
    C. The code accommodates 24 different amino acids.
    D. The code is redundant.

22. A single base substitution in the DNA causes a severe hemoglobin disorder in which oxygen stressed red blood cells collapse resulting in
    A. sickle-cell anemia.
    B. Tays-Sachs disease.
    C. cystic fibrosis.
    D. hemolytic disease of the newborn.

23. A change in one base of a codon may produce a change in the hereditary information. This is called a
    A. point mutation.
    B. chromsomal reversal.
    C. chromosomal inversion.
    D. synapsis.

24. What is the characteristic number of chromosomes in human somatic cells?
    A. 23
    B. 46
    C. 48
    D. 78

25. A genetically normal human female has
    A. 23 pairs of autosomes
    B. 23 pairs of autosomes and two X chromosomes
    C. 22 pairs of autosomes and two X chromosomes
    D. 22 pairs of autosomes, one X chromosome, and one Y chromosome.

26. The end result of mitosis in humans is
    A. two identical "daughter" cells.
    B. four haploid cells.
    C. two cells with 23 chromosomes.
    D. two cells with mutations.

27. Which of the following is true for meiosis?
    A. It involves only one division which duplicates the parent cell exactly.
    B. It produces gametes.
    C. When a mutation occurs it affects only the individual.
    D. It has no effect on evolution.

28. Crossing over is a process in which
    A. segments of DNA are exchanged between homologous chromosome arms.
    B. two different chromosomes are fused together.
    C. a mutation occurs.
    D. two strands of DNA from two different species are allowed to combine.

29. Which of the following is **not** an example of nondisjunction?
    A. Down syndrome
    B. Sickle-cell anemia
    C. Turner syndrome
    D. Trisomy X

30. If chromosomes or chromosome strands fail to separate during meiosis serious problems can arise. This failure to separate is called
    A. Turner's syndrome.
    B. nondisjunction.
    C. a monosomy.
    D. random assortment.

31. The multinational effort to sequence all of the genes of the human body is called
    A. UNESCO.
    B. cloning.
    C. polymerase chain reaction.
    D. Human Genome Project.

32. An organism that is genetically identical to another organism is known as a
    A. clone.
    B. recombinant.
    C. genomic twin.
    D. random assortment.

33. A process in which genes from the cell of one species are transferred to the cell of another species is known as
    A. the polymerase chain reaction.
    B. recombinant DNA technology.
    C. meiosis.
    D. protein synthesis.

SHORT ANSWER QUESTIONS (& PAGE REFERENCES)

1. List and briefly describe the functions of three different components of the animal cell. (pp. 42-43)

2. What are the differences between DNA and RNA? (p. 47)

3. What is transcribed during protein synthesis and why? (p. 47-48)

4. How do the end-products of mitosis and meiosis differ? (pp. 57-58)

5. What is nondisjunction? (pp. 61-62)

ESSAY QUESTIONS (& PAGE REFERENCES)

1. What is a gene? Why are the concepts of exons and introns important in this regard? (pp. 48-52)

2. What is the evolutionary significance of meiosis? (pp. 60-61)

3. Why would it not be an exaggeration to say that this is the most exciting time in the history of evolutionary biology since Darwin published *On the Origin of Species*? (pp. 62-64)

ANSWERS, *CORRECTED STATEMENT* IF FALSE & REFERENCES TO TRUE/FALSE QUESTIONS

1. FALSE, p. 43, Mitochondria and ribosomes are found *outside of* the nucleus of the cell.

2. TRUE, p. 45.

3. FALSE, pp. 47-48, The mRNA message transcribed from the DNA is read in *3-letter* words called *codons* at the site of protein synthesis, the *ribosomes*.

4. TRUE, pp. 48-49

5. FALSE, p. 52, Sickle-cell anemia results from a *point* mutation *affecting the beta chain for the allele that produces hemoglobin*.

6. FALSE, p. 54, Humans have *46* chromosomes while chimps and gorillas have *48*.

7. FALSE, p. 56, A *karyotype* is the chromosomal complement of an individual or that which is typical for a species.

8. TRUE, p. 58

9. TRUE, p. 60

10. FALSE, p. 63, *The Polymerase Chain Reaction* is a method for producing thousands of copies of a DNA segment using the enzyme DNA polymerase.

ANSWERS & REFERENCES TO MULTIPLE CHOICE QUESTIONS

1. A, p. 42
2. C, p. 42
3. D, p. 42
4. B, p. 43
5. D, p. 43
6. B, p. 43
7. B, p. 44
8. D, p. 44
9. A, p. 44
10. A, p. 46
11. C, p. 45
12. C, p. 46
13. D, p. 47
14. A, p. 47
15. B, p. 50
16. C, p. 47

17. B, pp. 46-48
18. C, p. 48
19. D, p. 48 & see fig. 3-5
20. C, p. 48
21. C, p. 51 (Box 3-2)
22. A, p. 52
23. A, p. 52 & see Fig. 3-6
24. B, p. 54 & see Table 3-2
25. C, p. 56
26. A, p. 57
27. B, pp. 57-61
28. A, p. 60
29. B, pp. 61-62
30. B, p. 61
31. D, p. 64
32. A, pp. 61-62
33. B, p. 63

CONCEPT APPLICATION SOLUTION

mRNA molecule:
    GUUAUACCUUCGGCUGAGUGGGAUUAA

Polypeptide chain:
    Valine-Isoleucine-Proline-Serine-Alanine-Glutamic acid-Tryptophan-Aspartic acid-STOP

Mutated mRNA molecule:
    GU**A**AUACCUUCGGCUGAGUGGGAUUAA

Resultant Polypeptide chain:
    Valine-Isoleucine-Proline-Serine-Alanine-Glutamic acid-Tryptophan-Aspartic acid-STOP

See Box 3-2, point #4 on p. 51 for an explanation of redundancy and an illustration of neutral mutation.

CHAPTER 4
HEREDITY AND EVOLUTION

LEARNING OBJECTIVES

After reading this chapter you should be able to

- Discuss Mendel's Principles of Segregation and Independent Assortment (pp. 71-76).
- Recognize the patterns of inheritance for autosomal dominant, autosomal recessive and sex-linked traits (pp. 79-83).
- Perform simple matings using a Punnett square (p. 74).
- Analyze a simple genealogy by pedigree analysis (pp. 79-83).
- Describe the difference between Mendelian traits and polygenic traits (pp. 84-87).
- Understand the complexity involved between genetic and environmental factors (pp. 86).
- Define biological evolution (pp. 89-90).
- Describe the factors that produce and distribute genetic variation (pp. 90-94).
- Discuss the role natural selection in the direction of evolution (pp. 94-97).
- Discuss how evolutionary change occurs as an integrated process. Illustrate through an example (pp. 96-97).

CHAPTER OUTLINE

Introduction

In the last chapter the structure and function of DNA was presented. In this chapter we look at the principles of heredity, originally studied by Gregor Mendel. We close with the synthesis of Darwinism, Mendelianism, and genetics into the comprehensive modern theory of biological evolution.

I. THE GENETIC PRINCIPLES DISCOVERED BY MENDEL.
    A. Introduction.
        1. Gregor Mendel (1822-1884) laid down the basic principles of heredity.
        2. Mendel crossed different strains of purebred plants and studied their progeny.
    B. Segregation.
        1. Mendel crossed purebred plants that differed in one trait.
            a. The plants used in this first cross were designated the parental, or P generation.
            b. One of the traits disappeared in the hybrid offspring.
            c. The trait that was present in the F_1 generation was not intermediate between the two traits as would be the case if blending inheritance was valid.
            d. When the F_1 generation self-fertilized the trait missing reappeared in the F_2 generation.
            e. Mendel obtained a constant ratio of 3 dominants to 1 recessive in the F_2 generation.
        2. Mendel's results could be explained if:
            a. The trait was the result of 2 units.
            b. These two factors segregated during gamete formation.

       c.   The idea that traits are controlled by two discrete units, which separate into different sex cells, was Mendel's principle of segregation.

       d.   Today we know that meiosis explains Mendel's principle of segregation.

C. Dominance and Recessiveness

    1. Mendel called the trait that disappeared in the F_1 generation, but reappeared in the F_2 generation, recessive.

    2. Mendel called the trait that was expressed in the F_1 generation dominant.

    3. When two copies of the same allele are present the individual is homozygous for that trait.

    4. When there are two different alleles at a locus the individual is heterozygous.

    5. Mendel's results can be illustrated by a Punnett square (see Fig. 4-3).

       a.   The Punnett square shows the proportions of offspring with specific genotypes.

       b.   The Punnett square does not show the actual number of offspring with a specific genotype.

       c.   The Punnett square is useful for predicting the proportions of F_2 generation genotypes.

D. Independent Assortment

    1. Mendel next crossed two different characters, which he considered simultaneously.

    2. The F_1 generation expressed only the dominant traits.

    3. The F_2 generation contained combinations of traits not present in either of the plants of the P generation.

    4. Mendel deduced that these traits were inherited independently of one another.

    5. Mendel's second principle of inheritance is the principle of independent assortment.

    6. By chance, Mendel did not use traits that were linked, i.e., genetic loci that are on the same chromosome.

       a.   If Mendel had used linked traits his results would have been considerably different.

       b.   Linked genes travel together during meiosis; consequently, they are not independent of one another and do not conform to the ratios predicted by independent assortment.

II. MENDELIAN INHERITANCE IN HUMANS

A. More than 9600 human traits are known to be inherited by simple Mendelian principles.

B. The human ABO blood system is an example of simple Mendelian inheritance.

    1. The A and B alleles are dominant to the O allele.

    2. Neither the A or B allele are dominant to one another; they are codominant and both traits are expressed.

C. Genetic disorders can be inherited as dominant or recessive traits.

    1. Dominant disorders are inherited when one copy of a dominant allele is present.

       a.   Such disorders include achondroplasia, brachydactyly, and familial hypercholesterolemia

    2. Recessive disorders require the presence of two copies of the recessive allele.

       a.   Heterozygotes for such disorders are not affected, but because they carry one copy of the recessive allele they are carriers.

          i.   Some recessive conditions that affect humans are phenylketonuria, cystic fibrosis, Tay-Sachs disease, and albinism.

D. Misconceptions regarding dominance and recessiveness.

1. A major misconception is that the presence of a recessive allele in heterozygotes has no effect on the phenotype
   a. Today we know this is not true.
2. We now know that recessive alleles exert an effect at the biochemical level in heterozygotes.
3. Another misconception is that dominant alleles are more common, or that they are "stronger" or "better."
   E. Patterns of Inheritance
   1. The principle technique used in human inheritance studies is the construction of pedigrees.
      a. Pedigree analysis helps determine if a trait is Mendelian.
      b. Pedigree analysis helps determine the mode of inheritance; six different modes of Mendelian inheritance are recognized. The three most important are:
         i. autosomal dominant.
         ii. autosomal recessive.
         iii. X-linked recessive.
      c. In pedigree charts squares represent males and circles represent females.
   2. Autosomal dominant traits
      a. These traits are governed by loci on autosomes.
      b. Because these traits are dominant, anyone who inherits a dominant allele will express the trait and almost all affected individuals are heterozygotes.
      c. Pattern of inheritance:
         i. Each affected individual has at least one affected parent.
         ii. Autosomal dominant traits do not skip generations.
      d. There is no sex bias in autosomal dominant traits; equal numbers of males and females are affected.
      e. Another characteristic of autosomal dominance is that about one-half of the offspring of an affected parent are also affected.
   3. Autosomal recessive traits.
      a. These traits are also controlled by loci located on the autosomes.
      b. Because these traits are recessive there must be two alleles present in an affected person.
      c. Pattern of inheritance:
         i. Recessive traits often appear to skip generations.
         ii. Affected individuals often have two unaffected parents who are carriers.
         iii. Affected individuals occur less often than with dominant traits
         iv. Since they are often the result of two heterozygous parents roughly one-fourth of the offspring express the trait.
   4. Sex-linked traits.
      a. The loci for sex-linked traits are found on the sex chromosomes.
      b. Almost all of the known sex-linked traits are on the X chromosome.
      c. One of the best-known sex-linked traits is hemophilia (see Figure 4-10 on p. 83).
      d. Because males are hemizygous for the X chromosome any allele on that chromosome is expressed.

III. NON-MENDELIAN PATTERNS OF INHERITANCE
   A. Polygenic Inheritance.
      1. Mendelian traits are discrete traits.

a. Discrete or discontinuous traits fall into clear categories.

b. Because discrete traits are discontinuous, there are no intermediate forms between discrete traits.

c. Mendelian traits are governed by a single genetic locus.

2. Polygenic traits are continuous traits governed by alleles at more than one genetic locus.

   a. Continuous traits show gradations.

      i. There is a series of measurable intermediate forms between the two extremes.

   b. The gradations formed by continuous traits produce a bell curve graphically.

3. Each locus in a polygenic trait contributes to the phenotype; we say these combined effects are additive, although the contribution of the alleles are not all equal.

   a. A well known example of a polygenic trait is human skin color, governed by perhaps 6 loci and at least 12 alleles.

4. Because polygenic traits <u>are</u> continuous they can be treated statistically.

   a. The mean is a summary statistic which gives the average of a sample or population.

   b. A standard deviation measures within-group variation

   c. Researchers are able to compare continuous traits between different populations to see if there are significant differences statistically.

   d. Mendelian characteristics are not as amenable to statistical analysis as polygenic characters are.

      i. However, Mendelian characteristics can be described in terms of frequencies within populations and compared between populations.

      ii. Mendelian characters can be analyzed for mode of inheritance from pedigree data.

      iii. Mendelian characters are valuable because the approximate or exact position of genetic loci for them is often known.

B. Genetic and environmental factors

1. The terms genotype and phenotype have both a narrow and broad definition.

   a. On the narrow level they both may be used in reference to a single trait, e.g., the genetic and physical expression of purple flowers vs. white flowers that Mendel studied on pea plants.

   b. At a broader level these two terms may refer to the individual's entire genetic makeup and all of its observable characteristics.

2. The genotype sets limits and potentials for development.

   a. The genotype also interacts with the organism's environment.

   b. Many aspects of the phenotype are influenced by the genetic/environmental interaction.

3. The environment influences many polygenic traits, such as height.

4. Mendelian traits are less likely to be influenced by the environment.

5. Even though polygenic traits are controlled by several loci and are more susceptible to environmental influences, they still obey Mendelian principles at the individual loci.

C. Pleiotropy

1. In pleiotropy a single gene influences more than one phenotypic expression.

2. Pleiotropy is probably the rule, rather than the exception.

3. Phenylketonuria (PKU) is an example of pleiotropy; because a particular enzyme is not produced a metabolic pathway is blocked with several consequences.

D. Mitochondrial inheritance
  1. Mitochondria, the cell's energy converters, contain ring-shaped DNA called mitochondrial DNA (mtDNA).
     a. mtDNA contains about 40 genes responsible for energy conversion.
  2. mtDNA is inherited only from the mother.
  3. mtDNA mutation rates have been used for constructing evolutionary relationships between species.

IV. MODERN EVOLUTIONARY THEORY
  A. Darwin and Mendel each discovered essential mechanisms for how evolution worked.
    1. Those who followed saw the work of these two men as incompatible in explaining evolution.
    2. By the 1930s biologists realized that Darwinian selection and Mendelian genetics were complementary factors that explained evolution - the fusion of these two ideas was called the modern synthesis.
  B. The Modern Synthesis partitioned evolution into two stages:
    1. Small, new changes in the genetic material were transmitted by Mendelian principles and resulted in variation.
    2. The genetic variation was acted on by natural selection.

V. DEFINITION OF EVOLUTION
  A. The modern definition of evolution is a change in allele frequency from one generation to the next.
    1. Allele frequencies are numerical indicators of the genetic makeup of a population.
    2. Only populations evolve -- individuals do not evolve over time.
  B. Microevolution consists of small-scale inherited changes that occur over a short period within a species.
  C. Macroevolution is major evolutionary change that occurs over geological time and may result in new species.

VI. FACTORS THAT PRODUCE AND REDISTRIBUTE VARIATION
  A. Mutation
    1. An actual molecular alteration in genetic material is called a mutation.
    2. For a mutation to have any evolutionary significance it must occur in a sex cell.
    3. Mutation rates for any given trait are quite low.
    4. Mutation is the only way to produce "new" variation; hence, mutation is the basic creative force in evolution.
  B. Gene Flow
    1. Gene flow is the exchange of genes between populations.
    2. Gene flow has been a consistent feature of hominid evolution and explains why speciation has been rare in humans.
  C. Genetic Drift
    1. A random factor that is due mainly to sampling phenomena.
       a. Genetic drift is directly related to the size of the population.
       b. Small populations are more prone to randomness in evolution, i.e. genetic drift.
    2. A special case of genetic drift is called founder effect (the Sewell Wright effect).
       a. In founder effect only a very small proportion of a population contributes alleles to the next generation.

  b. Founder effect can result when a small group migrates and founds a new population.

  c. Through founder effect an individual who carries an allele, rare in the parent population, can make a disproportionate genetic contribution to the next generation.

 3. Genetic drift has probably played an important role in human evolution.

  a. Nevertheless, the effects of drift have been irregular and nondirectional.

  b. Drift, along with gene flow, probably results in microevolutionary changes within a species.

  c. However, there is some evidence that our species experienced a genetic bottleneck in the last 100,000 to 200,000 years; if this is the case genetic drift would have played a very important role in our evolution.

 D. Recombination.

  1. Sexual reproduction is, in itself, a recombination, or reshuffling, of genetic material coming from two different parents.

  2. The reshuffling of chromosomes, including crossing-over, during meiosis can produce trillions of gene combinations.

VII. NATURAL SELECTION ACTS ON VARIATION

 A. Without natural selection there is no long-term direction to evolution.

  1. Mutation, gene flow, genetic drift, and recombination produce variation.

  2. Natural selection acts on the variation and provides direction.

 B. Selection acting on variation enables populations to adapt.

  1. Selection results in a change in allele frequency relative to specific environmental factors.

  2. If the environment changes, selection pressures change also.

 C. Hemoglobin S (Hb^S) is the best-documented case of natural selection in humans.

  1. Hemoglobin S is the result of a point mutation in the gene coding for the hemoglobin beta chain.

  2. Inherited in a double dose the individual will suffer the severe manifestations of sickle-cell anemia.

  3. The mutation for Hb^S occurs in all human populations, but does not have a high frequency most places.

   a. Nevertheless, the sickle-cell allele (Hb^S) is frequent in some populations, especially in west and central Africa; there are also high frequencies in Greece and India.

   b. Associated with higher frequencies of Hb^S is the presence of malaria.

    i. Malaria has exerted enormous selection pressures on human populations.

  4. The malarial *Plasmodium* parasite invades red blood cells where they obtain oxygen.

   a. An experiment was done in the 1950's in which carriers (heterozygotes) and individuals homozygous for normal hemoglobin were compared in their response to infection by malaria.

   b. Heterozygotes were much more resistant to malaria.

    i. Heterozygote red blood cells do not provide a conducive environment for the malarial parasite to reproduce.

  5. Hence, the parasite often dies before infecting the body of a carrier.

a. "Normal" individuals were more likely to have their reproductive success lowered due to malarial infections.

VIII. REVIEW OF GENETICS AND EVOLUTIONARY FACTORS

A. The different levels at which evolutionary factors operate are all related and integrated.

B. Evolution works on a population; it is the population that will, or will not, change over time.

C. If the allele frequencies in a population have changed, then evolution has occurred.

D. If evolution has occurred, why has it occurred?
   1. A new allele can only arise through mutation.
   2. Mutations must spread; this could occur in a small population through genetic drift.
   3. Long-term evolutionary trends can only occur due to natural selection.

Key terms

allele: the alternative form of a gene.

allele frequency: the proportion of a particular allele to all the other alleles at a given locus in a population.

antigens: large molecules found on the surface of cells. Several different loci governing antigens on red and white blood cells are known. Foreign antigens provoke an immune response in individuals.

autosome: any of the chromosomes excluding the two sex chromosomes.

carrier: an individual who is a heterozygote for a recessive genetic disorder; the individual is unaffected.

codominance: both alleles are expressed in the phenotype.

continuous traits: traits which have measurable gradations between the two end points, such as height in humans.

discrete traits: traits which fall into clear categories, such as a purple flower vs. a white flower in a garden pea.

dominant: the genetic trait that is expressed in the heterozygous state.

evolution (biological): a change in allele frequencies between generations.

F_1 generation: the hybrid offspring of purebreeding parents

Founder effect: a type of genetic drift in which allele frequencies are altered in small populations that are taken from, or are remnants of, larger populations.

gene flow: exchange of genes between different populations of a species.

genetic drift: evolutionary changes in the gene pool of a small population due to chance (random factors).

gamete: a sex cell, in humans these are ova (eggs) and sperm.

genotype: the genetic makeup of an organism.

hemizygous: condition where there is only one allele present (on the X chromosome) instead of two.

heterozygous: the presence of two different alleles for a given genetic trait in an individual.

homozygous: the presence of the same alleles for a given genetic trait in an individual.

hybrid: parents who are in some ways genetically dissimilar. This term can also be applied to heterozygotes.

linked: describing genetic loci or genes located on the same chromosome.

mean: a summary statistic which gives the average of a sample or of a population.

macroevolution: evolutionary changes on a large scale, encompassing many generations, and involving change above the species level.

Mendelian traits: traits that are inherited at a single locus on a single chromosome

microevolution: small, short-term changes in the gene pool of a population occurring over just a few generations.

mutation: an alteration in the genetic material (a change in the base sequence of DNA).

natural selection: the evolutionary factor that causes changes in the allele frequencies in populations due to differential net reproductive success of individuals. The force of evolution that gives direction in response to environmental factors.

pedigree chart: a diagram showing family relationships in order to trace the hereditary pattern of particular genetic traits.

phenotype: the physical expression of an organism's genotype

phenotypic ratio: the proportion of one phenotype to other phenotypes.

pleiotropy: a situation whereby several, seemingly unrelated, phenotypic effects are influenced by the action of a single gene.

population: a community of individuals, all of the same species, that occupy a particular area and breed among themselves.

polygenic: referring to traits that are influenced by genes at two or more loci.

principle of independent assortment: Mendel's principle that states that alleles for different traits sort independently during gamete formation

principle of segregation: the principle expounded by Mendel that alleles occur in pairs which separate (segregate) during gamete formation. At fertilization the full number of alleles is restored.

recessive: the genetic trait that is not expressed in a heterozygous state

sex chromosome: the chromosomes that determine sex. In humans these are the X and Y chromosomes.

sickle-cell trait: a condition resulting from a point mutation of the gene coding for production of the beta-chain hemoglobin. A red blood cell with this trait is subject to collapse during periods of extreme stress or low blood oxygen levels.

standard deviation: a summary statistic which measures within-group variation.

variation (genetic): inherited differences between individuals. The basis of all evolutionary change.

INTERNET & *INFOTRAC COLLEGE EDITION* EXERCISES

Go online to the National Center for Biotechnology Information's "Online Mendelian Inheritance in Man" website (http://www.ncbi.nlm.nih.gov/omim/). Scroll down and click the link titled: "Search the OMIM Morbid Map". This will take you to a search page. In the "View" box, type one of the Mendelian traits listed in Table 4-2 on p. 77 of your text. For example, if you enter "Albinism" and click the "View" button you will be taken to the database listing all of the Mendelian conditions that are associated with albinism. Click on a numbered hyper-link in the "Disorder" column to read more about the condition.

In *InfoTrac* do keyword searches on these three individuals who were central to the construction of the modern synthesis of evolutionary biology: Sewall Wright, Ernst Mayr and George Gaylord Simpson. Read an article on each that describes their major contributions.

CONCEPT APPLICATIONS

Punnett squares

Fill in the Punnett squares below to figure out the ABO blood type ratios for the next generation.

	A	O
B		
O		

	A	B
A		
B		

	B	O
A		
B		

Now fill in the Punnett square for one of Mendel's dihybrid cross experiments. Both parents are heterozygous for plant height ("T" is dominant for "Tall", "t" is recessive for "short") and seed shape ("R" is dominant for "Round", "r" is recessive for "wrinkled"). Each gamete in this example will have **2** alleles: one for plant height and one for seed shape. What are the possible phenotypes produced by this mating and what will the phenotypic ratios of the offspring be?

	TR	Tr	tR	tr
TR				
Tr				
tR				
tr				

Pedigree Chart for X-Linked Recessive Trait

The pedigree chart below illustrates a couple who had four children (a son and 3 daughters labeled 1-4). The mother is a carrier of an X-linked recessive trait (such as hemophilia) and her carrier status is indicated by the circle (indicating "female") enclosing a dot. The conditions of the couple's grandchildren are given: open shapes are unaffected individuals, carriers are the circle/dots and those afflicted with the genetic disease are indicated by the filled-in shapes. Given the grandparents' and grandchildren's conditions, figure out the conditions of the four offspring of the original pair (labeled 1-4 in the dotted shapes).

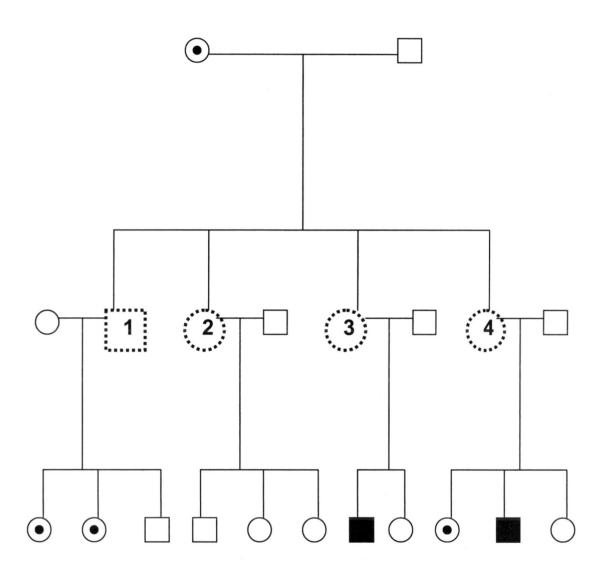

Now answer the True/False, Multiple Choice and Short Answer sample test questions. Following completion of the tests correct them with the answers and textbook page references at the end of this Study Guide chapter. Note the areas in which you are strong and weak to guide you in your studying. Finally, answer the sample Essay Questions.

TRUE/FALSE QUESTIONS

1. Mendel's principle of segregation states that members of a pair of hereditary factors controlling a trait separate into different sex cells.
   TRUE   FALSE

2. Genes controlling different traits are inherited independently of one another.
   TRUE   FALSE

3. Dominant alleles are always more common and better adapted to the environment than recessive alleles.
   TRUE   FALSE

4. Hemophilia is an example of an autosomal dominant trait.
   TRUE   FALSE

5. Polygenic traits are influenced by genes at multiple loci and often by environmental factors.
   TRUE   FALSE

6. Outside of the nucleus, the only cellular organelles that contain their own DNA are the ribosomes.
   TRUE   FALSE

7. A change in the frequency of alleles from one generation to the next is the modern definition of evolution.
   TRUE   FALSE

8. Genetic drift is the exchange of alleles between populations.
   TRUE   FALSE

9. One of the best-documented cases of natural selection in humans is the relationship between achondroplasia and the ABO blood group system.
   TRUE   FALSE

10. Populations evolve, individuals do not.
    TRUE   FALSE

MULTIPLE CHOICE QUESTIONS

1. In a cross between two purebred strains of garden peas Mendel found that in the offspring
    A. both traits were represented in the F₁ generation.
    B. they were homozygous for the traits being studied.
    C. one of the traits disappeared.
    D. the traits were intermediate between the two parental traits.

2. Mendel used the term dominant for
    A. plants that were larger than others of the same variety.
    B. a trait that prevented another trait from appearing.
    C. a variety of pea plants that eliminated a weaker variety.
    D. a trait that "skipped" generations.

3. When Mendel crossed peas with Rr and Rr genotypes, the phenotypic ratio of the offspring was _____ (hint: you may want to use a Punnett square to figure this out)
    A. 1:1.
    B. 3:1.
    C. 1:2:1.
    D. 2:2.

4. Genes exist in pairs in individuals; during the production of gametes, the pairs are separated so that a gamete has only one of each kind. This is known as the
    A. principle of segregation.
    B. principle of independent assortment.
    C. mitosis.
    D. unification theory.

5. What physiological process explains Mendel's principle of segregation?
    A. mitosis.
    B. meiosis.
    C. metamorphosis.
    D. metastasis.

6. Which of the following is characteristic of dominant alleles
    A. dominant alleles are expressed in heterozygous genotypes.
    B. dominant alleles are the alleles which are most common in a population.
    C. dominant alleles always cause more serious defects than recessive alleles.
    D. dominant alleles drive recessive alleles out of a population.

7. A trait which is inherited as a recessive is expressed in the
    A. homozygous recessive individual.
    B. homozygous dominant individual.
    C. heterozyous individual.
    D. codominant individual.

8. An alternative form of a gene is called a(n)
    A. nucleotide.
    B. locus.
    C. allele.
    D. epistasis.

9. Which of the following genotypes is homozygous?
    A. AB
    B. OO
    C. ABO
    D. BO

10. The principle of independent assortment states that
    A. a pair of genes segregate during the production of gametes.
    B. genes recombine in a predetermined way.
    C. the distribution of one pair of genes does not influence the distribution of other pairs of genes on other chromosomes.
    D. mutations come from independent sources.

11. A heterozygous genotype would be written as
    A. AA.
    B. Aa.
    C. aa.
    D. AA and aa.

12. Mendelian traits are
    A. also known as traits of simple inheritance.
    B. controlled by alleles at more than one genetic locus.
    C. the product of several alleles on different chromosomes.
    D. only known for about 160 human traits.

13. When there are two different alleles present in a heterozygote and both of these alleles are expressed, this condition is called
    A. recessive.
    B. dominance.
    C. codominance.
    D. sex-linked.

14. Geneticists call the diagram that shows the matings that have taken place in a family, going back several generations, a
    A. karyotype chart.
    B. pedigree chart.
    C. genotype.
    D. syndrome.

15. Which of the following are modes of Mendelian inheritance?
    A. autosomal recessive
    B. autosomal dominant
    C. sex-linked
    D. all of the above

16. Which sex is more likely to suffer from X-linked recessive disorders such as hemophilia?
    A. females
    B. males
    C. males and females are equally likely
    D. neither sex

17. Polygenic traits are produced by the interaction between multiple genes and
    A. proteins.
    B. the environment.
    C. the sex chromosomes.
    D. recombination.

18. Males have only one X chromosome. This condition is called
    A. heterozygous.
    B. homozygous.
    C. hemizygous.
    D. autozygous.

19. Polygenic traits can often be graphically illustrated as
    A. a bell curve.
    B. a simple indication of presence or absence.
    C. an ellipse.
    D. a 2-bin histogram.

20. In many polygenic traits the various loci each influence the phenotype producing
    A. a discrete trait.
    B. a discontinuous trait.
    C. an additive effect.
    D. a new allele.

21. The modern synthesis integrates Darwinian natural selection with
    A. paleontology.
    B. embryology.
    C. genetics.
    D. ecology.

22. The modern genetic definition of biological evolution is
    A. change.
    B. a change in allele frequency from one generation to the next.
    C. mutation.
    D. survival of the fittest.

23. Which of the following is the **only** evolutionary force that can create brand-new genetic variation within a population?
    A. mitosis.
    B. natural selection.
    C. mutation.
    D. recombination.

24. The introduction of alleles from one population into another population is known as
    A. genetic drift.
    B. gene flow.
    C. founder effect.
    D. bottleneck effect.

25. An example of gene flow would be
    A. the Amerasian children of Vietnam.
    B. the isolated Amish of Pennsylvania.
    C. the American colonization of Antarctica.
    D. a small hunting and gathering society in Siberia with little outside contact.

26. The force of evolution which is significant when small human populations become isolated is
    A. gene flow.
    B. mutation.
    C. genetic drift.
    D. random mating.

27. In Tenth Century Norway, Eric the Red and his followers were banished for murders and general rowdiness (even by Viking standards). This small group, which had a higher representation of the red-hair allele than the rest of the population of Norway, sailed west and established a colony on Iceland. Within several centuries the colony had a population of several thousand. This would **best** be explained as
    A. gene flow.
    B. natural selection.
    C. mutation.
    D. founder effect.

28. In any sexually reproducing species both parents contribute genes to the offspring. This is
    A. mutation.
    B. genetic drift.
    C. recombination.
    D. natural selection.

29. The hemoglobin S allele
    A. is present only in "black" populations.
    B. reaches its highest frequencies in areas where malaria is present.
    C. is powerful enough to produce sickle-cell anemia in heterozygotes.
    D. originated in the first place by genetic drift.

30. The unit of evolutionary change is the
    A. family.
    B. individual.
    C. population.
    D. pedigree.

31. Scientists including Ronald Fisher, J.B.S. Haldane, Sewell Wright, Ernst Mayr and George Gaylord Simpson were responsible for the development of the
    A. Mendelian theory of inheritance.
    B. Darwinian theory of natural selection.
    C. Lamarckian theory of the inheritance of acquired characteristics.
    D. modern synthesis of evolutionary biology.

32. This ring-shaped DNA molecule is found outside of the nucleus and is transmitted exclusively through the maternal line.
    A. ribosomal DNA (rDNA)
    B. nuclear DNA (nDNA)
    C. mitochondrial DNA (mtDNA)
    D. all of the above

SHORT ANSWER QUESTIONS (& PAGE REFERENCES)

1. What is Mendel's principle of segregation? (pp. 71-74)

2. Describe three Mendelian traits manifested in humans. (p. 77, Box 4-2)

3. Why does hemophilia affect males more often than females? (pp. 81-83)

4. What are the differences between polygenic and pleiotropic traits? (pp. 84-87)

5. What is founder effect? (pp. 92-93)

ESSAY QUESTIONS (& PAGE REFERENCES)

1. Describe one of Mendel's pea plant experiments. How does the experiment's results illustrate the principles of segregation and independent assortment? (pp. 71-75)

2. What is the modern genetic definition of evolution? In this context, define and state the significance of the following terms: population, allele frequency, microevolution and macroevolution. (pp. 89-90)

3. What are the factors that produce and redistribute genetic variation? (pp. 91-93)

ANSWERS, *CORRECTED STATEMENT* IF FALSE & REFERENCES TO TRUE/FALSE QUESTIONS

1. TRUE, p. 72

2. TRUE, p. 75.

3. FALSE, pp. 78-79, Dominant alleles are *not* always more common and *may or may not be* better adapted to the environment than recessive alleles.

4. FALSE, pp. 81-83, Hemophilia is an example of a *sex-linked* trait.

5. TRUE, p. 84

6. FALSE, p. 87, Outside of the nucleus, the only cellular organelles that contain their own DNA are the *mitochondria*.

7. TRUE, p. 89

8. FALSE, p. 90, *Gene flow* is the exchange of alleles between populations.

9. FALSE, p. 94, One of the best-documented cases of natural selection in humans is the relationship between *malaria* and *hemoglobin S*.

10. TRUE, p. 89

ANSWERS & REFERENCES TO MULTIPLE CHOICE QUESTIONS

1. C, pp. 71-72	17. B, p. 86
2. B, p. 72	18. C, p. 82
3. B, p. 72	19. A, p. 84
4. A, pp. 71-72	20. C, pp. 84-85
5. B, p. 72	21. C, pp. 87-88
6. A, pp. 78-79	22. B, p. 89
7. A, pp. 72-73	23. C, p. 90
8. C, p. 72	24. B, pp. 90-92
9. B, p. 73	25. A, p. 91
10. C, pp. 74-76	26. C, pp. 92-93
11. B, pp. 73-74	27. D, p. 92
12. A, p. 76	28. C, p. 93
13. C, pp. 76-77	29. B, pp. 94-95
14. B, p. 79	30. C, p. 96
15. D, pp. 79-83	31. D, p. 88 (Box 4-1)
16. B, p. 82	32. C, p. 87

CONCEPT APPLICATION SOLUTIONS

<u>Punnett Squares</u>

	A	O
B	AB	BO
O	AO	OO

	A	B
A	AA	AB
B	AB	BB

	B	O
A	AB	AO
B	BB	BO

Square 1 - ¼ Blood Type AB : ¼ Blood Type B : ¼ Blood Type A : ¼ Blood Type O
Square 2 - ¼ Blood Type A : ½ Blood Type AB : ¼ Blood Type B
Square 3 - ¼ Blood Type AB : ½ Blood Type B : ¼ Blood Type A

	TR	Tr	tR	tr
TR	TTRR	TTRr	TtRR	TtRr
Tr	TTRr	TTrr	TtRr	Ttrr
tR	TrRR	TtRr	ttRR	ttRr
tr	TtRr	Ttrr	ttRr	ttrr

Dihybrid cross:
9/16 Tall/Round : 3/16 Tall/wrinkled : 3/16 short/Round : 1/16 short/wrinkled

Pedigree Chart for X-Linked Recessive Trait

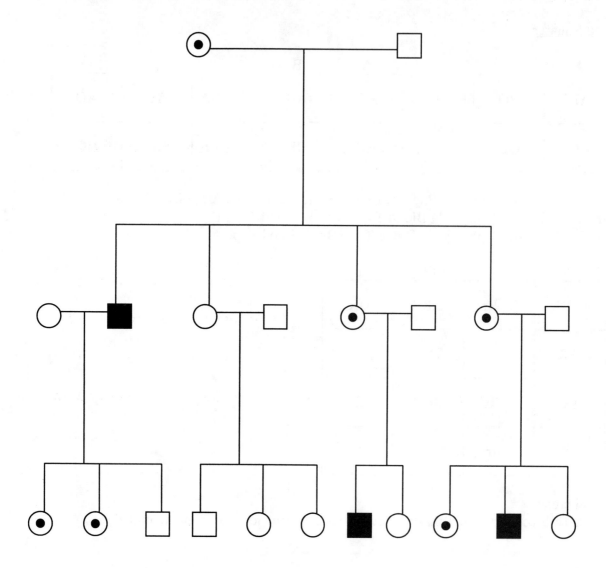

CHAPTER 5
AN OVERVIEW OF THE PRIMATES

LEARNING OBJECTIVES

After reading this chapter you should be able to

- list and discuss primate evolutionary trends (pp. 103-105).
- describe the influence of the arboreal environment on primate evolution (pp. 106-108).
- compare and contrast the "arboreal hypothesis" with the "visual predation hypothesis" (p. 108).
- work out a dental formula (p. 109).
- describe the major forms of locomotion found among primates and be able to name one type of primate for each form of locomotion (pp. 112-114).
- explain how taxonomic classification reflects biological relationships (114-115).
- explain how new genetic technologies have been used to deduce evolutionary relationships of the hominoids and tarsier (pp. 114-117).
- name, compare, and contrast the two major subdivisions of the primates (pp. 117-120).
- name the major groupings of the anthropoids (pp. 119-124).
- discuss the differences between New World monkeys and Old World monkeys (pp. 120-123).
- name the two subdivisions of the Old World monkeys and the features that distinguish these two groups (p. 122-123).
- explain why New World monkeys and Old World monkeys appear so similar (p. 123-124).
- explain how monkeys and apes differ (pp. 124).
- describe the major characteristics of the various apes that comprise the hominoids (pp. 124-130).
- discuss the primate conservation challenges facing primatologists today (pp. 130-132).

CHAPTER OUTLINE

Introduction

The preceding chapters have focused on the basic biological background for understanding human evolution. Now we will look at human evolution in more detail. In order to understand any organism it is important to have a frame of reference as to where that organism belongs - how it is similar and how it is different from other closely related organisms. This is done through a comparative approach. The organisms that are most useful to study, in this regard, are the other 190 species in the Order Primates. In this chapter we look at the physical characteristics that define the primates, an overview of the living members of the order, the molecular techniques that are used to deduce evolutionary relationships between primate species, and finish with a discussion of the conservation of our closest relatives.

I   Primate As Mammals
  A. Primates belong to the vertebrate class, Mammalia.
    1. There are over 4,000 species of mammals.
    2. Primates belong to the subgroup of placental mammals.
  B. As mammals, primates share a number of traits in common with other mammals.
    1. These are called primitive, or generalized, traits. These include:
      a. Fur, or, as it is referred to in humans, body hair.
      b. A relatively long gestation period followed by live birth.
      c. Different types of specialized teeth, or heterodontism.
      d. Homeothermy, the ability to maintain a constant body temperature through physiological mechanisms.
      e. Increased brain size leading to a greater capacity for learning and behavioral flexibility.
II   Characteristics of Primates
  A. As an Order, primates have retained many primitive mammalian traits and remain quite generalized.
    1. On the other hand, many other mammals have become increasingly specialized.
    2. This leads to the modification of anatomical structures for the particular function that they become specialized for, e.g. the reduction of digits in horses.
    3. Some mammals have specialized structures that are not found in any other mammalian group. An example is the four carnassial teeth found only in the Order Carnivora.
  B. Because primates are generalized mammals they cannot be defined by one or two common traits.
    1. Primates are defined by evolutionary trends.
      a. Evolutionary trends are traits that characterized the entire order to a greater or lesser degree.
    2. It is important to note that primate evolutionary trends are a set of general tendencies not equally expressed in all primate species.
      a. The evolutionary trends that have been traditionally used by primatologists are a combination of primitive mammalian traits and common primate specialized traits.
      b. These traits characterize the Order Primates.
  C. Limbs and locomotion
    1. Primates exhibit a tendency towards erect posture, especially in the upper body, whether sitting, leaping, or standing.
    2. Primates possess a flexible, generalized limb structure which does not lock them into a specialized form of locomotion.
    3. Primate hands and feet possess a high degree of prehensility (grasping ability).
      a. Other features of the hands and feet include retention of five digits on hand and feet.
      b. An opposable thumb and, in most species, a divergent and partially opposable great toe.
      c. Primates possess nails on at least some digits.
      d. Primates have tactile pads enriched with sensory nerve fibers at the ends of digits which enhance the sense of touch.

D. Diet and teeth
   1. Primates, for the most part, lack dietary specializations and tend to eat a wide variety of foods.
   2. Primates possess a generalized dentition.
E. The senses and the brain
   1. All primates rely heavily on vision. Primate evolutionary trends in vision include
      a. Color vision in all diurnal primates. Nocturnal primates lack color vision.
      b. Depth perception or stereoscopic vision is made possible, in part, by eyes that are positioned in the front of the skull, providing over-lapping fields of vision (known as binocular vision).
      c. Visual information from each eye is transmitted to the visual centers in both hemispheres of the brain.
      d. Visual information is organized into three-dimensional images by specialized structures in the brain itself.
   2. Primates have a decreased reliance on the sense of smell (olfaction).
   3. The primate brain has expanded in size and has become increasingly complex.
F. Maturation, learning, and behavior
   1. Primates possess the mammalian characteristic of the placenta, which provides for a more efficient means of fetal nourishment. Primates are marked by longer periods of gestation, fewer numbers of offspring, delayed maturation, and elongation of the entire life span.
   2. Primates exhibit a greater dependence on flexible, learned behavior.
   3. Primates tend to live in social groups. Males are permanent members of many primate social groups, a situation unusual among mammals.
   4. Primates tend to be diurnal.
III   PRIMATE ADAPTATIONS
A. Evolutionary factors: the Arboreal Adaptation
   1. Traditionally, the arboreal adaptation was thought to be the most important factor in the evolution of the primates.
   2. Arboreal life selected for stereoscopic vision in a three-dimensional environment.
   3. The primate grasping, prehensile hand is adapted to climbing in the trees.
   4. The tropical arboreal environment provided a variety of foods which led to the primate omnivorous diet and generalized dentition.
   5. Other challenges of the arboreal environment may have led to increased brain size and complexity as well as increased behavioral flexibility.
   6. This view that the arboreal environment was the major factor influencing primate evolution is called the arboreal hypothesis.
B. The visual predation hypothesis
   1. The visual predation hypothesis is an alternative to the arboreal hypothesis.
   2. This hypothesis states that primates may have first evolved in the bushy forest undergrowth.
      a. In this environment forward-facing, close-set eyes enabled early primates to judge distance when grabbing for insects.
   3. Early primates would have to travel on small vertical limbs which grasping hands would enable them to do.

C. The visual predation and the arboreal hypotheses are not necessarily mutually exclusive explanations.
   1. Many primate features may have begun in nonarboreal settings.
   2. Nevertheless, primates did move into the trees and, if they did have characteristics that evolved in another setting, they were "preadapted" for life in the trees.
D. Geographical distribution and habitats
   1. Most living nonhuman primates live in the tropical or semitropical areas of the New and Old Worlds.
   2. Most primates are arboreal, living in forest or woodland habitats.
   3. Some Old World monkeys have adapted to life on the ground.
   4. Gorillas and chimpanzees spend considerable time on the ground.
   5. However, no nonhuman primate is adapted to a fully terrestrial environment – all spend some time in the trees.
E. Diet and teeth
   1. Primates are generally omnivorous and this is reflected in their generalized dentition.
   2. Although the majority of primate species emphasize some food items over others, most eat a combination of fruit, leaves and insects.
      a. Some primates (baboons and chimpanzees) occasionally kill and eat small mammals.
      b. Some primates, such as the colobine monkeys, are dietary specialists on leaf.
   3. Most primates have four types of teeth.
      a. Incisors and canines function in biting and cutting.
      b. Premolars and molars are used for crushing and grinding.
   4. A dental formula describes the number of each type of tooth that typifies a species.
      a. A dental formula is read in the following order: incisor(s), canine(s), premolar(s), and molar(s).
      b. The number of each type of tooth is presented for a quarter of the mouth. If these teeth are added up and multiplied by four the result is the number of teeth characteristic of that species.
         i) For example, New World cebid monkeys have a dental formula of 2.1.3.3, therefore this species has 36 total teeth (4 X 9).
         ii) In comparison, the primitive dental formula for all placental mammals is 3.1.4.3 which totals 44 teeth.
      c. Primates, as well as other mammals, have fewer teeth than the primitive mammalian condition because of evolutionary trends in those lineages.
   5. The primate dentition is characterized by a lack of dental specialization.
      a. Unlike carnivore or herbivore specialists, primates possess low, rounded cusps that enable them to process most foods.
F. Locomotion
   1. Almost all primates are, to some degree, quadrupedal - using all four limbs in their locomotion.
      a. Many primates are able to employ more than one form of locomotion, a product of their generalized limb structure.
      b. The majority of quadrupedal primates are arboreal, but terrestrial quadrupedalism is also fairly common.
      c. Limb ratios of quadrupeds differ.

          i)   The limbs of terrestrial quadrupeds are approximately equal in length, with forelimbs being 90 percent as long as hind limbs.

          ii)   In arboreal quadrupeds, forelimbs are proportionately shorter and may only be 70-80 percent as long as hind limbs.

    d. Quadrupeds are also characterized by a relatively long and flexible lumbar spine which positions the hind limbs well forward and enhances their ability to propel the animal forward.

  2. Vertical clinging and leaping is found in many prosimians.

  3. Brachiation (arm swinging) employs the forearms and is found among the apes.

    a. Only the small gibbons and siamangs of Southeast Asia use this form of locomotion exclusively.

    b. Brachiators are characterized by:

          i)   arms shorter than legs.

          ii)   a short stable lumbar spine.

          iii) long curved fingers.

          iv) reduced thumbs.

    c. Brachiator characteristics have been inherited by the great apes from their ancestors who were either brachiators or climbers.

    d. Some monkeys that use a combination of leaping with some arm swinging are termed semibrachiators.

  4. An aid to locomotion is a prehensile tail.

    a. Among the primates prehensile tails are found only among the New World monkeys.

    b. A prehensile tail is capable of wrapping around a branch and supporting the animal's weight.

IV   PRIMATE TAXONOMY

  A. See Fig. 5-6 for primate classification.

  B. In taxonomic systems organisms are organized into increasingly narrower categories.

    1. All of the primates are grouped together in the Order Primates.

    2. This primate order is subdivided into two large suborders.

      a. The Prosimii include lemurs, lorises and, traditionally, tarsiers.

        i) By grouping these primates together an evolutionary statement is implied - these animals are more closely related to each other than they are to any of the anthropoids.

      b. The other suborder, Anthropoidea, includes monkeys, apes, and humans.

    3. At each succeeding level finer distinctions are made until the species level is reached.

      a. In this manner, classifications not only organize diversity into categories, but also illustrate evolutionary and genetic relationships between species and groups of species.

  C. Primate chromosomes, proteins, and DNA

    1. Karyotypes show that orangutan chromosomes are distinct from African large-bodied hominoids (gorillas, chimps and humans).

      a. This implies that the latter group's members are more closely related to each other than any are to the orangutan.

      b. Karyotype studies are more ambiguous about the relationships among gorillas, chimps and humans.

      c.   Nevertheless, the traditional grouping of the orangutan, chimp and gorilla into the family Pongidae is challenged by this evidence.

   2. Other genetic techniques, such as amino acid sequencing and DNA hybridization, have confirmed the basic tenets of traditional primate classification.

      a.   However, it is now accepted on the basis of these biochemical analyses that humans and chimps are more closely related to each other that either is to other apes.

      b.   Therefore, some primate taxonomists have changed their classifications to reflect this closeness of relationship by placing chimps, humans (and sometimes gorillas) in the same taxonomic family.

   3. The place of tarsiers among the primates has also been hotly debated by primate taxonomists.

      a.   Tarsiers are highly derived and display several unique characteristics.

      b.   Traditionally they have been classified as prosimians because they possess a number of primitive primate traits.

      c.   However, they also share several traits with the anthropoids.

      d.   Regarding their chromosomes, they are distinct from both groups, but other genetic comparisons have aligned them with the anthropoids.

      e.   The problem of where to place tarsiers has resulted in a taxonomic scheme which replaces the traditional taxonomy with alternative suborders.

         i)   Lemurs and lorises are placed in the suborder Strepsirhini (wet-nosed primates).

         ii)   The tarsiers and anthropoids are placed in the suborder Haplorhini (dry-nosed primates).

V   A SURVEY OF THE LIVING PRIMATES

  A. Prosimians (lemurs and lorises)

   1. Prosimians are the most primitive of the primates.

   2. Primitive characteristics include:

      a.   Greater reliance on olfaction compared to the other primates.

         i)   This is reflected in the moist rhinarium at the end of the nose and the relatively long snout.

         ii)   Prosimians mark their territories with scent.

      b.   Prosimians have more laterally placed eyes.

      c.   Their reproductive physiology, as well as the shorter gestation length and maturation period, differs from the other primates.

   3. Many prosimians possess a dental specialization called the "dental comb".

      a. This structure is formed by forward-projecting lower incisors and canines.

      b. The dental comb is used in both feeding and grooming.

  B. Lemurs

   1. Lemurs are found only on the island of Madagascar and several other nearby islands off the east coast of Africa.

      a.   On Madagascar the lemurs diversified into numerous and varied ecological niches without competition from higher primates.

      b.   Lemurs became extinct elsewhere in the world.

   2. Characteristics of lemurs

      a.   Body size ranges from the small mouse lemur (5 inches in length, 2 ounces in weight) to the indri (over 2 feet long, approximately 22 pounds).

b. The larger lemurs are diurnal and exploit a wide variety of vegetable foods ranging from fruit to leaves, buds, bark, and shoots.
c. Smaller lemurs are nocturnal and insectivorous (insect-feeding).
3. There is great variation in lemur behavior from species to species.
a. Many forms are arboreal but some, such as the ring-tailed lemur, are more terrestrial.
b. Some arboreal forms are quadrupedal, while others, such as the sifaka, are vertical clingers and leapers.
c. Some species (e.g. ring-tailed lemurs and sifakas) live in groups of 10 to 25 animals, which includes both males and females of all ages.
d. Others, such as the indri, live in monogamous family units.
e. Most of the nocturnal species are solitary.
C. Lorises
1. Lorises are very similar in appearance to lemurs.
2. Lorises were able to survive in continental areas by adopting a nocturnal activity pattern.
a. This enabled the lorises to avoid competition with the more recently evolved monkeys.
3. Loris species are found in tropical forests and woodlands of India, Sri Lanka, Southeast Asia, and Africa.
4. A member of the loris family is the galago, or bushbaby, which is found in forests and woodlands of sub-Saharan Africa.
5. Characteristics of lorises
a. Locomotion
i) Lorises employ a slow cautious climbing form of quadrupedalism.
ii) Galagos are active vertical clingers and leapers.
b. Diet
i) Some lorises are almost completely insectivorous.
ii) Others supplement their diet with combinations of fruit, leaves, gums, and slugs.
c. These animals frequently forage alone.
i) Ranges overlap and females frequently form associations for foraging or in sharing the same sleeping nest ("dormitories").
6. Both lemurs and lorises represent the same general primate adaptive level.
a. Vision is stereoscopic, but not to the extent found in anthropoids.
i) Color vision exists in some diurnal species, but not in the nocturnal species.
b. Nails are present, but not on all digits. Most have a "grooming claw" on the second toe.
c. These animals have longer life spans compared to other similar-sized mammals.
i) This is an important primate characteristic associated with longer developmental and learning periods.
D. Tarsiers
1. Tarsiers are small nocturnal primates found in the islands of Southeast Asia.
2. Tarsiers eat insects and small vertebrates which they catch by leaping from branches.
3. The basic social pattern appears to be a family unit consisting of a mated pair and their offspring.
4. Tarsiers exhibit a combination of anatomical traits not seen in other primates.

a. Primitive (prosimians-like) traits include small size, grooming claws, and an unfused mandible (lower jaw bone).
b. Traits shared with anthropoids include the lack of a rhinarium and orbits completely enclosed by bone. Biochemically tarsiers are also closer to the anthropoids.
E. Anthropoids (monkeys, apes and humans)
1. Anthropoid characteristics that distinguish them from prosimians include:
a. Generally larger body size.
b. Larger brains both in absolute size and in relation to body size.
c. Reduced reliance on the sense of smell.
d. Increased reliance on vision with forward-facing eyes placed at the front of the face.
e. Greater degree of color vision.
f. Bony plate at the back of the eye socket.
g. Different pattern of blood supply than found in the prosimians.
h. Both halves of the mandible are fused at the midline.
i. Less specialized dentition.
j. Internal female reproductive anatomy is different from the prosimian condition.
k. Longer gestation and maturation periods.
l. Increased parental care.
m. More mutual grooming.
2. Monkeys represent about 70 percent of all primate species and are divided into two large groups: New World monkeys and Old World monkeys.
F. New World monkeys
1. A characteristic that distinguishes the New World monkeys from the Old World monkeys is the shape of the nose.
a. New World monkeys have widely flaring noses with nostrils that face outward.
b. New World monkeys are placed in the infraorder Platyrrhini (meaning "flat-nosed").
c. Old World monkeys have narrower noses with downward facing nostrils. They are placed in the infraorder Catarrhini, which means "downward-facing nose."
2. New World monkeys are almost exclusively arboreal.
3. Like Old World monkeys all species, with the exception of the owl monkey, are diurnal.
4. The New World monkeys are divided into two families: the Callitrichidae and the Cebidae.
5. The callitrichids are the small marmosets and tamarins.
a. The marmosets and tamarins are considered to be the most primitive monkeys.
i) They retain claws instead of nails. The claws assist these quadrupedal monkeys in squirrel-like climbing of vertical trees trunks.
ii) They give birth to twins (a prosimian trait among primates) instead of single infant.
b. Socially these monkeys live in family groups composed of either a mated pair, or a female and two adult males, plus the offspring. Males are heavily involved with infant care.
6. There are 30 different cebid species.
7. Cebids are larger than callitrichids.

a. Cebid diets vary with most eating a combination of fruit and leaves supplemented by insects.
b. The locomotor pattern of most cebids is quadrupedalism.
   i) Spider monkeys are semibrachiators.
   ii) Spider and howler monkeys possess prehensile tails.
c. Socially most cebids live in groups of both sexes and all ages, or as monogamous pairs with subadult offspring.

G. Old World monkeys
1. Old World monkeys are found from sub-Saharan Africa to the islands of Southeast Asia.
   a. Their habitats range from tropical forests to semiarid desert and even extend to seasonally snow-covered highland forests in northern Japan.
2. General characteristics of Old World monkeys.
   a. The locomotor pattern of most Old World monkeys is quadrupedal.
   b. They are primarily arboreal, although some have adapted to life on the ground.
   c. Old World monkeys sit erect and associated with this posture are areas of hardened skin, ischial callosities, that serve as sitting pads.
3. All of the Old World monkeys belong to one family, the Cercopithecidae, which is divided into two subfamilies, the cercopithecines and the colobines.
4. Cercopithecines
   a. Cercopithecines are more generalized than the colobines.
   b. Cercopithecines have a more omnivorous diet.
   c. A dietary adaptation is the presence of cheek pouches which enable these monkeys to store food while foraging.
   d. Geographical distribution
      i) Most cercopithecines are found in Africa.
      ii) However, a number of species of macaques are also found in Asia.
5. Colobines
   a. These animals are dietary specialists on leaf.
   b. Geographical distribution
      i) The colobus monkeys are exclusively African.
      ii) Langurs are found in Asia and proboscis monkeys on Borneo.
6. Locomotor behavior is varied among Old World monkeys.
   a. Guenons, macaques, and langurs are arboreal quadrupeds.
   b. Baboons, patas monkeys, and macaques are terrestrial quadrupeds.
   c. Colobus monkeys practice semibrachiation and leaping.
7. Many Old World monkey species show a marked difference in size or shape between the sexes.
   a. This is called sexual dimorphism and is particularly pronounced in terrestrial species such as baboons.
8. Females of several species exhibit pronounced cyclical changes of the external genitalia that advertise to males that they are sexually receptive.
   a. This hormonally initiated period is called estrus.
9. Several types of social organization characterize Old World monkeys.
   a. Colobines tend to live in small groups that contain only one or two adult males.
   b. Savanna baboons and most macaques live in large groups containing adults of both sexes and offspring of all ages.

H. Old and New World monkeys: a striking case of homoplasy
    1. The evolutionary principle that explains the similarities between New World and Old World monkeys is homoplasy.
        a. Homoplasy results from geographically distinct populations responding to similar environmental pressures.
    2. Despite several differences between New World and Old World monkeys, they are nevertheless, recognizable as monkeys.
    3. New World and Old World monkeys have been separated for at least 30 million years.
    4. It was once believed that both groups evolved from separate prosimian ancestors.
    5. Current consensus is that both groups evolved from a common monkey ancestor in Africa.
    6. New World monkeys would have reached South America, then an island continent, by "rafting."
        a. "Rafting" is the dispersal of organisms on chunks of land that have broken off from mainland areas and float on currents to another landmass.
            i) These "floating islands," with their biological communities, are still seen today.
        b. At the time that the ancestors of New World monkeys would have rafted to South America it was in closer proximity to Africa than it is today.
I. Hominoids (apes and humans)
    1. The superfamily Hominoidea includes the "lesser" apes (family Hylobatidae: gibbons and siamangs), the great apes (family Pongidae), and the humans (family Hominidae).
    2. Hominoid characteristics that distinguish them from monkeys include:
        a. Larger body size (gibbons and siamangs are exceptions).
        b. Absence of a tail.
        c. Shortened trunk (the lumbar area is relatively shorter and more stable).
        d. Differences in position and musculature of the shoulder joint (adapted for suspensory locomotion).
        e. More complex behavior.
        f. More complex brains and enhanced cognitive abilities.
        g. Longer period of infant development and dependency.
J. Gibbons and siamangs
    1. Gibbons and siamangs are found in the tropical areas of southeast Asia.
    2. They are the smallest of the apes - gibbons weigh 13 pounds and siamangs 25 pounds.
    3. Gibbons and siamangs have anatomical features adapted for brachiation that include
        a. Extremely long arms.
        b. Curved fingers.
        c. Reduced thumbs.
        d. Powerful shoulder muscles.
    4. The highly specialized locomotor adaptations may be related to feeding behavior while hanging beneath branches.
    5. Diet is composed largely of fruit with supplements of leaves, flowers, and insects.
    6. The basic social unit is a monogamous pair with their dependent offspring.
        a. Males are very involved with the rearing of the offspring.
        b. The mated pair are territorial and delineate their territories with elaborate siren-like whoops and "songs."

K. Orangutans (*Pongo pygmaeus*)
1. Orangutans are found only in heavily forested areas of Borneo and Sumatra.
2. They are slow, cautious climbers.
3. They are almost completely arboreal.
    a. They do sometimes travel quadrupedally on the ground (especially the larger males).
4. They are large animals (males = 200 pounds, females = 100 pounds) with pronounced sexual dimorphism.
5. Socially these animals are solitary.
6. They are principally frugivorous (fruit-eating).
L. Gorillas (*Gorilla gorilla*)
1. Gorillas are the largest of the living primates and are confined to forested regions of central and western Africa.
2. Gorillas exhibit marked sexual dimorphism, males can weigh up to 400 pounds, females 200 pounds.
3. Because of their large size gorillas are primarily terrestrial employing a semi-quadrupedal posture called knuckle-walking.
4. Gorillas live in groups that consist of one (sometimes two) large silverback males, a few adult females, and their subadult offspring.
5. All gorillas are exclusively vegetarian.
    a. Their diets consist primarily of leaf, pith and stalks.
M. Chimpanzees (*Pan troglodytes*)
1. Chimpanzees are found in equatorial Africa.
2. Chimpanzees anatomically resemble gorillas in many ways particularly in limb proportions and upper body shape.
    a. These similarities are due to their common mode of terrestrial locomotion: knuckle-walking.
3. The ecological adaptations of chimps and gorillas differ with chimps spending more time in the trees.
4. In size chimps are smaller than orangutans and gorillas; although they are also sexually dimorphic, it is not to the degree seen in the orangutans and gorillas.
5. Locomotion includes quadrupedal knuckle-walking on the ground and suspensory behavior (including brachiation, especially among younger chimps) in the trees.
6. Chimpanzees are omnivorous.
    a. They eat a large variety of both plant and animal foods.
    b. Chimps hunt and the hunting parties include both males and females.
        i) Chimps kill and eat young monkeys, bushpigs, and antelope.
        ii) Prey is grudgingly shared among the group members.
7. Chimpanzees live in large, fluid communities of as many as 50 individuals.
    a. The core of the community are bonded males who never leave the group into which they were born.
    b. Chimp communities are fluid (individuals come and go) and consist of animals who occupy a particular territory, but the individual members are usually dispersed into small foraging parties.
    c. Females frequently forage alone or in the company of their offspring.
8. Females may leave the community either permanently or temporarily while in estrus.

a. This latter behavior reduces the risk of mating with close male relatives (recall that males do not leave their birth group).

N. Bonobos (*Pan paniscus*)
1. Bonobos are another species of *Pan* and are only found in an area south of the Zaire River in Zaire.
2. Bonobos are the least studied of the great apes and their population is believed to number only a few thousand individuals.
3. Bonobos differ from chimpanzees in several features.
   a. A more linear body build with longer legs relative to arms.
   b. A relatively smaller head, a dark face from birth, and tufts of hair at the side of the face.
4. Bonobo behavior:
   a. Bonobos are more arboreal than chimpanzees.
   b. They are less aggressive among themselves.
   c. Like chimps they live in fluid communities.
   d. Bonobos exploit many of the same foods as chimps, including occasional meat from killing small mammals.
5. Among bobonos it is male-female bonds that constitute the societal core.
   a. This may be due to bonobo sexuality in which copulations are frequent and occur throughout the female's estrous cycle.

O. Humans (*Homo sapiens*)
1. Humans represent the only living species belonging to the family Hominidae.
2. The primate heritage of humans is shown in a number of features including:
   a. Dependence on vision for orientation to the world.
   b. Lack of reliance on olfactory cues.
   c. Flexible limbs and grasping hands.
3. In diet, humans are omnivorous.
4. Unique among animals, are the human cognitive abilities that are the result of dramatic increases in brain size and other neurological changes.
5. Humans are also completely dependent on culture; however, none of the technologies we have developed would have been possible without a biology that produced our highly developed cognitive abilities.
6. Another unique characteristic of our species is the development of spoken language.
   a. This is an elaboration of our primate heritage.
   b. Research with apes has revealed that these primates, while anatomically not capable of producing speech, can communicate with symbols.
7. Aside from our cognitive abilities, the most distinctive characteristic that sets humans apart from other primates is our unique habitual bipedal locomotion.
   a. Bipedal locomotion has required significant structural modifications of the pelvis and the limbs.
   b. As primates, our ancestors were already behaviorally preadapted for bipedalism.

VI ENDANGERED PRIMATES
A. Probably the greatest challenge facing primatologists today is the urgent need for conservation.
B. Over half of all living primates are endangered and many face immediate extinction.
C. Three main factors threaten endangered primate species.

1. Habitat destruction; most primates live in tropical rain forests that are being logged or destroyed for their natural resources or for farm land.
        2. Hunting for their meat.
        3. Live capture for either the local pet trade or to export to collectors.
    D. Encompassing all of these factors is the burgeoning human population, which leads to competition between non-human primates and humans for scarce resources.
        1. Ninety percent of all primates live in the tropical forests of Africa, Asia, and Latin America.
        2. These nations, with an estimated 1.5 billion people, are suffering from a fuelwood shortage leading to forest destruction.
        3. In addition, tropical hardwoods are in high demand by developed nations such as the United States, Japan, and European nations.
    E. Hunting of primates
        1. In West Africa the most serious problem is hunting to provide "bush meat" to feed the growing human population.
        2. It is estimated that thousands of primates, including gorillas and chimpanzees, are killed and sold for meat every year; primates are also killed for commercial products.
    F. Primates have also been live captured for zoos, biomedical research, and the exotic pet trade.
        1. Live capture has declined dramatically in recent years.
        2. The implementation of the Convention on Trade in Endangered Species of Wild Flora and Fauna (CITES) in 1973 has made a difference, 87 countries have signed this treaty.
    G. Conservation Efforts
        1. Many developing countries such as Madagascar and Costa Rica have designated areas as national parks or biological reserves.
        2. Private organizations, such as the Rain Forest Information Center in Ecuador, have purchased land to set up biological reserves.
        3. It is only through such practices and through educational programs that many primate species have any chance at escaping extinction.

KEY TERMS

adaptive niche: the entire way of life of an organism: where it lives, what it eats, how it obtains food, etc.

amino acid sequencing: a molecular technique in which amino acid sequences in proteins are mapped. They can then be compared between species in order to deduce evolutionary relationships.

anthropoid: any of the members of the primate suborder Anthropoidea. This suborder includes the monkeys, apes, and humans.

arboreal: living in the trees.

arboreal hypothesis: the view that primate characteristics, such as stereoscopic vision and grasping hands, are the result of evolutionary adaptation to arboreal habitats.

auditory bulla: a bony structure surrounding the middle-ear cavity that is partially formed from the temporal bone.

binocular vision: vision that results from forward facing eyes, hence overlapping visual fields. Binocular vision is a requirement for stereoscopic vision.

brachiation: a form of suspensory locomotion involving arm swinging. Found mainly among the apes.

bush meat: term used for primates and other game that are killed for food.

Callitrichidae: the family of New World monkeys that consists of the small marmosets and tamarins.

Cebidae: the family of New World monkeys that includes the capuchin, howler, squirrel, and spider monkeys. These monkeys are usually larger than the callitrichids.

Cercopithecidae: the one taxonomic family of the Old World monkeys.

cercopithecinae (cercopithecines): the subfamily of Old World monkeys that includes the baboons, macaques, and guenons.

colobinae (colobines): the subfamily of Old World monkeys that have evolved anatomical specializations in their teeth and in a large sacculated stomach for consuming a diet of leaves.

Convention on Trade in Endangered Species of Wild Flora and Fauna (CITES): a treaty aimed at the conservation of endangered organisms. This treaty has been signed by 87 nations.

cusps: the elevated portions (bumps) on the chewing surfaces of premolar and molar teeth.

dental formula: a morphological formula that gives the number of each kind of tooth for one-quarter of the mouth for a mammal. If the upper and lower dentition is different the dental formula will be presented for one-half of the mouth.

derived: refers to specialization found within a particular evolutionary lineage.

diurnal: an animal that is active during the day.

DNA hybridization: a molecular technique in which two single strands of DNA from two different species are combined to form a hybrid molecule of DNA. Evolutionary relationships can be deduced from the number of mismatched base pairs between the two strands of DNA.

estrus: period of sexual receptivity in female mammals that corresponds with ovulation. It differs from menstruation, the condition found in human females, in that the endometrial lining is reabsorbed rather than shed.

evolutionary trends: overall characteristics of an evolving lineage, such as the primates. Such trends are useful in helping categorize the lineage as compared to other lineages.

frugivory, -ous: a diet that consists mainly of fruit.

Hominoid: a member of the superfamily Hominoidea. This group includes apes and humans.

homoplasy: separate evolutionary development of similar characteristics in different groups of organisms.

intelligence: mental capacity; ability to learn, reason, or comprehend and interpret information, facts, relationships, meanings, etc.

ischial callosities: a pad of callused skin over the bone of the ischial tuberosity (a part of the pelvic bone) that serves as a sitting pad in Old World monkeys and gibbons.

Mammalia: the technical term for the formal grouping (class) of mammals.

morphology: the form (size, shape) of anatomical structures. This can include the entire organism.

nocturnal: an animal that is active during the night.

postorbital bar: a ring of bone that encloses the eye sockets in the primate skull.

postorbital plate: a plate of bone at the back of the eye orbit in primates.

primates: members of the mammalian order Primates. This includes prosimians, monkeys, apes and humans.

primatologist: a scientist that studies the biology of primates, including primate evolution.

primitive: in evolutionary terms, an organism that is most like the ancestor from which its lineage was derived. A more general member of its group. In primates the prosimians are the most primitive members.

prosimian: any of the members of the primate suborder Prosimii. Traditionally, this suborder includes lemurs, lorises, and galagos.

quadrupedal: using all four limbs to support the body during locomotion. This is the basic mammalian (and primate) form of locomotion.

rhinarium: the moist, hairless pad at the end of the nose seen in most mammalian species.

sexual dimorphism: differences in physical features between males and females of the same species. Examples among primates include larger body size of males (baboons, gorillas among others) and larger canine teeth in males (baboons and chimpanzees are representative).

specialized traits: traits that have evolved to perform a particular function. Particular specialized traits are found in a specific lineage and serve to elucidate evolutionary relationships.

stereoscopic vision: a condition, due to binocular vision, in which visual images are superimposed upon one another. This is interpreted by the brain and results in the perception of depth or three-dimensional vision.

INTERNET & *INFOTRAC COLLEGE EDITION* EXERCISES

Take an online visit to the wonderful Primate Info Net (http://www.primate.wisc.edu/pin/), hosted by the Wisconsin Regional Primate Research Center of the University of Wisconsin – Madison. Click on the "AV Resources" button on the left and you are taken to the site's audiovisual archives. From there you can browse through the primate world of sight and sound. Listen to numerous primate vocalizations (the gibbon "songs" and howler "howls" are particularly cool), and view hundreds of images of primates stored in their fully searchable online slide collection.

In *InfoTrac* do a keyword search on "primate extinction." Read a couple of articles and summarize what is currently being done to prevent specific species of endangered primates from going extinct.

Fill in the 18 numbered blanks in the simplified primate taxonomy below with the 18 lettered choices provided.

A. ischial callosities	J. the great apes
B. species include *troglodytes* and *paniscus*	K. stereoscopic vision and prehensility
C. reliance on olfaction more than other primates	L. dental comb shared with lorises
D. largest eyes among the primates	M. bigger, brainier than prosimians
E. acrobatic ape brachiators	N. language, reliance on culture
F. not nearly as ferocious as popularly perceived	O. means "flat-nosed"
G. all have a 2-1-2-3 dental formula	P. suspensory locomotion
H. includes the galagos, or bushbabies	Q. bipedalism
I. some can hang by their tails	R. only found on Borneo and Sumatra

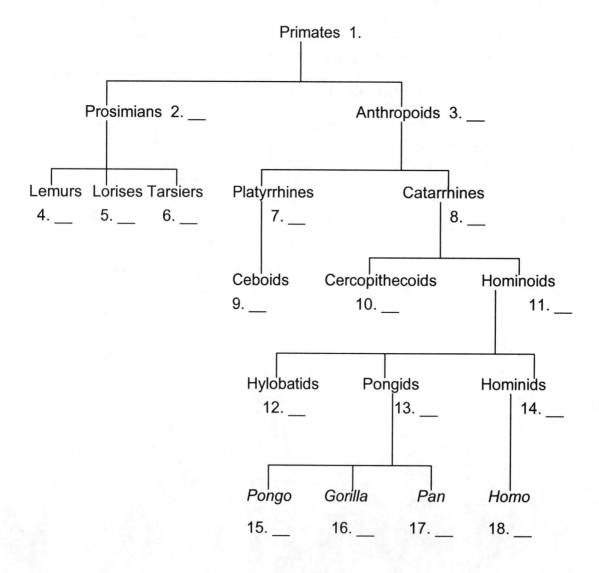

Primates 1.

Prosimians 2. __   Anthropoids 3. __

Lemurs   Lorises   Tarsiers   Platyrrhines   Catarrhines
4. __   5. __   6. __   7. __   8. __

Ceboids   Cercopithecoids   Hominoids
9. __   10. __   11. __

Hylobatids   Pongids   Hominids
12. __   13. __   14. __

Pongo   *Gorilla*   *Pan*   *Homo*
15. __   16. __   17. __   18. __

Now answer the True/False, Multiple Choice and Short Answer sample test questions. Following completion of the tests correct them with the answers and textbook page references at the end of this Study Guide chapter. Note the areas in which you are strong and weak to guide you in your studying. Finally, answer the sample Essay Questions.

TRUE/FALSE QUESTIONS

1. Scientists who study the evolution, anatomy and behavior of nonhuman primates are forensic anthropologists.
   TRUE   FALSE

2. Primates are characterized by binocular (overlapping) vision and stereoscopic vision (depth perception).
   TRUE   FALSE

3. Traditionally, primate evolutionary trends have been explained by invoking the terrestrial adaptation -- primates are adapted to a life on the ground.
   TRUE   FALSE

4. Primates are found throughout the temperate zones of North America, Europe and Australia.
   TRUE   FALSE

5. Genetic and biochemical analyses have shown that chimps are more closely related to humans than they are to orangutans.
   TRUE   FALSE

6. The prosimian suborder includes the lemurs, lorises and tarsiers.
   TRUE   FALSE

7. Monkeys are generally smaller-bodied, smaller-brained and rely more on the sense of smell than do prosimians.
   TRUE   FALSE

8. The separate evolutionary development of similar characteristics in different groups of organisms is known as homoplasy.
   TRUE   FALSE

9. Typically gibbons knuckle-walk, chimps and gorillas brachiate and monkeys are bipedal.
   TRUE   FALSE

10. In September 2000, scientists declared that Miss Waldron's red colobus from West Africa was the first new monkey species to be discovered this millennium.
    TRUE   FALSE

MULTIPLE CHOICE QUESTIONS

1. Which of the following is **not** an evolutionary trend of primates?
    A. Increasing reliance on the sense of smell.
    B. A tendency for most species to be active during the day, i.e. diurnal.
    C. A trend towards omnivory.
    D. A tendency to develop color vision.

2. Primate evolutionary trends developed because most primates
    A. spend their lives in the trees.
    B. spend their lives on the ground.
    C. eat meat.
    D. are bipedal.

3. Binocular vision in primates results in
    A. color vision.
    B. dichromatic vision.
    C. panoramic vision.
    D. stereoscopic vision.

4. The dental formula 2-1-2-3 corresponds to what order of teeth?
    A. molar, pre-molars, canines, incisors.
    B. premolars, incisors, molars, canines.
    C. canines, premolars, incisors, molars.
    D. incisors, canines, premolars, molars.

5. All Old World monkeys, apes and humans share which of the following features?
    A. tails
    B. 2-1-2-3 dental formula
    C. arms that are relatively longer than their legs
    D. all of the above

6. The tarsier has a dental formula of 2-1-3-3/1-1-3-3. How many incisors does a tarsier have?
    A. 2
    B. 3
    C. 4
    D. 6

7. On which of the following continents would you **not** find any non-human primates living in the wild?
    A. Australia
    B. Asia
    C. Africa
    D. South America

8. Which of the following statements is correct?
    A. Most apes are arboreal quadrupeds.
    B. Terrestrial quadrupeds generally have much longer arms compared to their legs.
    C. Brachiators have longer hindlimbs than forelimbs.
    D. Prehensile tails are only found in some New World monkeys.

9. A form of locomotion found among some of the smaller lemurs and tarsiers is
    A. knuckle-walking.
    B. quadrupedalism.
    C. vertical clinging and leaping.
    D. bipedalism.

10. In what part of the world would you find a primate that has huge eyes, is exclusively carnivorous and is a spectacular clinger and leaper?
    A. South America.
    B. Africa.
    C. Madagascar.
    D. the islands of Southeast Asia.

11. In the traditional taxonomy, tarsiers are classified with the _____, but we now know that they share a more recent common ancestor with the _____.
    A. insectivores; rodents
    B. prosimians; anthropoids
    C. New World monkeys; Old World monkeys
    D. gibbons; lemurs

12. Prosimians are considered to be the most primitive of the primates. What does "primitive" mean in evolutionary biology?
    A. most like the ancestor
    B. poorly adapted
    C. inferior
    D. evolved later in time

13. In which type of primate would you find a "dental comb?"
    A. Old World Monkey.
    B. New World Monkey.
    C. lemur.
    D. gibbon.

14. Lemurs are found exclusively in
    A. Borneo.
    B. India.
    C. Madagascar.
    D. Sri Lanka.

15. Why are lemurs so diverse compared to lorises?
    A. Lemurs evolved much earlier than did lorises.
    B. Lemurs were isolated from competition with higher primates.
    C. Lemurs are much more geographically widespread.
    D. Lemurs live exclusively on the ground.

16. Which of the following traits is/are characteristic of the ring-tailed lemur?
    A. dental comb
    B. post-orbital bar
    C. 2-1-3-3 dental formula
    D. all of the above

17. Which of the following is **not** true of tarsiers?
    A. They are nocturnal.
    B. They are insectivorous.
    C. The live in large social groups.
    D. They can rotate their heads almost 180°.

18. Which of the following is **not** characteristic of anthropoids?
    A. a bony plate that encloses the orbit
    B. relatively shortened gestation period
    C. a relatively larger brain
    D. increased parental care

19. The only nocturnal anthropoid is the
    A. baboon.
    B. chimpanzee.
    C. howler monkey.
    D. owl monkey.

20. Which of the following is **not** true regarding New World monkeys?
    A. Some species have prehensile tails.
    B. Their nostrils face downward.
    C. Almost all species are arboreal.
    D. They include marmosets, spider monkeys and howler monkeys.

21. Which of the following structures are found in cercopithecines?
    A. ischial callosities
    B. prehensile tail
    C. claws
    D. dental comb

22. The term "sexual dimorphism" refers to
    A. differences in size and structure between males and females.
    B. differences in behavior between males and females.
    C. differences in reproductive physiology between males and females.
    D. parallel evolution between males and females of different species.

23. The period of sexual receptivity in non-human, female primates is called
    A. estrus.
    B. menarche.
    C. menstruation .
    D. hylobates.

24. New World monkeys and Old World monkeys have been geographically separated for a minimum of 30 million years, yet they are clearly recognizable as monkeys. This is an example of the evolutionary principle of
    A. reciprocal evolution.
    B. homoplasy.
    C. evolutionary reversal.
    D. Dollo's Law.

25. Which of the following hominoids demarcate their territories by sound?
    A. gibbons and siamangs.
    B. orangutans.
    C. gorillas.
    D. Humans.

26. A frugivore is standing in front of a vending machine. Which item will he select?
    A. Koala Brother's Eucalyptus Cough Drops.
    B. Rainbow Fruit Bar.
    C. Rigney's Chewing Gum.
    D. Rip Tyle's Chocolate-Covered Ants.

27. Which of the following statements are accurate in describing chimpanzees?
    A. They are exclusively insectivorous.
    B. They live in monogamous family units.
    C. They are almost always bipedal on the ground.
    D. They occasionally hunt and eat young monkeys.

28. In what way do bonobos differ from chimpanzees?
    A. They are more terrestrial than chimps.
    B. Their have relatively larger heads.
    C. Their legs are relatively longer.
    D. They have larger body sizes.

29. The prime-age male that dominates gorilla social groups is known as
    A. a redtail.
    B. a silverback.
    C. a blackback.
    D. the big Kahuna.

30. What biochemical and/or genetic methods have been used to determine the evolutionary relationships of the great apes and humans?
    A. chromosome banding patterns
    B. amino acid sequencing
    C. DNA hybridization
    D. all of the above

31. Which of the following is **not** a reason that many nonhuman primates are endangered?
    A. habitat destruction for logging, mining, and agriculture uses
    B. hunting for food and commercial products
    C. live capture for either the exotic pet trade or biomedical research
    D. establishment of biological reserves

32. In 1973, the implementation of what international agreement caused a dramatic decline in live capture of non-human primates?
    A. NASA
    B. OPFOR
    C. CITES
    D. UNESCO

SHORT ANSWER QUESTIONS (& PAGE REFERENCES)

1. Describe five features that can be used to distinguish primates from other mammals. (pp. 103-105)

2. Describe three different modes of primate locomotion. (pp. 112-114)

3. What do the banding patterns of chromosomes tell us about chimp and human evolutionary relationships? (pp. 115-116)

4. How do apes differ from monkeys? (p. 124)

5. In what ways are chimps and gorillas similar? How do they differ? (pp. 126-128)

ESSAY QUESTIONS (& PAGE REFERENCES)

1. Compare and contrast the traditional arboreal hypothesis for the evolution of the primates to the visual predation hypothesis. (pp. 106-108)

2. Why do some primate taxonomists classify tarsiers as prosimians while others refer to them as haplorhines? (pp. 114-115, 117)

3. What are the major challenges facing primate conservationists? What approaches to primate conservation appear to be the most promising? (pp. 130-132)

ANSWERS, *CORRECTED STATEMENT* IF FALSE & REFERENCES TO TRUE/FALSE QUESTIONS

1. FALSE, p. 103, Scientists who study the evolution, anatomy and behavior of nonhuman primates are *primatologists*.

2. TRUE, p. 104.

3. FALSE, pp. 106-108, Traditionally, primate evolutionary trends have been explained by invoking the *arboreal* adaptation -- primates are adapted to a life *in the trees*.

4. FALSE, pp. 108, 110-111, Primates are found throughout the *subtropical and tropical* zones of *South America, Africa and Asia*.

5. TRUE, p. 116

6. TRUE, pp. 115, 117-119

7. FALSE, p. 119, Monkeys are generally *larger*-bodied, *larger*-brained and rely *less* on the sense of smell than do prosimians.

8. TRUE, pp. 123-124

9. FALSE, pp. 124, 126-130, Typically gibbons *brachiate*, chimps and gorillas *knuckle-walk* and *humans* are bipedal.

10. FALSE, p. 130, In September 2000, scientists declared that Miss Waldron's red colobus from West Africa was the first monkey species to be *officially declared extinct* this millennium.

ANSWERS & REFERENCES TO MULTIPLE CHOICE QUESTIONS

1. A, pp. 103-105	17. C, p. 119
2. A, pp. 106-107	18. B, p. 120
3. D, p. 104	19. D, p. 120
4. D, p. 109	20. B, p. 120
5. B, p. 109	21. A, pp. 121-122
6. D, p. 109	22. A, p. 123
7. A, p. 108	23. A, p. 123
8. D, pp. 112-114	24. B, pp. 123-124
9. C, p. 113	25. A, p. 124
10. D, p. 119	26. B, p. 125
11. B, p. 117	27. D, p. 128
12. A, p. 117	28. C, p. 128
13. C, pp. 117-118	29. B, p. 126
14. C, p. 118	30. D, pp. 115-116
15. B, pp. 118-119	31. D, p. 130
16. D, p. 118	32. C, p. 131

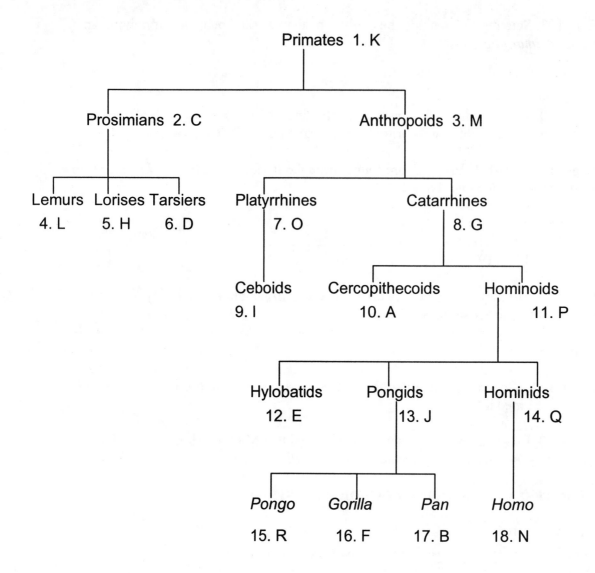

Primates 1. K

Prosimians 2. C   Anthropoids 3. M

Lemurs Lorises Tarsiers   Platyrrhines   Catarrhines
4. L   5. H   6. D   7. O   8. G

Ceboids   Cercopithecoids   Hominoids
9. I   10. A   11. P

Hylobatids   Pongids   Hominids
12. E   13. J   14. Q

Pongo   Gorilla   Pan   Homo
15. R   16. F   17. B   18. N

CHAPTER 6
FUNDAMENTALS OF PRIMATE BEHAVIOR

LEARNING OBJECTIVES

After reading this chapter you should be able to:
- understand why anthropologists study nonhuman primate behavior. (p. 139-140)
- understand the importance of behavioral ecology is explaining the evolution of primate behavior. (pp. 141-144)
- describe different types of non-human primate social groups. (p. 146-147)
- discuss aspects of social behavior found among all nonhuman primates, i.e., dominance hierarchies, communication, grooming, aggression, reproductive strategies, mother-infant relationship, and alloparenting. (pp. 148-157)

CHAPTER OUTLINE
Introduction
 In the last chapter you were introduced to the primate order and some of the biological characteristics that distinguish different groups of primates. In this chapter we look at behavioral characteristics found among primates including dominance, grooming, reproductive strategies and mother-infant relationships. We discuss field methods in primatology and the complexity of interpreting data from a behavioral ecology perspective.

I PRIMATE FIELD STUDIES
 A. Animals living in their natural habitat are referred to as free-ranging.
 B. To understand the adaptations and behaviors of nonhuman primates it is necessary to study them in their natural habitat.
 C. It is difficult to study arboreal primates.
 D. Most systematic information on primates comes from free-ranging animals that spend considerable time on the ground.
  1. Another approach is to study provisioned colonies of primates.
  2. Cayo Santiago Island off the coast of Puerto Rico is an example of a large provisioned colony of primates.
 E. Primatologists are gaining a fuller understanding of primate adaptation and behavior.
  1. Data on primate life history is becoming more plentiful because of long-term studies.
  2. Life history traits are characteristics or developmental stages that influence reproductive rates of individuals in a species.
II THE EVOLUTION OF BEHAVIOR
 A. Scientists studying free-ranging primate behavior do so within an ecological and evolutionary framework.
  1. This approach is known as behavioral ecology.
  2. It is based on the premise that all components of an ecosystem evolved in concert.
 B. Behavioral ecology looks at the evolution of behavior through natural selection
  1. Behavioral ecology views behavior as a phenotypic expression.
  2. Individuals whose genotypes influence behavioral phenotypes may have higher reproductive success.

C. A criticism of behavioral ecology is the simplistic perception that single genes code for specific behaviors.
   1. Controversy arises when attempts are made to apply this paradigm to humans.
   2. The fear is that if behaviors are explained in terms of genetics it could be used to support racist views.
D. Among insects and lower vertebrates behavioral patterns are innate.
   1. Among primates and humans most behavior results from learning.
   2. In higher organisms some behaviors are influenced by gene products, such as hormones.
   3. Increased levels of testosterone has been shown to increase aggressive behavior in many non-human species.
E. Behavior is a highly complex trait and is the product of interactions between genetic and environmental factors.
   1. There is considerable variation in behavioral plasticity between species.
      a. Plasticity refers to the capacity for change, how flexible within-species behavior can be in differing situations.
   2. Not only the ecological setting, but a species' evolutionary history, shapes its behavioral repertoire.
F. Problems arise when trying to apply the mechanics of behavioral evolution in complex social animals.
   1. There is a need to determine which behaviors have a genetic basis and how they affect reproductive success.
   2. This is difficult because we must learn more about genotype-phenotype interactions in complex traits and we need accurate long-term data on reproductive success in primate groups.
   3. Thus an evolutionary approach such as behavioral ecology offers hypotheses to be tested, not precise explanations of primate behavior.
G. Behavioral ecology grew out of two different approaches to studying animal behavior.
   1. Socioecology studies animals and their habitats.
   2. Sociobiology emphasizes natural selection's influence on behavior, but largely neglects ecological factors.
H. Sarah Blaffer Hrdy's explanation of infanticide among Hanuman langurs of India is cited as one of the best examples of sociobiological theory among primates.
   1. Infanticide is found in many primate species. It usually occurs in conjunction with the transfer of a new male into a group.
   2. When a new male takes over a Hanuman langur harem, he will often attempt to kill the nursing infants in the group.
   3. If the infanticidal male is successful, the mother who just lost her infant ceases to lactate and becomes sexually receptive within 2-3 months.
   4. This system benefits the infanticidal male because he does not have to wait for the females to wean their offspring.
      a. If he did wait, he would be unlikely to sire any offspring because male tenure in harems is only 2-3 years and he would be supplanted before any of his offspring were weaned.

        b. If he was supplanted by an infanticidal male, he would likely not contribute any genes to the next generation because all of his offspring would be at risk of attack from the new male.
    5. Some dispute the sociobiological explanation for infanticide.
        a. Other explanations include competition for resources, aberrant behavior caused by human overcrowding and questioning the actual prevalence of infanticide in primates.

I. Behavioral ecology explanations incorporate ecological interactions that have been largely ignored by sociobiology's focus on individual reproductive success.
    1. A behavioral ecological perspective on one behavioral element, for example the social structure of a given primate species, would have to take into account:
        a. Quality and quantity of diet
        b. Food resource distribution.
        c. Body size
        d. Basal metabolic rate
        e. Water distribution
        f. Predator distribution and types
        g. Sleeping site distribution
        h. Activity patterns
        i. Relationships with other primate and non-primate (non-predatory) species.
        j. Human activity and its impacts
    2. The complex interrelationships of ecology, social structure and behavior are not yet fully understood.
        a. Nevertheless, numerous factors suggest that group structure is related to problems in finding food and avoiding predators.
        b. For example, it has been traditionally understood that multimale, multifemale primate groups are common in areas where predation rates are high.
        c. More animals in the group are more likely to spot predators and warn their group-mates.
    3. Solitary foraging may be related to diet and distribution of resources.
        a. The loris is an example of a solitary feeder which avoids competition.
        b. Solitary foraging may also be related to predator avoidance.
    4. Large-bodied females foraging alone or with offspring may have little to fear from predators.
        a. Feeding alone may maximize access to food and minimize dietary competition from other females in the same species.

III   FIVE MONKEY SPECIES IN THE KIBALE FOREST, UGANDA
  A. Five monkey species have been studied in detail in the Kibale Forest of western Uganda.
  B. Sympatric refers to different species living in the same area.
    1. Black and white colobus monkeys are found in one-male groups.
    2. Red colobus monkeys are found in multimale/multifemale groups.
  C. Many primate species are exceedingly flexible regarding group composition.
    1. Omnivores move about more than folivores.
    2. The smaller individual body sizes are, the larger the groups tends to be.
    3. The area exploited by an animal or social group is called the home range.

IV   PRIMATE SOCIAL GROUPS
    A. Primates solve their major adaptive problems within the context of social groups.
    B. Typically, primate social groups include both sexes and all ages.
    C. One possible explanation for permanent social groups among primates is predator avoidance.
        1. Primates are preyed upon by eagles, snakes, leopards, other non-human primates and humans.
    D. Another theory for group living is defense of resources.
    E. One of the disadvantages of group living is intragroup competition resulting in an increase in aggression.
    F. The actual make-up of a social group is its group composition.
    G. The composition of social groups is influenced by diet, body size, activity patterns, availability of resources and mating patterns.
    H. Dispersal refers to members of one sex leaving their natal group around the time they reach puberty.
        1. One common theme in dispersal is that those individuals who leave usually find mates outside their natal group.
        2. Two possible explanations for dispersal are reduced competition for mates and the decreased likelihood of close inbreeding.
    I. The philopatric sex remains in their natal group.
    J. The roles played by dispersal and philopatry are not yet fully understood.
    K. In social groups individuals must be able to evaluate a situation before acting.
V   PRIMATE SOCIAL BEHAVIOR
    A. Dominance
        1. Dominance hierarchies impose a degree of order within the group.
        2. Dominant animals have priority access to food and mating partners.
        3. Rank is not permanent.
            a. Many factors influence one's status including sex, age, level of aggression, time spent in group, intelligence, motivation and mother's social position.
        4. Position in the hierarchy is learned.
        5. Gestures and behaviors are indications of dominance and subordination.
        6. Young primates learn how to negotiate through social interactions by early contact with their mother and exposure to their peers' behavior.
    B. Communication
        1. Any act that conveys information to another individual, either intentionally or unintentionally, is communication.
            a. Raised body hair or enhanced body odor are examples of autonomic communication.
            b. Vocalizations, intense staring and branch shaking are examples of deliberate modes of communication.
        2. Threat gestures might include a quick yawn to expose canines or bobbing back and forth in a crouched position.
        3. Reassurance can take the form of touching, patting, hugging or holding hands.
        4. The fear grin is seen in all primates to indicate fear and submission.
        5. Mounting among baboons is used to express dominance.
        6. Vocalizations are used to inform others that predators may be present.

7. Displays serve to communicate emotional states.
8. Communication is what makes social living possible.
C. Aggressive and affiliative interactions
   1. Affiliative interactions promote group cohesion.
      a. Affiliative behaviors pertain to amicable associations between individuals.
      b. Affiliative behaviors reduce levels of aggression.
      c. Most affiliative behaviors involve physical contact.
   2. Grooming is one of the most important affiliative behaviors among primates.
      a. Grooming is not only hygienic but it is immensely pleasurable.
      b. Grooming reinforces social bonds.
   3. Aggressive interactions can lead to group disruption.
      a. Conflict within a group is often caused by competition for resources, such as mating partners or food.
      b. Often these conflicts can be resolved by gestures and displays within the context of the dominance hierarchy.
   4. But oftentimes violence is a consequence of aggressive interactions.
      a. Hugging, kissing and grooming are all forms used in reconciliation after aggressive encounters.

VI REPRODUCTION AND REPRODUCTIVE STRATEGIES
   A. Females are sexually receptive when they are in estrus.
      1. Visual cues to a female's sexual readiness include swelling and changes in color of the skin around the genital area.
   B. The temporary relationship between male and female savanna baboons for mating purposes is called a consortship.
   C. Male and female bonobos may mate even when the female is not in estrus.
      1. This behavior is not typical of chimpanzee males and females.
   D. Reproductive strategies
      1. The goal is to produce and rear to adulthood as many offspring as possible.
      2. K-selection refers to the production of a few young with a large investment of parental care.
      3. R-selection refers to the production of many offspring with little parental care.
      4. Males and females have different strategies to meet life's challenges.
      5. Metabolic demands on female primates due to pregnancy, lactation and caring for offspring are enormous.
         a. Many female primates are viciously competitive to protect valuable food resources from other females.
      6. To increase his genetic contribution to the next generation, male primates will secure as many mates as possible.
      7. Male competition for mates and mate choice in females are both examples of sexual selection.
         a. Female birds frequently select males with vividly colored plumage.
         b. Males of many primate species are larger than females.
         c. The testes in males of multi-male groups are larger than males in other types of groups.
         d. In groups where mating is monogamous sexual dimorphism is reduced.

VII MOTHERS AND INFANTS

    A. Except in those species in which monogamy or polyandry occurs, males do not participate in rearing offspring.

    B. For a non-human primate mother to properly care for her offspring she should have had a normal upbringing with her own mother.

    C. In an experiment where monkeys were raised with no mother, they were incapable of forming lasting positive emotional ties to their own offspring.

    D. Monkeys need to learn rules of social behavior.

    E. The close mother-infant relationship does not always end with weaning.

    F. Social isolation can have devastating effects on subsequent development and behavior of many primate species.

    G. In some species adult males are involved in the care of offspring.

    H. Alloparenting is a term used for individuals other than the mother holding and interacting with an infant.

KEY TERMS

affiliative: friendly relations between individuals.

agonistic: aggressive or defensive social interactions

alloparenting: individuals other than the parents take care of infants.

autonomic: involuntary physiological responses

behavioral ecology: the study of the evolution of behavior, emphasizing the role of ecological factors as agents of natural selection

consortships: temporary relationship between one adult male and an estrous female

conspecifics: members of the same species

core areas: a portion of a home range where reliable resources are found such as food, water and sleeping trees

dispersal: members of one sex leave the natal group at puberty

displays: physical movements that convey an emotional state

diurnal: active during the day

dominance hierarchies: systems of social organization wherein individuals are ranked relative to one another based on priority access to food and sex.

ecological: the relationship between organisms and all aspects of their environment

estrus: period of sexual receptivity in female mammals (except humans) correlated with ovulation.

evolutionary ecology: behavioral attributes that have evolved due to demands imposed by a particular environment.

free-ranging: noncaptive animals living in their natural habitat

grooming: picking through fur to remove dirt, parasites or any other material that may be present.

home-range: the geographic area, usually permanent, exploited by an animal or social group for food, water and sleeping areas.

inclusive fitness: the total contribution of an individual's genes to the next generation, including those genes shared by close relatives.

infanticide: the killing of infants

inter: between (i.e., intergroup)

intra: within (i.e., intragroup)

K-selected: a reproductive strategy wherein the individuals produce fewer offspring but increase parental investment of care, time and energy

monogamous pair: a mated pair and its young.

natal group: the group in which an individual is born.

nocturnal: active at night

philopatric: remaining in one's natal group or home range as an adult.

physiology: the physical and chemical phenomena involved with the functions and activities of an organism or any of its various parts

polyandry: one female with multiple males.

presenting: a subordinate animal presents his/her rear to a dominant animal

reproductive strategies: behavioral patterns that contribute to an individual's reproductive success, i.e., producing and successfully rearing to adulthood as many offspring as possible.

R-selected: a reproductive strategy wherein individuals produce many offspring and provide relatively little parental investment of care, time and energy.

sexual selection: a type of natural selection operating on one sex (usually males). It may be the result of males competing for mates or female preference in choosing sexual partners.

social grooming: grooming done for pleasure. Common among primates and reinforces social relationships.

social structure: the composition, size and sex ratio of a group of animals.

sociobiology: a theoretical framework which looks at behavior within an evolutionary context. If a behavior has a genetic basis it will be subject to natural selection.

socioecology: attempts to find patterns of relationship between environment, biological needs and social behaviors when studying animals

sympatric: two or more species who live in the same area.

territory: the part of the home range that animals will defend

INTERNET & *INFOTRAC COLLEGE EDITION* EXERCISES

Are you interested in a potential career in primatology? Primate Info Net, the excellent web site you visited last chapter (http://www.primate.wisc.edu/pin/), has contributions from professionals in the field discussing what it takes to forge a career studying primates. Read what Dr. Kevin Hunt (Indiana University) has written concerning field research in primatology (http://www.primate.wisc.edu/pin/careers/hunt.html) or what Helena Fitch-Snyder of the Zoological Society of San Diego's Center for the Reproduction of Endangered Species (CRES) has to say about zoo careers (http://www.primate.wisc.edu/pin/careers/fitch.html).

Primate Info Net also has a comprehensive list of resources concerning primate behavior and ecology (http://www.primate.wisc.edu/pin/behavior.html). Browse through the categories listed and click on a few of the hyperlinks under "Social Behavior" to learn more about non-human primate behavior from the researchers themselves.

In *InfoTrac* do a keyword search on "chimpanzee behavior." Read a couple of the listed articles (by DeWaal, Vogel, Bower and/or Stanford) in order to answer the question: Do chimpanzees have culture?

Now answer the True/False, Multiple Choice and Short Answer sample test questions. Following completion of the tests correct them with the answers and textbook page references at the end of this Study Guide chapter. Note the areas in which you are strong and weak to guide you in your studying. Finally, answer the sample Essay Questions.

TRUE/FALSE QUESTIONS

1. The primary goal of primate field studies is to collect information on captive animals that are generally influenced by human activity.
    TRUE   FALSE

2. The study of the evolution of behavior, emphasizing the role of ecological factors as agents of natural selection is known as behavioral ecology.
    TRUE   FALSE

3. Infanticide in Hanuman langurs has been regarded as one of the best examples of a sociobiological explanation of primate behavior.
    TRUE   FALSE

4. The sex that transfers out of its natal group is known as the philopatric sex. In most primate species the philopatric sex is male.
    TRUE   FALSE

5. Many (but not all) primatologists postulate that the primary benefit of dominance is the increased reproductive success of the individual.
    TRUE   FALSE

6. Aggressive interactions pertain to amicable associations between individuals. Aggressive behaviors, such as grooming, reinforce social bonds and promote group cohesion.
    TRUE   FALSE

7. Behaviors that are removed from their original context and sometimes exaggerated to covey information are known as ritualized behaviors.
    TRUE   FALSE

8. In most primate species, sexual behavior is not tied to the female's reproductive cycle, with females sexually receptive to males at any time throughout the cycle.
    TRUE   FALSE

9. R-selection is a type of natural selection that operates only on one sex within a species, that results from competition for mates.
    TRUE   FALSE

10. Alloparenting is a common behavior in many primate species in which individuals other that the parent(s) hold, carry and interact with infants.
    TRUE   FALSE

MULTIPLE CHOICE QUESTIONS

1. Which of the following disciplines has **not** been concerned with the study of nonhuman primates?
    A. Psychology
    B. Zoology
    C. Geology
    D. Anthropology

2. Studies of free-ranging primates
    A. in their natural habitats has become a focus of anthropology.
    B. is generally very challenging because most are arboreal and can move swiftly through dense vegetation.
    C. are not necessarily uninfluenced by human activities.
    D. all of the above

3. Characteristics or developmental stages that influence reproductive rates of individuals are
    A. dominance hierarchies.
    B. life history traits.
    C. K-selected.
    D. polyandrous.

4. Among primates, _____ can be viewed as adaptive responses to environmental demands.
    A. behaviors
    B. blood types
    C. dental formulas
    D. all of the above

5. One of the underlying assumptions of behavioral ecology is that
    A. intelligent organisms can manipulate their environment.
    B. the various components of ecological systems evolved together.
    C. social structures are completely independent of ecological structures.
    D. the distribution of sleeping sites determines a species activity pattern.

6. The social structure of a given primate species is influenced by
    A. distribution of food resources.
    B. the types of predators inhabiting the environment.
    C. relationships with other sympatric primate species.
    D. all of the above

7. Where predation pressure is high we generally find group composition to be
    A. multimale/multifemale.
    B. one male harem.
    C. a monogamous pair.
    D. solitary.

8. Savannah baboons are an excellent example of
    A. monogamous pair social structure.
    B. solitary social structure.
    C. multimale/multifemale social structure.
    D. one male harem social structure.

9. The excellent example of a solitary, insectivorous, nocturnal forager is the
    A. loris.
    B. Diana monkey.
    C. gibbon.
    D. all of the above

10. The detailed study of monkeys in the Kibale Forest of Uganda reveals that
    A. colobus, mangabeys and red-tailed monkeys all follow a similar pattern in exploiting the environment.
    B. all monkeys eat the same foods.
    C. male and female reproductive strategies are identical.
    D. there is little correlation between social organization and feeding strategies.

11. The sympatric species studied in the Kibale Forest of Uganda
    A. differ with regard to anatomy.
    B. differ with regard to behavior.
    C. differ with regard to dietary preference.
    D. all of the above

12. In the Kibale study
    A. omnivores are more mobile than folivores.
    B. the smallest omnivores live in the smallest groups.
    C. omnivore population density is greater than that it folivores.
    D. all of the above

13. Behavioral ecology grew out of which two different approaches to animal behavior?
    A. genetics and cultural anthropology
    B. paleontology and ethnology
    C. socioecology and sociobiology
    D. psychology and linguistics

14. Unlike in primates, the behavior of insects is
    A. primarily innate.
    B. learned.
    C. culturally transmitted.
    D. none of the above

15. Sociobiology is narrower than behavioral ecology because the former does not strongly emphasize
    A. ecological factors.
    B. the effects of natural selection in explaining animal behavior.
    C. the input of genetics on the manifestation of behavior.
    D. that behaviors are the result of the interactions between genotype and phenotype.

16. Among non-human primates a polyandrous social group would include
    A. one female with two males
    B. one male with one female
    C. one male with two females
    D. none of the above

17. Which of the following do **not** prey on primates?
    A. Bears
    B. Eagles
    C. Humans
    D. Other primates

18. Group living in primates helps individuals to primarily defend resources from
    A. predators.
    B. other members of the same species.
    C. members of different primate species.
    D. domestic livestock.

19. The philopatric sex
    A. does not reproduce.
    B. protects the group from predators
    C. remains in the natal group.
    D. transfers out of the natal group.

20. Dispersal in primate behavior refers to
    A. food distribution in the home range.
    B. the manner in which males and females exploit the environment.
    C. spreading seeds to germinate.
    D. one sex leaving the natal group.

21. Nonhuman primates must be able to evaluate a situation before acting. To this end, selective pressure has been placed on
    A. social intelligence
    B. a more complex brain
    C. the ability to store information
    D. all of the above

22. Dominance hierarchies
    A. increase aggression and fighting within a group.
    B. have no apparent function in social groups.
    C. provide a degree of order in social groups.
    D. are limited to adult males.

23. Dominance hierarchies
    A. likely give dominant males a reproductive advantage.
    B. do not result in dominant females having priority access to food.
    C. are found only in monogamous and solitary primates.
    D. are permanent and inflexible.

24. Unintentional modes of communication among primates (including humans) might include
    A. enhanced body odor ("fear sweat").
    B. raised body hair ("goose bumps").
    C. blushing.
    D. all of the above.

25. Which of the following is not a threat gesture among nonhuman primates?
    A. a quick yawn to expose canines
    B. an intense stare
    C. bobbing back and forth
    D. mounting

26. Displays
    A. communicate an emotional state.
    B. reassure others in the group.
    C. console others.
    D. all of the above

27. Affiliative behaviors
    A. are amicable associations between individuals.
    B. defuse potentially dangerous situations.
    C. promote group cohesiveness.
    D. all of the above

28. Grooming
    A. rarely occurs in primate social groups.
    B. often causes aggression between primate individuals.
    C. is only a hygienic activity.
    D. none of the above

29. Primate reproductive strategies
    A. are similar for males and females.
    B. are K-selected.
    C. are r-selected.
    D. none of the above

30. Sexual selection
    A. is a type of natural selection.
    B. operates on only one sex.
    C. is the result of competition for mates.
    D. all of the above

31. The larger testes seen in males of some multimale groups may be the result of
    A. monogamy.
    B. "sperm competition."
    C. consort pairing.
    D. dominance.

32. In which of the following species do males **not** participate in the rearing of the young?
    A. gibbons
    B. marmosets
    C. orangutans
    D. tamarins

33. Mothering among primates appears to be
    A. completely innate.
    B. of minor importance in the development of offspring.
    C. dependent on a normal experience with one's own mother.
    D. all of the above

34. Alloparenting
    A. is not as common in primates as in other mammals.
    B. may help young females train for motherhood.
    C. does not often occur since female primates are extremely possessive of their offspring.
    D. is the adoption of an orphan primate by a female of another primate species.

SHORT ANSWER QUESTIONS (& PAGE REFERENCES)

1. What are the goals of primate field studies? (pp. 139-140)

2. Describe three different kinds of primate social groups. (Box 6-1, p. 146)

3. What is the difference between autonomic and deliberate forms of primate communication? (p. 149)

4. What are the various functions of grooming in primate societies? (pp. 152-153)

5. Explain the difference between K-selection and R-selection. (p. 154)

ESSAY QUESTIONS (& PAGE REFERENCES)

1. Compare and contrast behavioral ecology to sociobiology as theoretical approaches to explaining primate behavior. (pp. 141-143)

2. How are dominance hierarchies in primates organized and what functions do they serve for individuals and primate groups? (p. 148, 151)

3. How and why do male and female reproductive strategies differ? (pp. 154-155)

ANSWERS, *CORRECTED STATEMENT* IF FALSE & REFERENCES TO TRUE/FALSE QUESTIONS

1. FALSE, p. 139, The primary goal of primate field studies is to collect information on *free-ranging* animals that are generally *uninfluenced* by human activity.

2. TRUE, p. 141.

3. TRUE, p. 142.

4. FALSE, p. 147, The sex that *remains in* its natal group is known as the philopatric sex. In most primate species the philopatric sex is *female*.

5. TRUE, p. 148

6. FALSE, p. 151, *Affiliative* interactions pertain to amicable associations between individuals. *Affiliative* behaviors, such as grooming, reinforce social bonds and promote group cohesion.

7. TRUE, p. 150

8. FALSE, p. 153, In most primate species, sexual behavior is ~~not~~ tied to the female's reproductive cycle, with females sexually receptive to males *only when they are in estrus*.

9. FALSE, p. 155, *Sexual selection* is a type of natural selection that operates only on one sex within a species, that results from competition for mates.

10. TRUE, p. 157

Answers and References to Multiple Choice Questions

1. C, p. 139
2. D, pp. 139-140
3. B, p. 140
4. A, p. 141
5. B, p. 141
6. D, pp. 142-143
7. A, p. 143
8. C, p. 143
9. A, p. 144
10. D, pp. 144-145
11. D, p. 144
12. A, p. 146
13. C, pp. 141-142
14. A, p. 141

15. A, p. 142
16. A, p. 155
17. A, p. 147
18. B, p. 147
19. C, p. 147
20. D, p. 147
21. D, p. 147
22. C, p. 148
23. A, p. 148
24. D, p. 149
25. D, p. 149
26. A, p. 150
27. D, p. 151
28. D, p. 152

29. B, p. 154
30. D, p. 155
31. B, p. 155
32. C, p. 157
33. C, p. 156
34. B, p. 157

CHAPTER 7
MODELS FOR HUMAN EVOLUTION

LEARNING OBJECTIVES

After reading this chapter you should be able to:
- describe characteristics that set humans apart from other primates (p. 162)
- understand the relationship between primate body size and diet (pp. 162-163)
- discuss the index of encephalization and its importance in hominid evolution (p. 164)
- give a brief overview of language studies done with nonhuman primates (pp. 164-167)
- understand the basics of neurobiology and its relationship to producing and understanding language (pp. 167-169)
- distinguish affiliative behaviors among nonhuman primates (pp. 176-177)
- analyze and debate the motivation and advantages of aggressive interactions among nonhuman primates and their possible implications for human evolution (pp. 173-175)
- discuss what makes chimpanzees good models for early hominid cultural evolution (pp. 170-173)

CHAPTER OUTLINE

Introduction

In the last chapter we looked at some behavioral patterns among primates, methodologies of primatology, and the underpinnings of behavioral ecology. In this chapter we explore the relationship between body size and brain size, language capabilities, nonhuman primate cultural behaviors, aggressive interactions, affiliation, altruism and cooperation. We then address what their adaptive significance might be and what this might imply about human evolution. We end the chapter with a comparison of human and nonhuman primate behavioral similarities.

I. INTRODUCTION
   A. Intelligence is another term for behavioral complexity.
   B. The predisposition for complex social life provided a foundation for the evolution of early hominids.
   C. The ability to learn is rooted in biological factors.
   D. Investigating behavioral patterns among human and nonhuman primates can be fruitful.
   E. Because behaviors have developed as a function of natural selection, they must be viewed within the context of behavioral ecology and as components of life history.

II. BEHAVIOR AND HUMAN ORIGINS
   A. When compared with other primates humans are not really that unique.
   B. Behavioral attributes set humans apart from other primates.
      1. Culture became key in our coping with environmental challenges.
      2. Our use of symbolic language also sets us apart from our closest relatives.
   C. Several other features distinguish us from other primates:
      1. Bipedality is the human mode of locomotion.

2. Humans live in permanent bisexual social groups.
3. Human brains are very large relative to body size.
4. Humans have an economic division of labor by sex.
5. There are no obvious signs of estrus in human females.
D. Modern African apes and humans last shared a common ancestor between 8 and 5 million years ago.
E. We study the behavior of our closest relatives to see what hominid behavior may have been like before culture became a significant factor.

III. ASPECTS OF LIFE HISTORY AND BODY SIZE
A. A crucial factor that influences all aspects of life history is body size.
1. Body size includes body mass and weight.
2. Primate body weight ranges from 66 g or 2.4 ounces to 117 kg. or 258 pounds.
B. Body size greatly influences diet.
1. Smaller bodied species primarily eat insects.
2. Larger bodied species primarily eat leaves.
3. Almost all species eat some fruit.
C. Body size is closely correlated with metabolic rates.
1. Small animals have higher energy needs than larger animals.
2. Larger animals expend relatively less energy.
D. Body size is also correlated with locomotion and habitat preference.
1. Small, arboreal primates generally leap through the trees.
2. Suspensory behavior is found among larger arboreal primates.
3. Monkeys that weigh over 10 kg (22 lbs) are usually terrestrial.
E. Body size and brain size
1. Brain size and body size are closely correlated.
2. Proportional brain size is more important than absolute brain size.
3. The index of encephalization is the predictable relationship between body and brain size in a species.
F. Modern humans are much more encephalized than early members of the genus *Homo* and the primitive hominids, the australopithecines.
1. In both humans and nonhuman primates the brain grows rapidly before or immediately after birth.
2. In humans rapid brain growth also occurs for at least the first year after birth.
3. Early hominids varied from *Homo sapiens* in body size.
4. Allometry refers to the relative growth of one anatomical part in relation to the entire organism.

IV. LANGUAGE CAPABILITIES
A. Nonhuman primates do not use language the same way humans do.
1. Vervet monkeys have three different vocalizations to indicate the presence of different predators.
B. Human language, as a mode of communication, is open.
1. Humans have the ability to think symbolically.
C. Humans and apes have differences in the anatomy of the vocal-tract and the language-related structures in the brain.

D. Different apes have demonstrated varying degrees of human-like language capabilities.
    1. Washoe, an infant female chimpanzee, learned ASL (American Sign Language for the deaf).
    2. Sara, another chimpanzee, learned to recognize plastic chips as symbols for objects.
    3. Koko, a female gorilla uses more than 500 signs of ASL.
    4. A male orangutan named Chantek learned to sign in reference to objects that were not present.
    5. Chimps have also shown that they can categorize unfamiliar objects.
    6. Kanzi, an infant male bonobo, spontaneously acquired language and used symbols by the age of 2½ years.
E. For human evolution communication became very important.
    1. For most humans the language center of the brain is located in the left hemisphere.
    2. Wernicke's area is involved with perception of speech.
    3. Broca's area is involved with production of speech.
    4. The reorganization of neurological structures enabled humans to develop language.

V.   PRIMATE CULTURAL BEHAVIOR
A. Most biological anthropologists feel that it is appropriate to use the term culture in referring to nonhuman primates as well as humans.
B. Cultural behavior is learned and passed on from one generation to the next.
    1. Young primate infants learn appropriate behaviors.
    2. Imo was a Japanese macaque who began washing her sweet potatoes in sea water before eating them.
    3. Imo also invented an efficient way to clean sand out of grain.
C. Chimpanzee cultural behaviors, including tool making and use, are very well documented.
    1. Examples of chimpanzee tools include termite fishing sticks, leaf sponges, twigs as toothpicks and stones as weapons.
    2. Chimpanzees exhibit regional variation in their tool use.
    3. Kanzi, the captive male bonobo, learned to make sharp-edged flakes by throwing the stone onto a concrete floor.
D. Evolution is not directed towards producing humans.
    1. Such a view is termed anthropocentric.
    2. Nonhuman primate behaviors that have been recently documented by humans are not newly-developed in our nonhuman primate relatives.

VI.   AGGRESSIVE INTERACTIONS BETWEEN GROUPS
A. Primate land-use and defense:
    1. Members of the same species are referred to as conspecifics.
    2. The home range is the area where a primate lives permanently.
    3. Territories are portions of the home range that are actively defended against conspecifics.
    4. The core area within the home range is richest in resources and is the area that a primate would most frequently defend.

5. Nonaggressive arboreal primates use vocalizations to avoid other groups in the canopy.
B. Chimpanzee territoriality is atypical for primates and males are particularly intolerant of strangers.
1. Before entering a peripheral area chimpanzees will hoot and display to see if any other animals are around.
2. Chimps are tense and quiet when they patrol their community's borders.
3. Chimpanzee border patrols have been observed and documented brutally attacking outnumbered individuals.
4. Chimpanzee males have strong affiliative bonds between adult males of the same group.
C. Humans and chimpanzees are the only known mammalian species where lethal and unprovoked aggression occurs between conspecific groups.
1. In chimpanzees and most traditional human cultures males are philopatric.
2. In most conflicts involving females the attacks are not fatal.
3. The apparent benefits to lethal aggressive behavior seems to be acquisition of mating partners and food.
4. Shared patterns of strife between populations may be a predisposition that chimpanzees and early hominids inherited from a common ancestor.
VII. AFFILIATION, ALTRUISM, AND COOPERATION
A. Some affiliative behaviors appear to be examples of care giving or compassion.
B. Little Bee, a chimpanzee from Gombe, brought food to her mother as she lay dying.
C. Altruism
1. Altruism refers to behaviors that benefit others with some risk or sacrifice to the performer.
2. Protecting dependent offspring is the most fundamental of altruistic behaviors.
3. Washoe once rescued an unrelated infant from a water-filled moat.
4. Among macaques, baboons and chimpanzees orphans are sometimes adopted.
D. Cooperation
1. Cooperative behaviors may benefit the participants.
2. It appears that chimpanzee groups may often hunt cooperatively.
3. Chimpanzee hunting is a highly goal-directed activity.
4. After the kill the meat is usually shared.
5. Cooperative hunting among chimpanzees may provide insights into how this behavior developed in the human lineage.
VIII. THE PRIMATE CONTINUUM
A. When traits or behaviors continuously grade into one another so that there are no discrete categories these characteristics are said to be part of a continuum.
1. Differences in many human and chimpanzee behaviors are therefore differences in degree, not kind.

KEY TERMS

affiliation: friendly relations between individuals.

allometry: the relative growth of a part of an organism in relation to the entire organism.

altruism: helping another individual at some risk or cost but with no direct benefit to oneself.

anthropocentic: interpreting nonhuman traits and behaviors from the perspective of human values and experiences. Viewing humans as the most important entity in the world.

biological continuum: traits and behaviors that continuously grade into one another with no discrete categories in organisms that are related through common ancestry.

bisexual: refers to both sexes

Broca's area: an area of the brain responsible for the production of speech.

conspecifics: members of the same species.

core areas: a portion of a home range where reliable resources are found such as food, water and sleeping trees.

encephalization: a predictable relationship between brain size and body size.

home range: a geographic area where a primate group remains permanently.

life history: components of an animal's development and physiology including body size, proportional brain size, metabolism, maturation, lifestyles and reproduction.

motor cortex: the outer layer of the brain. In humans movement of the mouth, larynx and tongue for language production are located in this area of the brain.

philopatric: remaining in one's natal group.

social intelligence: the ability to assess a social situation before acting and storing information related to social interactions.

territory: the part of the home range that animals will defend.

Wernicke's area: an area of the brain responsible for perception of speech.

INTERNET & *INFOTRAC COLLEGE EDITION* EXERCISES

Revisit Primate Info Net's comprehensive list of resources concerning primate behavior and ecology (http://www.primate.wisc.edu/pin/behavior.html). Under the heading "Learning (Language, problem solving, tool use)" click on a few of the hyper-links to learn more about some of the famous "language-using" apes discussed in the chapter such as Koko, Chantek and Kanzi. Review these sites critically, focusing on the question of whether or not apes have been demonstrated to master human-like language.

In *InfoTrac* do a keyword search on "chimpanzee hunting" and read the article by Craig Stanford titled "Chimpanzee hunting behavior and human evolution." What information did you learn from this article that was not offered in the text? Are the perspectives of Stanford and your textbook authors similar or different? Does Stanford make a compelling case for using the behavior of modern chimpanzees as a model for the subsistence behavior of our earliest human ancestors?

Now answer the True/False, Multiple Choice and Short Answer sample test questions. Following completion of the tests correct them with the answers and textbook page references at the end of this Study Guide chapter. Note the areas in which you are strong and weak to guide you in your studying. Finally, answer the sample Essay Questions.

TRUE/FALSE QUESTIONS

1. In the last two decades there has been a growing consensus that certain human predispositions are absolutely unique when compared to other primates.
   TRUE   FALSE

2. Like many other primates, humans rely upon culture and spoken, symbolic language.
   TRUE   FALSE

3. Smaller primates have relatively faster metabolisms than larger primates and therefore have relatively higher energy needs.
   TRUE   FALSE

4. Modern humans have a brain size that is expected for a primate of similar body size.
   TRUE   FALSE

5. Work with captive apes has confirmed that they can learn to interpret visual signs and use them in communication.
   TRUE   FALSE

6. Non-human primates have the capacity for culture, learned behaviors that are transmitted from generation to generation.
   TRUE   FALSE

7. Lethal, unprovoked aggression between groups of conspecifics is only know to occur among baboons and howler monkeys.
   TRUE   FALSE

8. The adoption of orphaned infants, reported in macaques, baboons and chimpanzees, is an example of anthropocentrism.
   TRUE   FALSE

9. An example of cooperation among primates is chimpanzee hunting behavior.
   TRUE   FALSE

10. Many of our behaviors are elaborate extensions of those of our hominid ancestors and close primate relatives.
   TRUE   FALSE

1. Primate
   A. neurological complexity is generally reduced when compared with other mammals.
   B. neurological complexity is increased compared with other mammals.
   C. instinctive behaviors are more important than learned behaviors.
   D. none of the above

2. Modern human behavior is
   A. no more complex than that of other primates.
   B. predominantly learned.
   C. predominantly genetic.
   D. similar to that of early hominids.

3. Viewing human behavior from a biological perspective
   A. concludes that all human behaviors are unique in the animal kingdom.
   B. may help to explain how certain behavior patterns may have evolved.
   C. is wrong because we are cultural beings.
   D. ignores the plasticity of human behavior.

4. Which of the following behavioral characteristics do **not** distinguish humans from other non-human primates?
   A. bipedalism
   B. symbolic, spoken language
   C. obtaining food through a male/female division of labor
   D. cultural differences between groups

5. Modern African apes and humans last shared a common ancestor
   A. 20 m.y.a.
   B. 15 m.y.a.
   C. 8 to 5 m.y.a.
   D. 11 m.y.a.

6. Small-bodied primate species
   A. have relatively high energy needs.
   B. have relatively high metabolisms.
   C. eat insects as quick sources of protein and energy.
   D. all of the above

7. Folivorous primates
   A. are generally larger-bodied than insectivores.
   B. primarily eat fruit.
   C. lack any gut specializations for eating leaf.
   D. all of the above

8. Suspensory behavior is more common in
    A. small, arboreal primates.
    B. large, arboreal primates.
    C. terrestrial primates.
    D. vertical clingers.

9. The predictable relationship between brain and body size has been called the index of
    A. anthropometry.
    B. allometric scaling.
    C. altruism.
    D. encephalization.

10. Vervet monkey communication
    A. confirmed the belief that primate vocalizations could not reference external events.
    B. is limited to scent marking and autonomic displays.
    C. includes specific alarm calls for different categories of predators (air, tree or ground).
    D. all of the above

11. Apes do not speak because
    A. they lack the intelligence.
    B. they lack the anatomical structures necessary for spoken language.
    C. they have nothing to say.
    D. none of the above

12. Sara is a chimpanzee who
    A. learned ASL from her mother.
    B. learned to recognize plastic chips as symbols for various objects.
    C. spontaneously began signing after observing others.
    D. taught an infant chimp ASL.

13. Koko
    A. is a female lowland gorilla.
    B. has learned over 500 signs of ASL.
    C. communicated with a male gorilla named Michael using ASL.
    D. all of the above

14. Kanzi
    A. is an orangutan who learned how to make bone and wooden tools.
    B. is a Ugandan nature preserve that is home to 300 lowland gorillas.
    C. is a bonobo who spontaneously learned language through observation.
    D. none of the above

15. Ape language experiments
    A. show that apes are not capable of symbolic thought.
    B. may suggest clues to the origins of human language.
    C. show that all ape species have the same understandings of symbols and the objects they represent.
    D. have no value in assessing the evolutionary relationship between humans and apes.

16. In most humans the language centers of the brain
    A. include Broca's area.
    B. are located in the right hemisphere.
    C. are localized in the cerebellum.
    D. all of the above

17. The study of comparative brain structure
    A. is a very simple task.
    B. indicates that absolute brain size is the only important factor in the development of language.
    C. suggests that reorganization of neurological structures is most important in the development of language.
    D. demonstrates that human brains are simply enlarged monkey brains.

18. Nonhuman primate culture
    A. is innately inherited from one generation to the next.
    B. is uniform between different groups within the same species.
    C. is learned through observation.
    D. includes regional variation in predator alarm calls.

19. A famous example of nonhuman primate cultural behavior is
    A. the Japanese macaque named Imo who taught her peers to wash sweet potatoes and separate grain from sand in sea water.
    B. the orangutan named Lana who learned ASL.
    C. the gorilla named Francine who learned how to say five spoken words in English.
    D. the bonobo named Bob who learned how to play the kazoo.

20. Which of the following tool uses have **not** been seen among free-ranging chimpanzees?
    A. termite fishing
    B. leaf sponging
    C. sweet potato washing
    D. tooth picking

21. Kanzi has shown abilities in all but which of the following areas?
    A. problem-solving capabilities
    B. cooperative hunting
    C. tool manufacturing
    D. goal-directed activities

22. A portion of the home range that is actively protected is known as the group's
    A. territory.
    B. biological continuum.
    C. allometry.
    D. conspecifics.

23. Chimpanzee border patrollers
    A. loudly display at their community's borders.
    B. are relaxed and playful during patrols.
    C. may attack a lone chimp from a neighboring community.
    D. are looking for other groups to join in the food quest.

24. When female macaques and baboons band together in aggressive encounters with other groups of females
    A. fatalities almost always result.
    B. are unusual because most primate group conflicts are between members of the opposite sex.
    C. they are usually the result of competition for resources.
    D. none of the above

25. The principle benefit to chimpanzees who engage in lethal attacks appears to be increased access to
    A. mating partners.
    B. sleeping sites.
    C. territory.
    D. affiliative relationships with male relatives in neighboring communities.

26. Affiliative behaviors
    A. are most common when there is competition for resources.
    B. enhance group cohesiveness.
    C. are rare among primates.
    D. often include aggressive displays.

27. Conspecific refers to
    A. cooperative hunters.
    B. a mating pair.
    C. members of the same species.
    D. those who remain in their natal community.

28. Altruistic behaviors
    A. are always aggressive in nature.
    B. never result in the helping of one animal by another.
    C. are absent in free-ranging primates.
    D. benefit another individual at some potential cost or risk to oneself.

29. Which of the following may reflect kin selection?
    A. Adoption of orphaned infants by older siblings among chimpanzees.
    B. Helping a family member rather than a non-family member.
    C. Enhancing one's own reproductive success by helping a family member.
    D. all of the above

30. Hunting among chimpanzees
    A. is unique in that they are the only non-human species that hunts.
    B. is always cooperative.
    C. is a highly goal-directed activity.
    D. focuses upon zebra and wildebeest as their favorite prey items.

31. Which of the following have lead to the awareness that humans are part of a biological continuum with other primates?
    A. neurological processes
    B. the need for physical contact
    C. dependence on learning
    D. all of the above

SHORT ANSWER QUESTIONS (& PAGE REFERENCES)

1. How does small primate body size correlate with diet, habitat preference and locomotion? (pp. 162-163)

2. What is encephalization? (p. 164)

3. Name three ways that apes have been taught to communicate symbolically. (pp. 166-167)

4. Describe three chimpanzee tools and how they are used. (pp. 170-172)

5. How is altruism explained evolutionarily? (p. 176)

ESSAY QUESTIONS (& PAGE REFERENCES)

1. How do the ape language studies demonstrate similarities between human and ape language capabilities? How do they illustrate ape limitations in this regard? (pp. 164-169)

2. Do chimpanzees have culture? What do field studies on chimp tool-use, diet and hunting have to contribute to the resolution of this issue? (p. 170-173)

3. How is chimpanzee and human inter-group aggression unique amongst mammals? What explanations have been offered to explain this troubling similarity? (pp. 173-175)

ANSWERS, *CORRECTED STATEMENT* IF FALSE & REFERENCES TO TRUE/FALSE QUESTIONS

1. FALSE, p. 161, In the last two decades there has been a growing consensus that certain human predispositions *reflect patterns also seen in* other primates.

2. FALSE, p. 162, *Unlike any* other primates, humans rely upon culture and spoken, symbolic language.

3. TRUE, p. 163.

4. FALSE, p. 164, Modern humans have a brain size *well beyond* that expected for a primate of similar body size.

5. TRUE, p. 166

6. TRUE, p. 170

7. FALSE, p. 174, Lethal, unprovoked aggression between groups of conspecifics is only know to occur among *chimpanzees and humans*.

8. FALSE, p. 176, The adoption of orphaned infants, reported in macaques, baboons and chimpanzees, is an example of *altruism*.

9. TRUE, p. 177

10. TRUE, p. 178

ANSWERS AND REFERENCES TO MULTIPLE CHOICE QUESTIONS

1. B, p. 161
2. B, p. 161
3. B, p. 161
4. D, pp. 162, 170-173
5. C, p. 162
6. D, p. 163
7. A, p. 163
8. B, p. 163
9. D, p. 164
10. C, p. 165
11. B, p. 166
12. B, p. 166
13. D, p. 166
14. C, p. 167
15. B, pp. 167-169
16. A, p. 168

17. C, p. 169
18. C, p. 170
19. A, p. 170
20. C, pp. 170-172
21. B, pp. 167, 172-173
22. A, p. 173
23. C, p. 174
24. C, p. 175
25. A, p. 175
26. B, p. 176
27. C, p. 173
28. D, p. 176
29. D, p. 176
30. C, p. 177
31. D, p. 178

CHAPTER 8
PROCESSES OF MACROEVOLUTION: MAMMALIAN/PRIMATE EVOLUTIONARY HISTORY

LEARNING OBJECTIVES
After reading this chapter you should be able to:
- Recognize the place of humans in nature (p. 185).
- Use the classification chart of animal taxonomy (p. 186).
- Understand the ways in which evolutionary biologists deduce relationships between organisms (pp. 187-192).
- Discuss various species concepts (pp. 192-193).
- Understand the processes of speciation (194-195).
- Discuss the problems of classifying fossil forms at both the species and genus levels (pp. 195-197).
- Recount the major events of vertebrate evolution (pp. 197-199).
- Discuss continental drift and its impact on evolution (pp. 198-199).
- List the characteristics that distinguish the mammals from other vertebrates (pp. 200-202).
- Discuss the difficulties of distinguishing the primates of the Paleocene from other placental mammals of that time (p. 204).
- Discuss the major events of primate evolution chronologically (pp. 204-209)
- Discuss adaptive radiation and give a primate example (pp. 209).
- Define generalized and specialized characteristics (p. 210).
- Compare and contrast modes and tempos of evolutionary change (pp. 210-211).

CHAPTER OUTLINE
Introduction.

In the preceding chapters we surveyed the genetic mechanisms that are the foundation of the evolutionary process. Chapters 5 -7 looked at our closest relatives, the nonhuman primates, and how their study helps us to understand ourselves. In this chapter the process of macroevolution is studied. We begin by looking at principles of classification and the meaning of species. We examine the basics of geological history and continental drift. A synopsis of the key innovations in vertebrate, and particularly mammalian, evolution is examined over the great depth of time of these major groups. We will look at the fossil history of the primates over the last 60 million years and, by so doing, look at our own evolutionary history as well. With what you have learned about primate anatomy, ecology, and social behavior, you will be able to "flesh out" the bones and teeth that make up the evolutionary record of primate origins. This chapter ends with a discussion of the processes of macroevolutionary change.

I   THE HUMAN PLACE IN THE ORGANIC WORLD
    A. Considering both living and extinct organisms the amount of biological diversity is staggering.
        1. In order to understand this diversity biologists have constructed a classification system.
        2. The classificatory system that biologists have devised organizes life into convenient groupings.

a. This helps to reduce the complexity.

b. These groupings indicate evolutionary relationships.

B. The place of humans in nature.

1. Humans belong to a broad group of organisms that move about and ingest food which are called animals.

2. Humans belong to the group of animals that are multicelled, the Metazoa.

3. Within the Metazoa humans belong to the phylum Chordata, animals that possess

   a. a notochord, a stiff supporting rod along the back, and

   b. pharyngeal gill slits (at some stage of development).

4. Within the chordates humans belong to the vertebrates.

   a. These animals are characterized by a vertebral column.

   b. Vertebrates have a well developed brain.

   c. Additionally, vertebrates have paired sensory structures for sight, smell, and balance.

5. Vertebrates are divided into six classes: bony fishes, cartilaginous fishes, amphibians, reptiles, birds and mammals.

II PRINCIPLES OF CLASSIFICATION

A. The field that specializes in delineating the rules of classification is taxonomy.

1. One criterion for classifying organisms is physical similarities.

2. The crucial criterion for classification, however, is evolutionary descent.

B. Taxonomic concepts

1. Structures that are shared through descent from a common ancestor are called homologies.

2. Structures in organisms that are used for the same function, but have developed independently and are not the result of common descent, are called analogies.

   a. Recall from Chapter 5 that homoplasy is the process by which similarities can develop in different groups of organisms.

   b. Analogies can develop through homoplasy in unrelated organisms.

C. Constructing classifications and interpreting evolutionary relationships

1. There are two major "schools" of thought by which evolutionary relationships and classifications are interpreted.

   a. Evolutionary systematics is the more traditional approach.

   b. Cladistics is more recent and is favored among many anthropologists.

2. There are similarities in both approaches.

   a. Both attempt to trace evolutionary relationships and construct taxonomies.

   b. Both compare organisms by the possession of certain characters (physical, genetic, or even behavioral features) some of which are considered more informative than others.

   c. Both focus exclusively on homologies.

3. There are important differences between the two approaches.

   a. Evolutionary systematics and cladistics differ in

      i.   how characters are chosen.

      ii. which groups are compared.

      iii. how the results are interpreted and incorporated into evolutionary explanations.

   b. Evolutionary systematists produce a phylogenetic tree that incorporates time and attempts to make hypotheses regarding ancestor-descendant relationships.

  c. Cladistic analysis produces a cladogram that does not indicate time nor suggest any ancestor-descendant relationships.

  d. The main difference is that cladistics precisely defines the types of homologies that yield useful information; some homologous characters are more informative than others.

    i. Traits that reflect the primitive condition of the organisms being studied are said to be ancestral.

    ii. Traits that are shared by all members of a group, but not present before the group's appearance, are said to be shared derived characteristics; these are the traits considered to be most important to cladistics.

 4. In practice, most physical anthropologists and other biologists combine the two approaches.

III DEFINITION OF SPECIES

 A. The most basic level of taxonomic classification is the species.

  1. Species form through speciation, the process by which descendant species evolve from ancestors.

 B. How do biologists define species?

  1. The Biological Species Concept is the one preferred by most zoologists

   a. It depicts species as groups of individuals capable of fertile interbreeding, but reproductively isolated from other such groups.

  2. The Recognition Species Concept focuses on mate recognition.

   a. It depicts the key aspect of species as the ability of individuals to identify members of their own species for purposes of mating.

  3. The Ecological Species Concept focuses on commonalities in adaptation.

   a. It depicts a species as a group of organisms exploiting a single ecological niche.

 C. Processes of speciation

  1. Biologists have hypothesized that speciation could occur in three different ways:

   a. allopatric, parapatric or sympatric speciation.

  2. Allopatric speciation is by far the most widely accepted view of speciation.

   a. This model requires complete reproductive isolation between populations, leading to a split in the species that ultimately results in two new species evolving.

  3. Parapatric speciation requires only partial reproductive isolation.

   a. A hybrid zone would form between the two partially isolated populations.

  4. Sympatric speciation, which does not require any geographic isolation, is not well supported by contemporary evidence.

 D. Interpretation of species and other groups in the fossil record

  1. Our study of fossil primates has introduced us to a number of taxonomic names for extinct primates.

   a. What do these names mean in evolutionary terms?

  2. Our goal is to make meaningful biological statements when we assign taxonomic names.

  3. All populations contain variation.

   a. Individual variation exists.

   b. Age-dependent variation exists.

    i. In hominoids there is a difference in the number of adult teeth vs. the milk teeth.

ii. It would be a mistake to not recognize that members of the same species may have different numbers of teeth at different ages; otherwise two species would be described when there should only be one.

   c. Sexual dimorphism can be a confounding factor when describing a fossil species; males and females may have different structural traits.

4. The most precise taxonomic level that we would like to assign fossil primates to is the species.
   a. Do fossil species meet the criteria for the modern Biological Species Concept?
   b. We cannot obviously cannot observe their behavior or the outcomes of their matings, so we cannot know for certain.

5. Therefore when we examine fossils we must ask: "What is the biological significance of the variation that is present?" There are two possible answers:
   a. variation is accounted for by individual, age, and sex differences, i.e., intraspecific variation.
   b. or, variation represents differences between reproductively isolated groups, i.e., interspecific variation.

6. How do paleontologists make the choice between intraspecific and interspecific variation?
   a. In order to make a choice between the two possibilities we must use living species as models and observe their reproductive behavior.
   b. If the amount of morphological variation observed in fossil samples is consistent with the variation of modern species of closely related forms, then we should not split our sample into more than one species.
   c. One serious problem with fossil species is that not only is there variation over space, but there is also variation over time.
      i. Even more variation is possible in paleospecies because individual specimens may be separated by thousands, perhaps millions, of years.
      ii. Standard Linnaean taxonomy is designed to account for the variation present at a particular time (in living species) and, basically, describes a static situation (no change, or evolution, occurring).

7. Definition of genus
   a. The next higher level of taxonomy from the species is the genus.
   b. The classification of fossils at the genus level presents its own set of problems.
   c. One definition of a genus is a group of species composed of members more closely related to each other than they are to species from another genus.
      i. This definition often becomes very subjective.
      ii. In order to have more than one genus there must be at least two species.
   d. Another definition of a genus is a number of species that share the same broad adaptive zone.
   e. This represents a general ecological lifestyle more basic than the particular ecological niches characteristic of species.
      i. This ecological definition is more useful for applying to fossil genera.
      ii. Teeth are the most often preserved parts and they are excellent ecological indicators.
   f. Cladistic analysis also provides assistance in making judgments about evolutionary relationships

        i.   Members of the same genus should all share derived characters not seen in members of other genera.

IV   VERTEBRATE EVOLUTIONARY HISTORY: A BRIEF SUMMARY

A. In addition to the great diversity of life, evolutionary biologists must also contend with vast periods of time.

B. Geologists have formulated the geological time scale.
1. This organizes time into hierarchies.
2. Very large time spans are subdivided into eras, periods, and epochs.

C. There are three geological eras: the Paleozoic, Mesozoic, and Cenozoic.

D. The first vertebrates
1. The earliest vertebrates are present in the fossil record early in the Paleozoic, around 500 m.y.a.
2. Later in the Paleozoic, several varieties of fishes, amphibians and reptiles appeared.
3. At the end of the Paleozoic (ca. 250 m.y.a.) several types of mammal-like reptiles are present, probably including the ancestors of modern mammals.

E. Continental drift
1. The evolutionary history of vertebrates was profoundly influenced by geographical events.
2. The position of the earth's continents have dramatically shifted during the last several hundred million years.
    a. This process is called continental drift.
3. Continental drift is explained by the theory of plate tectonics which posits that the earth's crust is a series of gigantic and colliding plates.
4. In the late Paleozoic the earth's continents constituted a single land mass, the colossal continent called Pangea.
    a. In the early Mesozoic Pangea began to break up forming a southern "supercontinent" Gondwanaland (consisting of modern South America, Africa, Antarctica, Australia, and India).
    b. The northern continent was called Laurasia, consisting of North America, Europe, and Asia.
    c. By the end of the Mesozoic (ca. 65 m.y.a.), the continents were beginning to assume their current positions.
5. The evolutionary ramifications of continent drift were profound.
    a. Groups of land animals became geographically isolated from one another.

F. The Mesozoic
1. During this era, the reptiles underwent an adaptive radiation, a rapid expansion into a variety of ecological niches.
2. The first mammals are known from fossil traces early in the Mesozoic.
3. The placental mammals do not appear until late in the Mesozoic, around 70 m.y.a.

G. The Cenozoic
1. The Cenozoic is divided into two periods.
    a. The Tertiary lasts for about 63 million years.
    b. The Quaternary begins 1.8 m.y.a. and continues to the present.
2. To be more precise, paleontologists usually refer to the seven epochs of the Cenozoic.

V   MAMMALIAN EVOLUTION

A. After the dinosaur extinctions mammals underwent an adaptive radiation in which they filled a wide variety of ecological niches.
1. This mammalian diversification was so successful that the Cenozoic is sometimes referred to as the Age of Mammals.
2. Mammals and birds replaced reptiles as the dominant terrestrial vertebrates.
B. Factors contributing to the mammalian success:
1. The cerebrum of the mammalian brain expanded, in particular the neocortex which controls higher brain functions, came to comprise the majority of brain volume.
   a. This increase in brain size led to a greater ability to learn and a general flexibility of behavior in mammals.
2. An efficient mode of prenatal internal development is found among the mammals.
   a. This is associated with the need for the longer development of the larger brain.
3. Mammals are viviparous, i.e. they give birth to live young.
4. Mammals have specialized teeth, a condition called heterodonty.
   a. Mammals have four basic type of teeth that are shaped differently to perform different functions.
   b. Incisors are used for cutting.
   c. Canines function in grasping and piercing.
   d. Premolars and molars are used for crushing and grinding.
   e. Teeth are particularly important in paleontology because there is a disproportionate representation of teeth in the fossil record.
      i.   The enamel that covers the teeth is the hardest substance in the body.
5. Mammals are homeothermic; this means that mammals are able to regulate and maintain a constant body temperature.
   a. Associated with homeothermy is endothermy, the ability to generate body heat by muscle action.
   b. Homeothermy and endothermy allows mammals to be active during colder times of the 24-hour day and throughout the year.

VI   MAJOR MAMMALIAN GROUPS

A. There are three major subgroups of living mammals: monotremes, marsupials, and placental mammals.
B. Monotremes are egg-laying and are extremely primitive; there are only two types existing today.
C. Marsupials
1. The young are born extremely immature.
2. The young complete birth in an external pouch, or marsupium.
D. Placentals
1. The placenta is a structure that prevents the mother's immune system from rejecting the fetus.
2. The longer gestation period allows the central nervous system to develop more completely in the fetus.
3. Mammals also have the "bond of milk" between the mother and the offspring.
   a. This period of association between the mother and the offspring provides for a wider range of learning stimuli.
   b. It is not sufficient that the young mammal has a brain capable of learning; mammalian social systems provide youngsters with ample learning opportunities.

VII   EARLY PRIMATE EVOLUTION.
   A. Primate origins begin in the placental mammal radiation at the start of the Cenozoic.
      1. Primates diverged very early from the primitive placental mammals.
      2. Discerning early primates from these very early generalized mammals is quite difficult.
   B. Plesiadapiforms
      1. Until recently plesiadapiforms were considered to be the earliest primates.
         a. Only fragmentary evidence of jaws and teeth were known.
         b. Subsequent fossil material, including elements of the hand and wrist (where primate characteristics would be obvious), suggest these mammals are more closely related to colugos.
      2. The plesiadapiforms have been removed from the Order Primates.
      3. Nevertheless, plesiadapiforms are probably closely linked to the early roots of the primates, but the primates had already diverged by the appearance of this group.
      4. The bottom line: we are left with extremely scarce traces of the beginnings of the primate radiation.
   C. The earliest undoubted primates appear in the Eocene.
      1. These forms are found in North America, Europe, and Asia, which were all geographically connected.
      2. A summary of Eocene primates:
         a. These are the first "primates of modern aspect."
         b. These animals were widely distributed.
         c. By the end of the Eocene most of these primates were extinct.
         d. Some of these forms are probably the ancestors of the prosimians.
            i. Others appear to have given rise to the tarsiers.
            ii. Some recent discoveries from North Africa, the Persian Gulf, and China have been claimed to be anthropoid ancestors from the late Eocene.
   D. The Oligocene (34-22.5 m.y.a.)
      1. Most of our knowledge of primate Oligocene evolution comes from a site in Egypt, the Fayum.
      2. It is believed that New World and Old World monkeys share a common ancestor.
         a. Some of the earliest Fayum primates appear to be close to the ancestry of both groups of monkeys.
         b. Monkeys may have reached South America by "rafting" from Africa.
         c. Regardless of how monkeys reached South America, New World and Old World forms have had a separate lineage since about 35 m.y.a.
      3. The Fayum forms
         a. Some paleontologists have suggested that the genus *Apidium* lies near, or even before, the evolutionary divergence of New and Old World anthropoids.
         b. *Aegyptopithecus* is the largest of the Fayum primates whose weight is estimated between 13 to 18 pounds.
         c. *Aegyptopithecus* had a small brain, large snout, and does not show any of the derived traits of either Old World monkeys or the hominoids.
         d. This primate may be close to the ancestry of both Old World monkeys and apes.
         e. *Aegyptopithecus* is found in geological beds dated between 35-33 m.y.a., suggesting that the evolutionary divergence of hominoids from other Old World anthropoids occurred after this time.

VIII   MIOCENE FOSSIL HOMINOIDS
   A. The Miocene (23-5 m.y.a.) was marked by a spectacular radiation of apelike forms and could be called "the golden age of hominoids."
   B. During the Miocene, significant changes in climate and geography occurred.
      1. The early Miocene was considerably warmer than the preceding Oligocene.
      2. By the Middle Miocene (ca. 16 m.y.a.), a geographic connection was established between Africa and Eurasia through Arabia.
         a. As a result, hominoids were able to spread from Africa throughout Eurasia after this land bridge was established.
   C. The Miocene hominoid assemblage is large and complex. Consequently, they are often treated geographically.
      1. African forms (23-14 m.y.a.)
         a. The best known of these fossils is *Proconsul* and this genus exhibits considerable variation.
         b. The geographic range for African hominoids extends over 1800 miles.
      2. European forms (13-11 m.y.a.)
         a. These forms are quite derived, yet not well understood.
         b. The best known of these forms are assigned to the genus *Dryopithecus*.
      3. Asian Forms (16-7 m.y.a.)
         a. This is the largest and most varied group from the Miocene fossil hominoid assemblage.
         b. These forms are highly derived.
         c. The best known genus is *Sivapithecus*.
   D. Four general points can be made about the Miocene hominoid fossils.
      1. They are widespread geographically.
      2. These hominoids were numerous.
      3. They span a considerable portion of the Miocene.
      4. These hominoids are poorly understood.
   E. However, we can make the following conclusions:
      1. These primates are definitely hominoids.
      2. They are mostly large-bodied hominoids.
      3. Most of the Miocene forms are so derived that they are improbable ancestors of any living form.
         a. *Sivapithecus* however, shows some highly derived facial features that suggest a close link to the modern orangutan.
      4. There are no definite hominids from any Miocene-dated locale.
         a. However, some very recently discovered fossils from sites dated to ca. 6 m.y.a. in Africa may in fact prove to be hominid.

IX   PROCESSES OF MACROEVOLUTION
   A. Adaptive radiation
      1. Adaptive radiation is the evolutionary process by which a species undergoes expansion and diversification in response to new ecological niches.
      2. An adaptive radiation will occur if the species, or group of species,
         a. has an adaptive potential, and
         b. has available ecological niches to occupy.
      3. A primate example of adaptive radiation is the diversification of lemurs on Madagascar.

a. The 61 living lemur species represent a diverse group of animals descended from a very generalized common ancestor that provided great adaptive potential.

b. Without competition from other mammals, the lemurs were able to fill a large number of niches on Madagascar.

B. Generalized and specialized characteristics

1. A trait that is adapted for many functions is generalized.

a. Usually, but not always, such a trait is ancestral.

2. A trait that is limited to a narrow set of ecological functions is specialized.

a. Usually, such a trait is derived.

C. Modes of evolutionary change

1. Until recently, it was thought that microevolutionary changes accumulating over time will result in macroevolution, or speciation.

a. In the last 20 years, this view has been seriously challenged.

b. Many researchers now accept that macroevolution can only be partly explained by microevolutionary factors.

D. Gradualism vs. punctuated equilibrium

1. The traditional view of evolution, as put forth by Darwin, is called phyletic gradualism.

a. According to gradualism, evolution works by gradual changes accumulating over vast periods of geologic time.

b. There should be a series of intermediate, or transitional, forms in any line.

c. The reason that such forms are rarely found is attributed to the incompleteness of the fossil record.

2. The concept of punctuated equilibrium challenges the idea of gradualism.

a. Punctuated equilibrium posits that species may persist for long periods with little or no change.

b. This period of "stasis" comes to an end with a "spurt" of speciation.

c. This uneven, nongradual process of long periods of stasis and quick evolutionary spurts is called punctuated equilibrium.

d. Punctuated equilibrium does not challenge that evolution has occurred; it challenges the mode and tempo of gradualist evolution.

e. Rather than long periods of gradual change, this alternate view postulates long periods of no change, punctuated only occasionally by sudden bursts of speciation.

f. Rather than gradual accumulation of small changes (microevolution) in a single lineage, an additional evolutionary mechanism, accelerated speciation, directs macroevolution in a way quite distinct from gradualism.

g. Speciation events and the longevity of these transitional species are so short that they are not preserved in the fossil record.

h. The fossil record and punctuated equilibrium.

    i.   The fossil record for marine invertebrates supports punctuated equilibrium.

    ii.   The primate evolutionary record, on the other hand, does not appear to support the model of punctuated equilibrium.

KEY TERMS

adaptive radiation: the rapid expansion and diversification of an evolving group of organisms adapting to a variety of new niches.

analogies: similarities between organisms based strictly on common function with no assumed descent from a common ancestor. E. g., the wings of an insect and the wings of a bat.

ancestral (primitive) trait: referring to a character that reflects the ancestral condition within a lineage.

Apidium: a fossil primate genus from the Fayum that has three premolars. It may be ancestral to, or closely related to the ancestry of, the New World monkeys.

classification: the ordering of organisms into categories, such as phyla, orders, and families to show evolutionary relationships.

Cenozoic: the geological era during which primate evolution occurred. It encompasses the last 65 million years.

cerebrum: the outer portions of the brain.

Chordata (Chordates): the phylum of the animal kingdom that includes the vertebrates.

cladistics: an approach to taxonomy that groups taxa based on shared derived characteristics.

cladogram: a chart showing evolutionary relationships as determined by cladistic analysis. It is based solely on interpretation of shared derived characters. No time component is indicated, and ancestor-descendant relationships are not inferred.

continental drift: the movement of continents on sliding plates of the earth's surface. This has resulted in dramatic movement of the earth's land masses over time.

derived trait: referring to a character that reflects specialization within a lineage and is more informative about the evolutionary relationship between organisms.

Dryopithecus: the Miocene hominoid genus that inhabited Europe. This hominoid was characterized by thin molar enamel.

ecological niche: the positions of species within their physical and biological environment.

endothermy: production of heat within the animal by means of metabolic processes within cell (mainly muscle cells). Birds and mammals are the endothermic animals.

epochs: categories of the geological time scale; subdivision of periods.

evolutionary (phylogenetic) systematics: a traditional approach to classification (and evolutionary interpretation) in which presumed ancestors and descendants are traced in time by analysis of homologous characters.

Fayum: a rich paleontological site in Egypt that yields late Eocene primates and is the only site for Oligocene primates.

genus: a group of closely related species.

geological time scale: the organization of earth history into eras, periods, and epochs.

Gondwanaland: the southern continents that broke off of Pangea. Gondwanaland (a.k.a. Gondwana) included South America, Africa, Antarctica, Australia, and India.

heterodonty: the condition in which there are different kinds of teeth specialized for different functions.

hominids: popular form of Hominidae, the family to which modern humans belong; includes all bipedal hominoids back to the divergence from African great apes.

homologies: similarities between organisms based on descent from a common ancestor. (E.g., the bones in the wing of a bird and the bones in the arm of a human).

homoplasy: separate evolutionary development of similar characteristics in different groups of organisms.

homeothermy: the ability to maintain a constant body temperature. Through physiological feedback mechanisms heat generated through endothermy is either dissipated or retained within the normal range of body temperature for the species.

interspecific: refers to between two or more species.

intraspecific: refers to within one species.

large-bodied hominoids: those hominoids including "great" apes and hominids, as well as all ancestral forms back to the time of divergence from small-bodied hominoids.

Laurasia: the northernmost continents that had been part of Pangea. Laurasia included North America, Europe, and Asia.

Metazoa: the multicellular animals, a major division of the animal kingdom. The metazoa are all of the animals except the sponges.

neocortex: the outer layer of brain tissue of the cerebrum, which has expanded during the evolution of the vertebrates, particularly in primates, and most especially in humans. The neocortex is associated with high mental functions.

paleospecies: groups of fossil organisms that are assigned to the same species. Paleospecies exhibit more variation than in living species. This is because of the time span involved; in humans *Homo erectus* covers more than one million years.

Pangea: the supercontinent that included all of the present-day continents. Pangea began to break up in the early Mesozoic.

phyletic gradualism: the evolutionary concept, first postulated by Charles Darwin, that evolutionary change takes place slowly with slight modifications in each generation.

phylogenetic tree: a chart showing evolutionary relationships as determined by phylogenetic systematics. It contains a time component and infers ancestor-descendant relationships.

***Proconsul*:** the genus of Miocene hominoid from Africa. *Proconsul* was the most primitive of the Miocene hominoids.

punctuated equilibrium: the evolutionary concept that there are long periods, in the history of a species, in which no change takes place (stasis) followed by a quick spurt of evolutionary change (speciation).

shared derived trait: referring to a character shared in common by two forms and considered the most useful for making evolutionary interpretations.

***Sivapithecus* :** the Miocene hominoid found in Asia that has several derived characteristics that link it to the orangutan.

speciation: the process by which new species are produced from earlier species. The most important mechanism of macroevolutionary change.

vertebrates: animals with bony backbones; includes fishes, amphibians, reptiles, birds, and mammals.

viviparity: the reproductive process in which the young are born live.

INTERNET EXERCISES

To see a colorful and fascinating animation of continental drift and seafloor spreading documenting the breakup of Pangea (ca. 200 m.y.a. to the present), go to http://www.scotese.com/sfsanim.htm. After the animation loads, click and drag your cursor across the image from left to right (as fast or as slowly as you'd like) to "playback" 200 million years of earth history!

Check out a couple of sites featuring the primate fossil discoveries of some important researchers working in the field today. Dr. Chris Beard of the Carnegie Museum of Natural History, responsible for the discovery in China of *Eosimias* (http://www.carnegiemuseums.org/cmnh/research/eosimias/) and Dr. Elwyn Simons, leader of the expeditions into the Fayum Depression of Egypt (http://www.baa.duke.edu/SIMONS/egypt.html).

CONCEPT APPLICATION

Use the "Events" labeled A-P below to fill in the Geological Time Scale table. (The first two are filled in because we have not gotten to those time periods yet…)

A. The first placental and marsupial mammals	I. Mammal-like reptiles
B. The first "Primates of Modern Aspect"	J. The beginning of the "Age of Mammals"
C. Hominids spread around the world	K. The first egg-laying mammals
D. First air-breathing animals	L. The "Age of Fish"
E. Modern insects diversify	M. The "Great Age of Dinosaurs"
F. First fish	N. After the last Ice Age
G. *Aegyptopithecus* and the Fayum Depression	O. The "Golden Age of Apes"
H. Trilobites abound	P. Hominids diversify

ERA	PERIOD/EPOCH	BEGAN M.Y.A.	EVENT
CENOZOIC	Holocene Epoch	0.01	N
	Pleistocene Epoch	1.8	C
	Pliocene Epoch	5	
	Miocene Epoch	23	
	Oligocene Epoch	34	
	Eocene Epoch	55	
	Paleocene Epoch	65	
MESOZOIC	Cretaceous Period	136	
	Jurassic Period	190	
	Triassic Period	225	
PALEOZOIC	Permian Period	280	
	Carboniferous Period	345	
	Devonian Period	395	
	Silurian Period	430	
	Ordovician Period	500	
	Cambrian Period	570	

Now answer the True/False, Multiple Choice and Short Answer sample test questions. Following completion of the tests correct them with the answers and textbook page references at the end of this Study Guide chapter. Note the areas in which you are strong and weak to guide you in your studying. Finally, answer the sample Essay Questions.

TRUE/FALSE QUESTIONS

1. Structures that are shared by species on the basis of descent from a common ancestor are called homoplasies.
   TRUE   FALSE

2. Cladistics is an approach to classification that seeks to make rigorous evolutionary interpretations based solely on analyses of derived characters.
   TRUE   FALSE

3. Evolutionary systematics is the most basic process of macroevolution wherein a new species evolves from a prior species.
   TRUE   FALSE

4. Most speciation is allopatric.
   TRUE   FALSE

5. A group of closely related species is known as a paleospecies.
   TRUE   FALSE

6. Due to continental drift, the positions of landmasses have shifted dramatically during earth's history.
   TRUE   FALSE

7. The Miocene hominoid *Sivapithecus* is most likely ancestral to the modern gorilla.
   TRUE   FALSE

8. The first "primates of modern aspect" date to the Eocene.
   TRUE   FALSE

9. The Oligocene, North African site of the Fayum is famous for its fossil apes and early hominids.
   TRUE   FALSE

10. Punctuated equilibrium states that evolutionary change proceeds by long periods of stasis interrupted by rapid periods of change.
    TRUE   FALSE

MULTIPLE CHOICE QUESTIONS

1. Humans are
   A. animals.
   B. vertebrates.
   C. chordates.
   D. all of the above.

2. The scientific discipline that delineates the rules of classification is
   A. paleontology.
   B. stratigraphy.
   C. homology.
   D. taxonomy.

3. The traditional approach to classifying organisms is based upon similarities in
   A. physical structure.
   B. analogies.
   C. diet.
   D. ecology.

4. Bats have wings that allow them to fly. So do birds and insects. Similarities such as wings in different animals that have a common function
   A. must mean they have a recent common ancestry.
   B. are called homologies.
   C. are called analogies.
   D. are always primitive traits.

5. Humans and apes have certain characteristics in common such as a broad sternum, a Y-5 cusp pattern on the molars, and the lack of a tail. Since these features are not found in monkeys and prosimians these characteristics are
   A. analogies.
   B. primitive traits.
   C. shared derived traits.
   D. general traits.

6. A major difference between a paleospecies and a biological species is that a paleospecies
   A. is more variable.
   B. adds a temporal component.
   C. is not yet extinct.
   D. is static.

7. Closely related species are grouped together in a
   A. paleospecies.
   B. subspecies
   C. genus.
   D. family.

8. Which of the following is **not** a species concept?
   A. Biological Species Concept
   B. Hybrid Species Concept
   C. Recognition Species Concept
   D. Ecological Species Concept

9. _____ speciation requires complete reproductive isolation, leading to the formation of a new species geographically separated from its ancestral population.
   A. Allopatric
   B. Sympatric
   C. Parapatric
   D. all of the above

10. In the early Mesozoic, Pangea broke into two large continents, Gondwana and Laurasia. Laurasia consisted of the present day continents of
    A. South America and Africa.
    B. South America, Africa, and Australia.
    C. South America, Africa, Australia, India, and Antarctica.
    D. North America, Europe, and Asia.

11. Continental drift has affected the evolution of organisms by
    A. forming water barriers.
    B. affecting long-term rainfall patterns.
    C. decreasing the opportunities for gene flow.
    D. all of the above

12. During the Mesozoic the dominant terrestrial life forms were
    A. crossopterygians.
    B. amphibians.
    C. reptiles.
    D. birds.

13. Which of the following is **not** one of the mammalian innovations that has led to their success?
    A. ectothermy.
    B. heterodonty.
    C. viviparity.
    D. endothermy.

14. The primary advantage of heterodont dentition is that it
    A. allows the animal to defend itself more efficiently.
    B. allows for processing a wide variety of foods.
    C. opens up news ways of interacting with potential mates.
    D. allows the animal to grab prey that it could not catch otherwise.

15. The vast majority of fossil material that is available from most vertebrates, including primates, consist of
    A. pelves.
    B. humeri and other arm bones.
    C. femurs, which are the largest bones in any vertebrate.
    D. teeth.

16. The group of mammals that reproduce by laying eggs and generally have more primitive traits than other mammals are the
    A. monotremes.
    B. marsupials.
    C. placentals.
    D. eutherians.

17. An important aspect of viviparity is a barrier that protects the fetal tissues from the mother's immune system. This barrier is the
    A. placenta.
    B. lymphatic system.
    C. hard-shelled egg.
    D. human lymphatic antigen.

18. After birth a young mammal has a period of neural development coupled with learning. This period of close association between the young mammal and its mother is known as the
    A. rehearsal period.
    B. placental connection.
    C. biosocial perspective.
    D. "bond of milk".

19. Early primate evolution during the Paleocene
    A. is well represented by the genus *Aegyptopithecus*.
    B. is quite fragmentary with no indisputable primates identified.
    C. is represented mainly by limb bones of monkeys and apes.
    D. none of the above

20. The Eocene "primates of modern aspect" are found mostly on the continents of
    A. Asia and Australia.
    B. Africa and South America.
    C. North America and Europe.
    D. Antarctica, Australia and South America.

21. The first prosimian-like primate radiation was during the
    A. Paleocene.
    B. Eocene.
    C. Oligocene.
    D. Miocene.

22. Which of the following statements about New World monkey evolution is **not** correct?
    A. It is very unlikely that the Old and New World primates have shared any evolutionary history since the early Oligocene.
    B. The fossil history of the New World monkeys is rich in Central and North America.
    C. In the early Oligocene, South America was an island continent, much closer to Africa than it is today.
    D. *Apidium* may be close to the ancestry of the New World monkeys.

23. According to most primate evolutionary biologists, *Aegyptopithecus*
    A. is the common ancestor of the lemurs and lorises.
    B. evolved after the divergence of Old and New World anthropoids.
    C. is the direct ancestor of the New World anthropoids.
    D. precedes the major split in catarrhine evolution.

24. Today's hominoids are
    A. the most diverse group of primates that has ever existed.
    B. the most diverse group of hominoids that has ever existed.
    C. a small remnant of a very successful Miocene radiation.
    D. confined to the tropical rain forests of Southeast Asia.

25. Which of the following is a Miocene African hominoid?
    A. *Dryopithecus*
    B. *Sivapithecus*
    C. *Proconsul*
    D. *Pliopithecus*

26. Which of the following is **not** true of Miocene hominoids?
    A. There are definite hominids dated to the Miocene.
    B. Most Miocene forms are large-bodied hominoids.
    C. The Miocene forms are more closely related to apes than monkeys.
    D. Most are so derived as to be unlikely ancestors of any living form.

27. The Miocene ape that bears a striking resemblance to the modern orangutan in the face, but not in the postcranium, is
    A. *Dryopithecus*.
    B. *Sivapithecus*.
    C. *Proconsul*.
    D. *Kenyapithecus*.

28. There are two bird species on a midwestern prairie that look very much alike physically and are probably descended from a common ancestor. During courtship, however, the males of one species stands on one leg while looking at the female. The males of the second species uses both feet to drum on the prairie floor. The females will only mate with those males who behave appropriately during courtship. This is an example of
    A. parallel evolution.
    B. convergent evolution.
    C. behavioral isolation.
    D. geographical isolation.

29. The fossil record of many marine invertebrates shows long periods where there is very little change in species. New species appear geologically suddenly without the occurrence of any transitions. These observations best support the idea of
    A. convergent evolution.
    B. punctuated equilibrium.
    C. phyletic gradualism.
    D. small microevolutionary changes that lead to transspecific evolution.

30. A relatively rapid expansion and diversification of life forms into new ecological niches is known as
    A. adaptive radiation.
    B. punctuated equilibrium.
    C. phyletic gradualism.
    D. convergent evolution.

SHORT ANSWER QUESTIONS (& PAGE REFERENCES)

1. What is the difference between homology and analogy? (p. 187)

2. Name three ways that have been hypothesized for speciation to occur. (p. 194)

3. What is continental drift? (p. 198)

4. How do mammals differ from reptiles? (pp. 200-202)

5. Why is the Miocene known as the "Golden Age of Apes"? (p. 207)

ESSAY QUESTIONS (& PAGE REFERENCES)

1. What are the differences between the traditional evolutionary systematic and newer cladistic approaches in trying to reconstruct evolutionary relationships between species? (pp. 187-192)

2. Compare and contrast the Biological, Recognition and Ecological Species Concepts. (pp. 192-193)

3. Compare and contrast phyletic gradualism versus punctuated equilibrium with respect to the mode and tempo of evolution. (pp. 210-211)

ANSWERS, *CORRECTED STATEMENT* IF FALSE & REFERENCES TO TRUE/FALSE QUESTIONS

1. FALSE, p. 187, Structures that are shared by species on the basis of descent from a common ancestor are called *homologies*.

2. TRUE, p. 188

3. FALSE, p. 192, *Speciation* is the most basic process of macroevolution wherein a new species evolves from a prior species.

4. TRUE, p. 194

5. FALSE, p. 196, A group of closely related species is known as a *genus*.

6. TRUE, p. 198

7. FALSE, p. 209, The Miocene hominoid *Sivapithecus* is most likely ancestral to the modern *orangutan*.

8. TRUE, p. 204

9. FALSE, p. 206, The Oligocene, North African site of the Fayum is famous for its *Old World anthropoids*.

10. TRUE, p. 211

ANSWERS AND REFERENCES TO MULTIPLE CHOICE QUESTIONS

1. D, p. 185	16. A, p. 203
2. D, p. 185	17. A, p. 203
3. A, p. 185	18. D, p. 203
4. C, p. 187	19. B, p. 205
5. C, p. 188	20. C, p. 204
6. B, p. 192	21. B, p. 204
7. C, p. 196	22. B, p. 206
8. B, pp. 192-193	23. D, p. 206
9. A, p. 194	24. C, p. 207
10. D, p. 198	25. C, p. 208
11. D, p. 199	26. A, p. 209
12. C, p. 199	27. B, pp. 208-209
13. A, p. 202	28. C, p. 193
14. B, p. 202	29. B, p. 211
15. D, p. 202	30. A, p. 209

ERA	PERIOD/EPOCH	BEGAN M.Y.A.	EVENT
CENOZOIC	Holocene Epoch	0.01	P
	Pleistocene Epoch	1.8	O
	Pliocene Epoch	5	G
	Miocene Epoch	23	B
	Oligocene Epoch	34	J
	Eocene Epoch	55	A
	Paleocene Epoch	65	M
MESOZOIC	Cretaceous Period	136	K
	Jurassic Period	190	I
	Triassic Period	225	E
PALEOZOIC	Permian Period	280	L
	Carboniferous Period	345	D
	Devonian Period	395	F
	Silurian Period	430	H
	Ordovician Period	500	P
	Cambrian Period	570	O

CHAPTER 9
PALEOANTHROPOLOGY: RECONSTRUCTING EARLY HOMINID BEHAVIOR AND ECOLOGY

LEARNING OBJECTIVES

After reading this chapter you should be able to:
- List the important distinguishing characteristics of a hominid (p. 215).
- Discuss what mosaic evolution is and the mosaic nature of human evolution (p. 215).
- Explain a biocultural approach to the study of human evolution (pp. 215-217)
- Explain how and why paleoanthropology is a multidisciplinary science (pp. 217-219).
- Outline the steps and the types of individuals involved in finding an early hominid site through the interpretation of the site (pp. 217-219).
- Discuss the significance of Olduvai Gorge to paleoanthropology (pp. 220-221).
- Compare relative dating techniques to chronometric techniques (p. 222).
- Describe the various dating techniques in terms of how they are used and for what time periods (if applicable) they can be used for (pp. 222-224).
- Discuss the application of dating methods at Olduvai Gorge (pp. 224-225).
- List and describe the types of early hominid sites found at Olduvai (pp. 226-227).
- Describe the purposes of experimental archaeology (pp. 229-231).
- Discuss how early hominid environments and behavior are reconstructed (pp. 232-234).
- Review theories explaining the origins of hominid bipedalism (pp. 235-237)

CHAPTER OUTLINE

Introduction.

We have seen in previous chapters that humans are primates and we share our evolution and even much of our behavior with other primates. At some point, however, our ancestors took their primate heritage and went off in another direction to become the unique species we are today. Some primitive hominoid may have begun this process before 10 m.y.a., but after 5 m.y.a. there is definite hominid fossil evidence in East Africa. One of the factors influencing hominid evolution was their behavior, once again emphasizing the biocultural nature of human evolution. This chapter looks at how scientists deduce early human behavior and the methods used by paleoanthropologists.

I   DEFINITION OF HOMINID
   A. Modern humans and our hominid ancestors are distinguished from our closest relatives in a number of characteristics.
   B. Various researchers have pointed to certain characteristics as being significant (at some stage) for hominids:
      1. large brain size.
      2. toolmaking behavior.
      3. bipedal locomotion.
   C. Mosaic evolution.
      1. All of the above mentioned characteristics did not evolve simultaneously.
      2. The evolutionary pattern in which different features evolve at different rates is called mosaic evolution.

3. The hallmark characteristic of hominid evolution is bipedal locomotion
   a. Bipedal locomotion predates other specialized traits that makes hominids unique.
   b. Thus, skeletal evidence for bipedal locomotion is the only truly reliable indicator of hominid status.
D. Biocultural evolution: the human capacity for culture.
   1. The most distinctive behavioral feature of modern humans is our extraordinary elaboration and dependence on culture.
   2. Culture encompasses much more than just toolmaking capacity.
      a. Culture integrates an entire adaptive strategy involving cognitive, political, social, and economic components.
      b. The material culture, tools and other items, is but a small portion of this cultural complex.
   3. The record of earlier hominids is almost exclusively remains of material culture, especially residues of stone tool manufacture.
      a. Thus, it is difficult to learn anything about the earliest stages of hominid cultural development before the regular manufacture of stone tools, circa 2.5 m.y.a.
      b. Without "hard" evidence we cannot know exactly what the earliest hominids were doing.
         i. Before they began making stone tools, hominids were probably using other types of tools (such as sticks) made of soft, perishable materials.
         ii. We also cannot know anything about the cultural behavior of these earliest humans.
   4. The fundamental basis for human cultural elaboration relates directly to cognitive abilities.
      a. When did the unique combination of cognitive, social, and material cultural adaptations become prominent in human evolution?
         i. Care must be taken to recognize the manifold nature of culture and to not expect it always to contain the same elements across species or through time.
      b. We know that the earliest hominids did not regularly manufacture stone tools.
         i. The earliest members of our lineage, the protohominids date back to approximately 7-5 m.y.a.
         ii. The protohominids may have carried objects such as naturally sharp stones or stone flakes, parts of carcasses, and pieces of wood.
         iii. At the least, we would expect them to have displayed these behaviors to the same degree as is found in living chimpanzees.
      c. Over the millions of years of hominid evolution, numerous components interacted, but they did not all develop simultaneously.
         i. As cognitive abilities developed, more efficient means of communications and learning resulted.
         ii. As a result of neural reorganization, more elaborate tools and social relationships also emerged.
         iii. More elaborate tools and social relationships selected for greater intelligence which in turn selected for further neural elaboration in a positive feedback loop.
         iv. These mutual dynamics are at the very heart of hominid biocultural evolution.

II   THE STRATEGY OF PALEOANTHROPOLOGY
- A. The task of recovering and interpreting the remains of early hominids is the province of paleoanthropology.
    1. Paleoanthropology is the study of ancient humans.
    2. Paleoanthropology is a diverse, multidisciplinary field that seeks to reconstruct the dating, anatomy, behavior, and ecology of our ancestors.
- B. Site survey
    1. Geologists do the initial survey work to locate potential early hominid sites.
    2. Paleontologists can generally give quick estimates of the geological age of a site based on faunal remains.
    3. In this way fossil beds of a particular geological age, in which we might find humans, can be isolated.
- C. Site excavation
    1. The search for hominid traces is conducted by archaeologists.
    2. Hominid sites do not need to contain fossilized skeletal material for us to know that they occupied the site.
        a. Artifacts provide behavioral clues of early hominid activities.
        b. There is no solid evidence of the earliest stages of hominid cultural modifications.
        c. At some point hominids began modifying stone and this indestructible material leaves us a preserved record of human activity.
            i. Stones are transported from one place to another.
            ii. Stones are used for a number of things such as throwing projectiles, cutting tools, or simply for use in windbreaks.
            iii. The oldest artifact sites now documented are from the Gona and Bouri areas of northeastern Ethiopia, dating to 2.5 m.y.a.
- D. Site interpretation
    1. In the laboratory materials recovered must be cleaned, sorted, and labeled.
    2. Animal and plant remains can help reconstruct the local, ancient environment.
    3. Paleoecological analysis can help in reconstructing early hominid diet.
    4. The paleoanthropologist interprets the chronology of the site, which includes:
        a. geological dating (based on stratigraphy).
        b. paleontological dating (based on such things as the known time periods for certain plants or animals recovered at the site).
        c. geophysical dating (based on dating techniques that measure radioactive decay).
    5. The paleoanthropologist also interprets the paleoecology of the site, which includes:
        a. paleontology (the recovery and study of fossil organisms).
        b. palynology (the study of fossil spores, pollen, and other microscopic plant parts).
        c. geomorphology (changes in the earth's land which, of course, affects climate).
        d. taphonomy (the study of the deposition of bones and other materials).
    6. The paleoanthropologist finally interprets the cultural and fossil hominid evidence, which includes:
        a. archeological traces of behavior.
        b. anatomical evidence from hominid remains.
    7. The paleoanthropologist attempts to tie all this information together to "flesh out" the kind of animal that may have been our direct ancestor.
        a. Primatologists may contribute information comparing humans and contemporary

nonhuman primates.

    b. Cultural anthropologists may contribute ethnographic information on the behavior of more recent humans, particularly the ecological adaptations of contemporary hunter-gatherer groups exploiting roughly similar environmental settings as reconstructed for a hominid site.

III   PALEOANTHROPOLOGY IN ACTION - OLDUVAI GORGE

  A. The greatest abundance of paleoanthropological information concerning the behavior of early hominids comes from Olduvai Gorge, Tanzania.

    1. Continuous excavations there were done by Louis and Mary Leakey between 1935 and 1984; others continue their work.

    2. Olduvai is a steep-sided valley with a deep ravine that resembles a miniature Grand Canyon.

      a. The semi-arid pattern of modern Olduvai is believed to be similar to most of the past environments preserved there over the last two million years.

      b. Olduvai is part of the Serengeti Plains and the surrounding countryside is a grassland savanna that supports vast numbers of mammals, representing a enormous supply of "meat on the hoof."

    3. Olduvai is located on the eastern branch of the Great Rift Valley of East Africa.

      a. The geological processes associated with the formation of the Rift Valley makes Olduvai extremely important to paleoanthropological investigation.

      b. Three results of geological rifting are most significant:

        i.   faulting (earth movement) exposes geological beds near the surface that are normally hidden by hundreds of feet of accumulated overburden.

        ii.   active volcanic processes cause rapid sedimentation, which often yields excellent preservation of bone and artifacts.

        iii.   volcanic activity provides a wealth of radiometrically datable material.

  B. The greatest contribution of Olduvai to paleoanthropological research is the establishment of an extremely well documented and correlated sequence of geological, paleontological, archeological, and hominid remains over the last two million years.

    1. At the very foundation of all paleoanthropological research is a well-established geological context.

      a. Another hominid site can be accurately dated relative to other sites in the Olduvai Gorge by cross-correlating known marker beds.

    2. Paleontological evidence includes more than 150 species of extinct animals.

      a. This evidence provides clues to the ecological conditions that the earliest humans lived in.

      b. Species present for known periods of time and dated at Olduvai can be used to estimate dates for sites that do not contain radiometrically datable materials.

        i.   These species are known as index fossils.

      c. Analysis of bones associated with artifacts yield information about hominid diets and bone-processing techniques.

    3. The archeological sequence is well documented for the last two million years.

      a. The earliest hominid site is from around 1.85 million years ago.

      b. There is already the well developed stone tool kit called Oldowan which includes choppers and some flake tools.

        c. The Oldowan tradition continues into later beds, being somewhat modified into what is called Developed Oldowan.

        d. Partial remains of several fossilized hominids have been recovered at Olduvai.

           i.   These range from the earliest occupation levels to recent *Homo sapiens*.

IV   DATING METHODS

  A. One of the essentials of paleoanthropology is putting sites and fossils into a chronological framework (i.e., how old are they?).

  B. The two types of dating methods used by paleoanthropologists are relative dating and chronometric (absolute) dating.

  C. Relative dating

    1. Relative dating tells you which object is older or younger than another object, but not in actual years.

    2. One type of relative dating is stratigraphy, the study of the sequential layering of deposits.

       a. Stratigraphy is based on the law of superposition, i.e., that the oldest stratum (layer) is the lowest stratum and higher strata are more recent.

       b. Problems associated with stratigraphic dating:

          i.   Earth disturbances such as volcanic activity, river activity, mountain building, or even modern construction companies, can shift strata making it difficult to reconstruct the chronology.

          ii.   The time period of a particular stratum is not possible to determine with much accuracy.

    3. Fluorine analysis

       a. This relative dating technique can only be used on bones.

       b. When a bone is buried, groundwater seeps into the bone and deposits fluorine during the fossilization process.

       c. The longer a bone is in the ground, the more fluorine it will contain.

       d. Fluorine analysis can only be done with bones found at the same location, i.e., this method is "site specific."

         i.   The amount of fluorine in groundwater is based on local conditions and varies from one area to another.

         ii.   Comparing bones from different localities is impossible.

       e. As in other relative techniques, actual ages in years cannot be obtained.

  D. Chronometric (absolute) dating.

    1. Chronometric dating provides an estimate of age in years and is based on radioactive decay.

       a. Certain radioactive isotopes of elements are unstable and they disintegrate to form an isotope of another element.

       b. This disintegration occurs at a constant rate.

         i.   By measuring the amount of disintegration in a particular sample, the number of years it took for the amount of decay may be calculated.

         ii.   The time it takes for one-half of the original amount of the isotope to decay into another isotope is referred to as the half-life.

    2. Uranium 238 decays with a half-life of 4.5 billion years to form lead.

       a. This chronometric technique has been used to date the age of the earth.

    3. Potassium/argon (K/Ar) dating involves the decay of potassium into argon gas.

a. K/Ar has a half-life of 1.3 billion years.
   b. It can be used to date a wide chronological range.
   c. This technique can only be done on rock matrix; it will not work on organic material such as bone.
   d. However, fossil bones are often associated with matrix and can be indirectly dated by its association.
   e. The best type of rock to perform K/Ar dating on is volcanic rock.
      i. When the lava is laid down in its molten state the argon gas present is driven off.
      ii. After solidification any argon that has been trapped in the rock is the result of potassium decay.
      iii. To obtain the date of the rock, it is reheated and the escaping argon is measured.
   f. The ^{40}Ar/^{39}Ar method is a more accurate variant of the potassium/argon technique.
      i. It allows analysis of smaller samples.
      ii. It reduces experimental error.
      iii. It has been used on a wide variety of hominid fossil sites.
      iv. It can date a much wider range than K/Ar, even up to modern times.
4. Carbon-14 is a radiometric method commonly used by archaeologists.
   a. Carbon-14 has a half-life of 5730 years.
   b. This method can be used to reliably date organic materials younger than 40,000 years.
   c. The probability of error using Carbon-14 increases after 40,000 years.
5. Each of the chronometric techniques have their own problems and none of these methods is absolutely precise.
   a. Chronometric analyses provide approximate dates with standard deviations that provide a time ranges.
E. Application of dating methods: examples from Olduvai.
   1. "Zinj" (OH 5) was dated at around 1.75 million years using potassium-argon.
   2. Due to potential sources of error, K/Ar dating must be cross-checked using other independent methods.
   3. Fission-track dating
      a. Uranium-238 decays at a constant rate through spontaneous fission which leaves microscopic tracks in crystals.
      b. By counting tracks, i.e., the fraction of uranium atoms that have fissioned, the age of a mineral can be estimated.
      c. One of the earliest uses of uranium-238 dating was at Olduvai, which yielded a date of 2.30 ($\pm$.28) m.y.a., compatible with the K/Ar dates.
   4. Another important means of cross-checking dates is paleomagnetism.
      a. This technique is based on the constantly shifting nature of the earth's magnetic pole.
      b. The earth's magnetic field, currently oriented in a northern direction, periodically shifts.
      c. Paleomagnetic dating involves taking samples of sediment that contains magnetically charged particles.
         i. Magnetically charged particles orient towards the magnetic pole.

    ii. These particles will be oriented towards the direction of the magnetic pole that existed when they were incorporated into rock; thus these particles serve as a "fossil compass."

  d. The paleomagnetic sequence is then compared against the K/Ar dates to check if they agree.

 5. Faunal correlation, or biostratigraphy, is another method for cross-checking dating methods.

  a. This involves correlating the evolutionary stages of well-known mammals from one site to another; some of these stages are very brief and such an animal serves as an "index fossil."

  b. When these animals are found at sites with chronometric dates, approximate ages can be assigned to sites where no suitable materials for chronometric dating are present.

 6. Because each dating technique has problems, it is important to use several in conjunction with one another in order to cross-check the results.

V EXCAVATIONS AT OLDUVAI

 A. The 70 miles of exposed vertical surface at Olduvai has provided several dozen hominid sites.

  1. An incredible amount of paleoanthropological information has come from these excavated areas.

  2. The data has been organized into three broad categories of site types (see below), depending on implied function.

 B. "Butchering" localities

  1. These are sites that contain one (or at most a few) individuals of a single species of large mammal associated with a scatter of archaeological traces.

 C. Quarry localities

  1. These sites are areas where early hominids extracted their stone resources and initially fashioned their tools.

  2. There are usually thousands of small stone fragments of a particular type of rock at quarry localities, but no or very little bone refuse.

 D. Multipurpose localities (aka "campsites")

  1. These are general-purpose areas where hominids possibly ate, slept, and put the finishing touches on their tools.

  2. The accumulation of living debris, including broken animal bones and many broken stones is a basic human pattern.

  3. One of the multipurpose areas excavated at Olduvai is over 1.8 million years old.

  a. This site has a circle of large stones forming what was at one time thought to be a base for a windbreak

  b. However, this interpretation is now considered unlikely.

 E. Context and association

  1. Archeologists derive their information from more than just the analysis of objects.

  2. It is the context and association of objects that give archeologists the data they require to understand the behavioral patterns of ancient human populations.

  a. Context refers to where the objects are found.

  b. Association refers to what is found with the objects.

VI EXPERIMENTAL ARCHAEOLOGY

A. We can learn more about our ancestors by understanding how they made and used their tools.
B. Stone tool (lithic) technology
   1. The smaller piece struck off of a stone is called a flake.
   2. The Oldowan is the earliest known stone tool industry.
   3. The object in making a tool is to produce a usable cutting surface.
   4. Tools flaked on both sides are bifacial.
   5. Tiny blades called microliths are found in the uppermost beds at Olduvai (circa 17,000 y.a.)
   6. Archaeologists successfully butchered an entire elephant using stone tools.
C. Analysis of bone
   1. Taphonomy is the study of how natural factors influence bone deposition and preservation.

VII RECONSTRUCTION OF EARLY HOMINID ENVIRONMENTS AND BEHAVIOR
   A. We always need to ask ourselves what kinds of evidence support a particular contention.
   B. Environmental explanations for hominid origins
      1. The earliest hominids do not appear until early in the Pliocene (4-5 m.y.a.)
      2. For most of the Miocene, Africa was generally tropical.
      3. The earliest evidence of hominid diversification comes from East Africa.
      4. 12-5 m.y.a. in East Africa "fringe" habitats were transitional zones between forests and grasslands.
      5. Our knowledge of the factors influencing the appearance of the earliest hominids is limited.
   C. Changing environments and later hominid diversifications
      1. Elizabeth Vrba of Yale University studied the appearance of new species of antelope and hominids in South and East Africa.
      2. She noticed a correlation between the appearance of new species and increased aridity.
      3. The evolutionary pulse theory is not yet clearly established.
   D. Why did hominids become bipedal?
      1. Bipedal locomotion was the most fundamental adaptive shift among the early members of our family.
      2. Early hominids almost certainly sought safety at night in the trees.
      3. The primary influences claimed to have stimulated the shift to bipedalism include:
         a. the ability to carry objects and offspring,
         b. hunting on the savanna,
         c. gathering seeds and nuts,
         d. feeding from bushes,
         e. a better view of open country to spot predators,
         f. long-distance walking,
         g. and provisioning by males of females with dependent offspring.
      4. All theories attempting to explain the origin of bipedalism in hominids have one deficiency or another.

5. Nevertheless, paleoanthropological interpretations are scientifically grounded in that they all:
   a. use interrelating lines of evidence,
   b. employ contemporary primate models,
   c. and generate predictions about future evidence.

KEY TERMS

absolute dating techniques: see chronometric dating techniques.

accuracy: refers to how close a measured quantity is to the true value of what is being measured. Generally, the true value is represented by a standard.

artifacts: material remnants of hominid behavior, usually of made of stone or, occasionally, bone, early in then archaeological record.

association: what an artifact or archeological trace is found with.

biostratigraphy: dating method based on evolutionary changes within an evolved lineage.

chronometric dating techniques: dating techniques that gives an estimate in actual number of years, based on radioactive decay. (i.e. absolute dating).

context: the environmental setting where an archeological trace is found. *Primary* context is the setting in which the archeological trace was originally deposited. A *secondary* context is one to which the archeological trace has been moved by some force such as the action of a stream.

faunal analysis: see biostratigraphy.

fluorine analysis: a relative dating technique in which the amount of fluorine deposited in bones is compared. Bones with the most fluorine are the oldest.

geomorphology: changes in the form of the earth's land, such as rifting of land, mountain building, development of ravines and canyons, etc.

half-life: in chronometric dating, the amount of time that it takes for one-half of the original (parent) isotope to decay into its daughter isotope.

mosaic evolution: the evolutionary pattern in which different characteristics evolve at different rates.

paleoecology: the study of fossil communities and environments.

paleomagnetism: dating methods based on the earth's shifting magnetic poles.

paleontology: the recovery and study of ancient organisms.

palynology: the study of fossil spores, pollen, and other microscopic plant parts.

precision: refers to the closeness of repeated measurements of the same quantity to each other.

protohominid: the earliest members of the hominid lineage. No fossils of this hypothetical group have yet been found.

relative dating: a type of dating in which objects are ranked by age. Thus, some objects can be said to be older than other objects, but no actual age in years can be assigned.

stratigraphy: study of the sequential layering of deposits.

taphonomy: the study of how bones and other materials came to be buried and preserved as fossils.

INTERNET EXERCISES AND *INFOTRAC COLLEGE EDITION* EXERCISES

Are you interested in experiencing paleoanthropology in action? Then perhaps you should check out a paleoanthropological field school. Here are a couple of those that are available:
- Koobi Fora Field School, northwestern Kenya (administered jointly by Rutgers U. & the National Museums of Kenya, http://www.rci.rutgers.edu/~mjr/HTML/indexbody.html)
- Summer Paleoanthropology Field School at Makapansgat, South Africa (administered jointly by the Institute of Human Origins at Arizona State University and The University of the Witwatersrand, South Africa, http://www.asu.edu/clas/iho/field.htm)

In *InfoTrac*, do a keyword search on "Olduvai Gorge." A couple of short, but informative, articles will be displayed from the September, 1999, issue of *Calliope* written by anthropologists Curtis Marean and Fiona Marshall. Read them to learn more about the Leakeys and life at the Gorge.

CONCEPT APPLICATION

Answer the following questions that refer to the cross-section of a paleoanthropological site on the next page.

1. What chronometric method was likely used to date the volcanic layers that are labeled "1.0 m.y.a." and "50,000 y.a."?

2. Put the three skulls labeled "X, Y & Z" in the correct chronological order, from youngest to oldest. Approximately how old are skulls "X, Y & Z"?

3. The vertebral column on the right side is most likely associated with which skull? Why?

4. Which two of the three fireplaces (labeled "1, 2 & 3") are most likely the same approximate age? What chronometric technique would you use to verify your answer? Can you use the same technique on the other fireplace? Why or why not?

5. Which two of the three sets of limb bones (labeled "A, B & C") are most likely the same approximate age? What dating technique would you use to verify your answer?

6. What geological event can probably account for the difficulty in interpreting this site's stratigraphy?

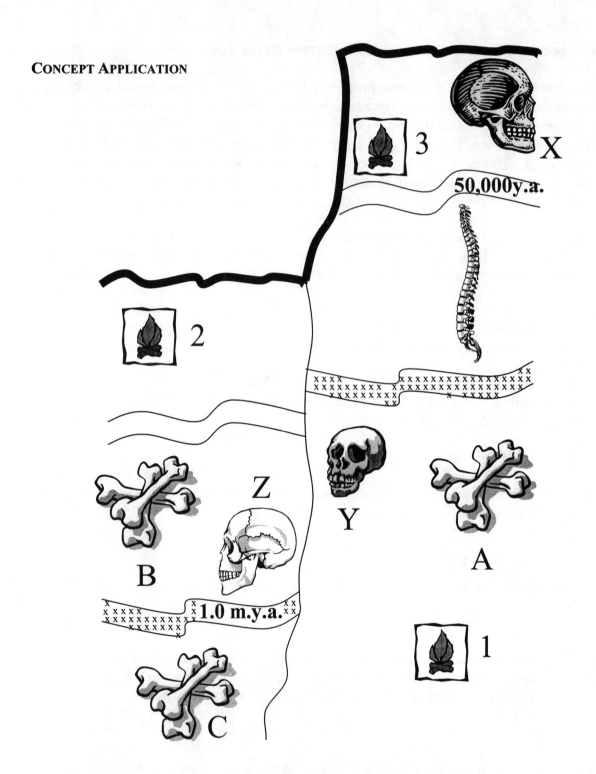

50,000 y.a.

1.0 m.y.a.

Now answer the True/False, Multiple Choice and Short Answer sample test questions. Following completion of the tests correct them with the answers and textbook page references at the end of this Study Guide chapter. Note the areas in which you are strong and weak to guide you in your studying. Finally, answer the sample Essay Questions.

TRUE/FALSE QUESTIONS

1. Mosaic evolution states that the hominid dental, locomotor and neurological systems evolved at remarkably uniform rates.
   TRUE FALSE

2. When compared with other animals, the most distinctive behavioral feature of humans is our extraordinary reliance on biological instinct.
   TRUE FALSE

3. Modern paleoanthropologists work independently of other scientists.
   TRUE FALSE

4. Olduvai Gorge is located in Ghana, in western Africa.
   TRUE FALSE

5. Potassium-argon dating only works on organic material, like charcoal.
   TRUE FALSE

6. Sites which contain one or only a few individuals from a single species associated with a scatter of archaeological traces are known as multipurpose localities.
   TRUE FALSE

7. The thin-edged fragment removed from another rock is called a core.
   TRUE FALSE

8. Vrba's evolutionary pulse theory suggests a gradual evolutionary change in hominid species around 5 m.y.a.
   TRUE FALSE

9. The most fundamental adaptive shift in hominid evolution was the development of a large brain.
   TRUE FALSE

10. Lovejoy's seed-eating hypothesis used the feeding behavior and ecology of lemurs as an analogy for early hominids.
    TRUE FALSE

MULTIPLE CHOICE QUESTIONS

1. Evolution in which structures evolve at different rates is termed
   A. convergent evolution.
   B. parallel evolution.
   C. mosaic evolution.
   D. punctuated equilibrium

2. Human evolution can be characterized as
   A. parallel.
   B. convergent.
   C. homologous.
   D. mosaic.

3. Which of the following is an aspect of material culture that could be a vestige of the earliest hominids?
   A. a fragment of a stone tool
   B. cognitive abilities
   C. economic systems
   D. social systems

4. Initial surveying and locating potential hominid sites is the primary task of
   A. physical anthropologists.
   B. geologists.
   C. paleoecologists.
   D. archaeologists.

5. The primary task of an archeologist at a paleoanthropological site is to
   A. search for hominid "traces."
   B. reconstruct the ancient environment of the site.
   C. establish the relationships of any fossil humans recovered.
   D. perform dating techniques to establish the time period.

6. The earliest documented artifact sites are
   A. Laetoli at 3.4 m.y.a.
   B. Gona and Bouri at 2.5 m.y.a.
   C. Olduvai at 1.85 m.y.a.
   D. Taung at 1 m.y.a.

7. The archeological setting where an artifact is found is called the
   A. microlith.
   B. context.
   C. quarry site.
   D. monolith.

8. Which of the following does a paleoanthropologist **not** use in the concluding stages of a site interpretation?
    A. information pertaining to dating.
    B. paleoecology.
    C. information from linguists.
    D. anatomical evidence from hominid remains.

9. The paleoanthropologist who discovered the best preserved *Proconsul* skull ever found and also discovered "Zinj," was
    A. Louis Leakey.
    B. Mary Leakey.
    C. Jane Goodall.
    D. Meg Weigel.

10. The earliest stone tool industry found at Olduvai is called
    A. Acheulean.
    B. Chellean.
    C. Oldowan.
    D. Developed Oldowan.

11. Which of the following statements is **not** correct?
    A. Earth disturbances may shift geological strata and the objects within them.
    B. Fluorine analysis can only be done on bones that come from the same location.
    C. Chronometric dating techniques are absolutely precise.
    D. Chronometric techniques are based on the phenomenon of radioactive decay.

12. A disadvantage to fluorine analysis is that it
    A. can only be done on volcanic beds.
    B. can only be done on bones found in the same area.
    C. is not effective for materials older than 50,000 years.
    D. has a range of error of 12,000 years.

13. Chronometric techniques are based on
    A. radioactive decay.
    B. superposition.
    C. stratigraphy.
    D. the works of Oldowan Kanobe.

14. A half-life
    A. differs for the isotopes of different elements.
    B. is the amount of time it takes for all of the original amount of an isotope to decay..
    C. is set at 5,730 years for K/Ar.
    D. All of the above.

15. The dating technique used extensively in paleoanthropology for the time period 1-5 m.y.a. is
    A. uranium-238.
    B. carbon-14.
    C. fluorine analysis.
    D. potassium-argon.

16. Chronometric dates are accompanied with a
    A. standard deviation.
    B. mean.
    C. analysis of covariance.
    D. regression slope.

17. If you found a fossil in East Africa and you suspected that it might be over a million years old, what type of dating technique would you use to obtain an actual date?
    A. Carbon-14 dating
    B. Biostratigraphy
    C. Potassium-Argon
    D. stratigraphy

18. Several different dating techniques are used to cross-check the age of a paleoanthropological site because
    A. no single one is perfectly reliable by itself.
    B. sources of error differ in the various techniques.
    C. sampling error, contamination and experimental error can cause imprecision.
    D. All of the above.

19. Areas from which early hominids extracted stone for their tools are referred to as
    A. butchering localities.
    B. quarry localities.
    C. multipurpose localities.
    D. campsites.

20. General-use areas where hominids possibly ate, slept, and made tools are
    A. butchering localities.
    B. quarry localities.
    C. multipurpose localities.
    D. assembly point.

21. Most of our information concerning early human behavior comes from
    A. living sites.
    B. stone tools.
    C. skeletal remains.
    D. cave paintings.

22. Knappers are
    A. thin-edged fragments.
    B. stones reduced by flake removal.
    C. those who flake stone tools.
    D. another word for hammerstones.

23. Microwear refers to
    A. microscopic changes on the edges of stone tools.
    B. microscopic structures in the cells of many plants.
    C. clothing associated with our smaller hominid ancestors.
    D. a method of removing flakes from a core.

24. The study of how natural factors influence bone deposition and preservation is
    A. osteology.
    B. paleontology.
    C. petrology.
    D. taphonomy.

25. Speculative and imaginative reconstructions of early hominid behavior are referred to as
    A. hypotheses.
    B. scenarios.
    C. theories.
    D. interpretations.

26. Environmental determinism refers to
    A. a single large environmental change producing a major adaptive change in a species.
    B. the environment influencing a species' evolutionary path.
    C. the destiny of a species being determined by its environment.
    D. a cause and affect relationship that exists between the environment and extinction.

27. The appearance of new species in Africa has been linked to
    A. increased rainfall.
    B. seasonal fluctuation.
    C. periodic episodes of aridity.
    D. cooler climates.

28. Which of the following has **not** been suggested as a factor that may have influenced the initial evolution of hominid bipedality?
    A. carrying objects, such as tools and infants
    B. seed and nut gathering
    C. the beginnings of agriculture
    D. hunting

29. Owen Lovejoy proposed that _____ was critical in the origins of bipedality in early hominids.
    A. seed eating
    B. visual surveillance
    C. feeding from bushes
    D. male provisioning

30. The most fundamental adaptive shift among early hominids was
    A. sleeping in trees.
    B. hunting.
    C. making tools.
    D. bipedal locomotion.

SHORT ANSWER QUESTIONS (& PAGE REFERENCES)

1. What is mosaic evolution? (p. 215)

2. What is the difference between relative and chronometric dating? (pp. 222-223)

3. How does a "Butchering" locality differ from a Multipurpose locality? (p. 226)

4. What is the difference between a flake and a core? (p. 229)

5. Why is a paleoanthropological scenario? (p. 232)

ESSAY QUESTIONS (& PAGE REFERENCES)

1. What have the long-term excavations at Olduvai Gorge taught us about the environments, chronology and subsistence of Plio-Pleistocene hominids? (pp. 220-221)

2. What is experimental archaeology and how does it help us understand early hominid behavior? (pp. 228-231)

3. Compare and contrast Jolly's seed-eating hypothesis with Lovejoy's provisioning model. (pp. 235-237)

ANSWERS, *CORRECTED STATEMENT* IF FALSE & REFERENCES TO TRUE/FALSE QUESTIONS

1. FALSE, p. 215, Mosaic evolution states that the hominid dental, locomotor and neurological systems evolved at *markedly different* rates.

2. FALSE, p. 215, When compared with other animals, the most distinctive behavioral feature of humans is our extraordinary reliance on *culture*.

3. FALSE, p. 217, Modern paleoanthropologists work *cooperatively with many* other scientists.

4. FALSE, p. 220, Olduvai Gorge is located in *Tanzania, in eastern* Africa.

5. FALSE, p. 223, Potassium-argon dating only works on *volcanic* material, like *lava*.

6. FALSE, p. 226, Sites which contain one or only a few individuals from a single species associated with a scatter of archaeological traces are known as *butchering* localities.

7. FALSE, p. 229, The thin-edged fragment removed from another rock is called a *flake*.

8. FALSE, p. 234, Vrba's evolutionary pulse theory suggests a *series of rapid environmental* changes around *2.5* m.y.a.

9. FALSE, p. 235, The most fundamental adaptive shift in hominid evolution was the development of *bipedal locomotion*.

10. FALSE, p. 236, *Jolly's* seed-eating hypothesis used the feeding behavior and ecology of *gelada baboons* as an analogy for early hominids.

ANSWERS AND REFERENCES TO MULTIPLE CHOICE QUESTIONS

1. C, p. 215	16. A, p. 224
2. D, p. 215	17. C, p. 223
3. A, p. 216	18. D, p. 225
4. B, p. 218	19. B, p. 226
5. A, p. 218	20. C, p. 226
6. B, p. 218	21. B, p. 227
7. B, p. 219	22. C, p. 230
8. C, p. 219	23. A, p. 231
9. B, p. 221	24. D, p. 231
10. C, p. 221	25. B, p. 232
11. C, p. 223	26. A, p. 232
12. B, p. 222	27. C, p. 234
13. A, p. 222	28. C, p. 236
14. A, p. 223	29. D, pp. 235-237
15. D, p. 223	30. D, p. 235

CONCEPT APPLICATION SOLUTION

1. What chronometric method was likely used to date the volcanic layers that are labeled "1.0 m.y.a." and "50,000 y.a."?
   Potassium-argon or better yet the $^{40}Ar/^{39}Ar$ method, particularly for the 50,000-year-old layer.

2. Put the three skulls labeled "X, Y & Z" in the correct chronological order, from youngest to oldest. Approximately how old are skulls "X, Y & Z"?
   "X" is younger than "Z" is younger than "Y". "X" is less than 50,000 years old, "Z" is between 50,000 and 1,000,000 years old, and "Y" is older than 1,000,000 years.

3. The vertebral column on the right side is most likely associated with which skull? Why?
   It is most likely associated with skull "Z" because they are both from the middle stratum, or layer.

4. Which two of the three fireplaces (labeled "1, 2 & 3") are most likely the same approximate age? What chronometric technique would you use to verify your answer? Can you use the same technique on the other fireplace? Why or why not?
   Fireplaces "3" and "2" are from the topmost layer so they are probably closest in age. Carbon-14 would be best to apply to these two fireplaces because this layer is younger than 50,000 years. Carbon-14 could not be applied to the Fireplace "1" because that layer is older than 1,000,000 years, well beyond the limits of the method.

5. Which two of the three sets of limb bones (labeled "A, B & C") are most likely the same approximate age? What dating technique would you use to verify your answer?
   Limb bones "A" and "C" are possibly of the same age because they are both found beneath the million-year-old volcanic layer. The fluorine method could check if the bones are similar to each other in age.

6. What geological event can probably account for the difficulty in interpreting this site's stratigraphy?
   An earthquake likely caused the faulting in the section that raised the right side in relation to the left.

CHAPTER 10
HOMINID ORIGINS

LEARNING OBJECTIVES
After reading this chapter you should be able to:
- List the major features of human bipedalism (pp. 243-247).
- Explain what is meant by habitual and obligate bipedalism (p. 245).
- Discuss bipedalism in reference to the early hominids of East and South Africa (pp. 248-268).
- Review the earliest East African hominids (pp. 249-253).
- Discuss the importance of australopithecines discoveries from Laetoli and Hadar (pp. 253-257).
- Compare and contrast the different types of early hominids found at Olduvai and Lake Turkana (pp. 259-260).
- Explain why the South African hominid finds were so important (pp. 263-265).
- Compare and contrast the "robust" and "gracile" australopithecines from South Africa (pp. 266-268).
- Understand the geological complexities and resultant dating problems in South Africa (pp. 269-271).
- Know the steps necessary to interpret fossil remains (p. 273).
- Discuss the current uncertainties in taxonomic interpretation for the Plio-Pleistocene hominids (pp. 274-277).
- Recount the four broad groupings for the Plio-Pleistocene African hominids as an alternative to a proposed phylogeny (pp. 277-278).
- Interpret various proposed phylogenies (pp. 278-279).

CHAPTER OUTLINE
Introduction

In the past, various researchers attempted to define hominids based mainly on dental characteristics or toolmaking behavior. Neither of these criteria work when applied to the earliest hominids. In this chapter, we review the large collections of early hominids recovered from East and South Africa encompassing the period from just before 4 m.y.a. to 1 m.y.a. Analysis of these several thousand specimens has led paleoanthropologists to conclude that bipedalism represents the primary functional adaptation that best distinguishes the hominid lineage. This chapter also explores the difficulties of trying to interpret this vast array of fossil material. We will look at the broader areas of interpretation where a general consensus can be found and end with the more specific interpretations of proposed evolutionary relationships.

I   THE BIPEDAL ADAPTATION
   A. Efficient bipedalism among primates is found only among hominids.
   B. The process of bipedal walking
      1. To walk bipedally a human must balance on the "stance" leg while the "swing" leg is off the ground.

2. During normal walking, both feet are simultaneously on the ground only about 25% of the time.
C. Structural/anatomical modifications for bipedalism
   1. To maintain a stable center of balance many drastic anatomical modifications in the basic primate quadrupedal pattern are required.
   2. The most dramatic changes occur in the hominid pelvis and its associated musculature.
      a. Compared to a quadruped's pelvis, the hominid pelvis is shorter and broader.
      b. This configuration helps to stabilize the line of weight transmission from the lower back to the hip joint.
      c. The result of the broadening of the two sides of the pelvis is to produce a basin-shaped structure that helps to support the abdominal organs.
   3. Hominid pelvic modifications also reposition the attachments of several key muscles that act on the hip and leg, changing their mechanical function.
      a. The gluteus maximus, the major muscle in bipedal walking is the largest muscle in humans (but not so in quadrupeds).
      b. The gluteus maximus is a powerful extensor of the thigh and provides additional force, particularly during running and climbing.
   4. The foramen magnum has been repositioned under the cranium so that the head balances on the spine.
      a. This arrangement also removes the need for robust neck muscles to hold the head erect.
   5. Unlike the straight great ape vertebral column, the human spine has curves that keep the trunk centered above the pelvis. This stabilizes weight transmission.
   6. The human hind limb is increased in length, increasing stride length.
      a. The femur is angled inward.
      b. This arrangement keeps the legs more directly under the body.
   7. There are several structural changes made in the human foot.
      a. The big toe is realigned so that it is in line with the other toes, losing its opposability.
      b. A longitudinal arch develops which helps to absorb shock and adds a propulsive spring.
   8. For these major anatomical changes to have been selected, there must have been a tremendous selective advantage to bipedalism.
      a. It bears repeating that we do not know what conditions led to bipedalism.
      b. The various ideas of what led to bipedalism should be considered scenarios rather than hypotheses.
      c. We do not have sufficient data to test any of these ideas.
D. Form follows function in structural modifications, exemplified by bipedalism.
   1. During evolution, organisms do not undergo significant structural change (i.e., form) unless these changes assist individuals in some functional capacity.
   2. Evolutionary changes such as bipedalism do not occur all at once, but probably evolve over a fairly long period of time.
E. Hominid bipedalism is habitual and obligate.
   1. Habitual bipedalism means that hominids move bipedally as their standard and most efficient mode of locomotion.

2. Obligate bipedalism means they hominids cannot locomote efficiently in any other manner.
3. When examining the earliest hominids it is crucial to identify those anatomical features that indicate bipedalism and to what degree these organisms were committed to bipedalism.
    a. All of the major structural changes required for bipedalism are seen in early hominids from East and South Africa.
    b. In particular, the pelvis shows dramatic remodeling to support weight in a bipedal stance.
    c. Other human structural characteristics are also present in these early hominids.
        i. The vertebral column shows the same curve as in modern humans.
        ii. The lower limbs were lengthened to almost the same degree as in modern humans (although the arms were longer).
        iii. The carrying angle of weight support from the hip to the knee was also very similar to modern humans.
    d. Early hominid foot structure is known from sites in both South and East Africa.
        i. These specimens indicate that the heel and longitudinal arch were well adapted for a bipedal gait.
    e. Some paleontologists suggest, however, that the great toe was divergent, unlike the pattern seen in later hominids.
        i. This would have aided the foot in grasping, enabling early hominids to more effectively exploit arboreal habitats.
        ii. This type of foot would not have been as efficient as a stable platform during bipedal locomotion.
    f. Consequently, some researchers believe that early hominids were not necessarily obligate bipeds.
        i. They believe that these early humans spent considerable amount of time in the trees.
        ii. Nevertheless, all the early hominids that have been identified from Africa are thought by most researchers to have been both habitual and obligate bipeds.

II EARLY HOMINIDS IN THE PLIO-PLEISTOCENE
    A. The beginnings of hominid differentiation have their roots in the late Miocene (ca. 10-15 m.y.a.)
        1. Sometime during the period 8-5 m.y.a. hominids began to adapt more fully to a ground-living niche.
        2. Unfortunately, fossil recovery for this time period is scant creating a significant 3 million year gap.
    B. The human fossil record increases beginning around 4.5 m.y.a.
        1. This encompasses the Pliocene and the earliest stages of the Pleistocene (5-1 m.y.a.)
        2. This span of time is usually referred to as the Plio-Pleistocene.

III THE EAST AFRICAN RIFT VALLEY
    A. The Great Rift Valley of Africa stretches 1,200 miles from the Red Sea in the north to the Serengeti Plain in the Tanzania.
        1. This area has experienced active geological processes over the last several million years in which the area is being rifted (separated).

2. Because of this geological activity earlier sediments are thrown to the surface where they become exposed and can be located by paleoanthropologists.
B. Rifting has stimulated volcanic activity.
   1. Volcanic sediments provide a valuable means for chronometrically dating many sites in East Africa.
   2. The datable hominid sites along the Rift Valley have yielded crucial information concerning the precise chronology of early human evolution.

IV   THE EARLIEST EAST AFRICAN HOMINIDS
A. Earliest traces
   1. Exciting new discoveries from the late Miocene and early Pliocene of Kenya and Ethiopia have recently come to light.
   2. Tugen Hills
      a. The oldest of these finds are from the Tugen Hills of central Kenya, near Lake Baringo, whose discovery was announced in 2000.
      b. These fossils, named *Orrorin tugenensis*, are dated to approximately 6 m.y.a.
      c. The scientists who discovered these fossils are convinced that they walked bipedally and are thus hominids.
   3. Middle Awash
      a. From the Middle Awash region of Ethiopia in 2001, other fossil hominids have been reported dating to 5.8-5.2 m.y.a.
      b. Again the researchers claim that fossil anatomy supports a claim of bipedality for these individuals.
B. *Ardipithecus* from Aramis (Ethiopia)
   1. This site has been chronometrically dated at 4.4 m.y.a., making the group of fossils from this site the oldest substantial collection of hominids yet discovered.
   2. Remains recovered include jaws, teeth, partial crania and upper limb bones, hand and foot bones.
      a. In addition, 40% of a single skeleton was recovered in 1995.
      b. As of now, however, this specimen has not yet been fully scientifically described.
   3. Because many of Aramis discoveries have only been partially described, only provisional interpretations are possible at this time.
      a. There is anatomical evidence of bipedalism, the criterion for hominid status.
      b. The foramen magnum is positioned further forward than in quadrupeds.
      c. Features of the humerus suggest that the forelimb was not weight-bearing.
   4. Tim White and his co-workers has suggested that the Aramis hominids be assigned to a new genus and species, *Ardipithecus ramidus*.
      a. The basis for this recognition of a new genus is that these specimens are much more primitive than *Australopithecus* (the other hominid genus closest to this time period).
      b. The thin enamel caps on the molars of *Ardipithecus* contrast to the thicker enamel caps typical for *Australopithecus.*
      c. *Ardipithecus* may represent the "sister-group" of *Australopithecus* and the root species for all later hominids.

V   *AUSTRALOPITHECUS* FROM EAST AFRICA
A. Most of these later East African fossils are included in the genus *Australopithecus*.
B. Kanapoi and Allia Bay (East Turkana).

1. These hominid sites had been dated between 4.2 and 1.4 m.y.a.
2. The thick enamel on the molars conform to the condition found in *Australopithecus*.
3. It has been suggested that these specimens be assigned to the genus *Australopithecus*, but to a separate species, i.e., *A. anamensis*.

C. Laetoli
1. This site is dated between 3.7-3.5 m.y.a.
2. An amazing find was made there in 1978: fossilized hominid footprints imprinted into a volcanic ash-fall!
3. We know for certain that there were bipedal hominids walking in East Africa at this time.
4. One group of footprints suggests two, possibly, three individuals.
   a. Analysis of the footprints indicate one individual was 4' 9" and the other was 4' 1".
5. Despite agreement that these individuals were bipedal, some researchers feel they were not bipedal in the same way as modern humans.
   a. They suggest that the Laetoli hominids moved in a "strolling" fashion with a short stride.

D. Hadar (Afar Triangle).
1. The most recent dating calibrations suggest a range of dates from 3.9-3.0 m.y.a.
2. Two of the most extraordinary discoveries of human paleontology were found at Hadar.
   a. Forty-percent of an *Australopithecus afarensis* female, nicknamed "Lucy," was recovered there in 1974.
      i. This is one of the two most complete hominid skeletons dating before 100,000 years ago.
   b. The "First Family," a group of bones representing at least 13 individuals, including 4 infants, was found at Hadar in 1975.
      i. It has been suggested that these individuals represented a single social unit that died at the same time in a catastrophe.
      ii. These individuals have been nicknamed the "first family."
      iii. The precise deposition of the site has not been completely explained and the assertion that these individuals were contemporaries must be viewed tentatively.
3. Considerable cultural material has been recovered.
   a. Some stone tools may be 2.5 million years old, making them the oldest cultural evidence yet found.

E. *Australopithecus afarensis* from Laetoli and Hadar
1. The hominids from Laetoli and Hadar are assigned to *Australopithecus afarensis*.
2. *A. afarensis* is more primitive than any of the later species of *Australopithecus*.
3. By "primitive" it is meant that *A. afarensis* is less evolved in any particular direction than are the later occurring hominid species.
4. *A. afarensis* shares more primitive features with other early hominoids (such as *Sivapithecus*) and living pongids than with later hominids.
5. The teeth of *A. afarensis*, for example, are quite primitive.
   a. The canines are often large, pointed teeth that overlap.
   b. The lower first premolar is semisectorial (i.e., it provides a shearing surface for

the upper canine).
   c. The tooth rows are parallel.
6. The cranial parts that are preserved also exhibit several primitive hominoid features.
   a. Cranial capacities are difficult to estimate but they seem to range from 375 cm^3 to 500 cm^3.
   b. It appears that the smaller cranial capacities are for the females and the larger cranial capacities are for males.
   c. One thing that is certain is that *A. afarensis* had a small brain; the mean for the pecies is probably 420 cm^3.
7. Postcrania
   a. Relative to the lower limbs, the upper limbs of *A. afarensis* are longer than in modern humans.
      i.   This is also a primitive hominoid condition.
   b. Note that this does not mean that the arms were longer than the legs.
   c. Wrist, hand, and foot bones show several differences from modern humans.
8. Stature has been estimated
   a. *A. afarensis* was shorter than modern humans.
   b. There appears to have been considerable sexual dimorphism.
      i.   If this is true, females were between 3.5 to 4 feet tall.
      ii. Males could be up to five feet tall.
   c. *A. afarensis* may have been as sexually dimorphic as any living primate.
9. *A. afarensis* is so primitive in the majority of dental and cranial features that if it were not for evidence of bipedalism this primate may not be classified as a hominid.
   a. However, these hominids were clearly obligate bipeds.

F. Another East African hominid
  1. In 1999, on the west side of Lake Turkana, Meave Leakey and her colleagues unearthed a new hominid skull.
  2. With a cranial capacity estimated between 400-500 cm^3 this specimen displayed a mosaic of cranial morphology and was interpreted as a completely new genus that was named *Kenyanthropus*.

G. Later East African australopithecine finds
  1. In 1999, at the Bouri site in the Middle Awash region of Ethiopia, yet another australopithecine species was recovered: *A. garhi*.
   a. These fossils, dated to 2.5 m.y.a., are suggested to be close to the ancestry of our own genus, *Homo*.
   b. Fossil animal bones that were clearly butchered were found nearby.
  2. There are up to 10 different hominid sites from 3-1 m.y.a. now known in East Africa.
  3. The three most important are:
   a. East Lake Turkana (Koobi Fora)
   b. West Lake Turkana
   c. Olduvai Gorge

H. Australopithecines from Olduvai and Lake Turkana.
  1. These include two different genera and up to six different species.
  2. The term "robust" is a term that paleoanthropologists use to describe an australopithecine that is heavily-built in its skull and dentition.
  3. "Gracile" has been applied to the lightly-built australopithecines.

4. The earliest representative of the robust group is WT 17000 ("the black skull").
   a. With a cranial capacity of 410 cm^3 WT 17000 has the smallest definitely ascertained brain volume of any hominid yet found.
5. WT 17000 also has other primitive traits reminiscent of *A. afarensis*, that include:
   a. a compound crest in the back of the skull.
   b. a projecting upper face.
   c. the upper dental row that converges in back.
   d. a cranial base that is extensively pneumatized (contains air pockets).
6. WT 17000 is a mosaic of primitive traits and very derived traits.
   a. These features seem to place it between *Australopithecus afarensis* and the later robust species.
   b. WT 17000 has been placed in a separate species, *Australopithecus aethiopicus*.
7. By 2 m.y.a., even more derived members of the robust lineage were on the scene in East Africa.
8. Robust australopithecines have
   a. relatively small cranial capacities (ranging from 510-530 cm^3) compared to later hominids.
   b. very large, broad faces.
   c. massive back teeth and lower jaws.
9. The larger (male?) individuals possess a sagittal crest.
10. These East African robust hominids are assigned to *Australopithecus boisei*.

VI EARLY HOMO
A. The earliest appearance of our genus, *Homo*, may be as ancient as the robust australopithecines.
   1. The earliest evidence of *Homo* may be skull and jaw fragments dating from 2.4-2.3 m.y.a. in Kenya and Ethiopia.
   2. Apparently these earliest humans were already beginning to diversify at the same time as the robust australopithecines.
B. *Homo habilis* at Olduvai ranges in time from 1.85-1.6 m.y.a.
   1. *H. habilis* differs from *Australopithecus* in cranial capacity and cranial shape.
      a. The average cranial capacity for *H. habilis* is estimated at 631 cm^3.
      b. The increase in cranial capacity is at a minimum 20% greater over the australopithecines.
   2. *H. habilis* has larger front teeth relative to back teeth and narrower premolars.
   3. When L. S. B. Leakey named these specimens *Homo habilis* (meaning "handy man") it was meaningful from two perspectives:
      a. It inferred that *Homo habilis* was the early Olduvai toolmaker.
      b. By calling this group *Homo*, Leakey was arguing for at least two separate branches of hominid evolution in the Plio-Pleistocene.
      c. By calling one group *Homo*, Leakey implied that they were our ancestors.
C. ER 1470 is an early *Homo* specimen from Koobi Fora, dating between 1.8-1.6 m.y.a.
   1. It has a cranial capacity over 750 cm^3, clearly out of the australopithecine range.
   2. The shape of the skull vault is not australopithecine-like either.
   3. However, the face and the back teeth were quite large, similar to australopithecines.
D. From the available evidence, it appears that one or more species of early *Homo* were present in East Africa by 2.5 m.y.a.

1. They would have developed in parallel with at least one line of australopithecines.
2. These hominid lineages lived contemporaneously for at least one million years.
3. After this time the australopithecine lineage became extinct.
4. The early *Homo* line evolved into a later form, *Homo erectus*, which itself eventually evolved into *H. sapiens*.

VII CENTRAL AFRICA
   A. A hominid mandible was discovered in Chad in 1995 dating from 3.5-3.0 m.y.a. (based on biostratigraphy)
   B. Preliminary analysis suggests that this fossil's closest affinities are to *Australopithecus afarensis*.
   C. This find is remarkable because it is over 1500 miles west of the known geographic range for early hominids.

VIII SOUTH AFRICAN SITES
   A. Earliest discoveries
       1. Darwin had predicted that the earliest humans would be found in Africa.
       2. The first australopithecine described was discovered in South Africa.
           a. This was a child from a quarry at Taung.
       3. Raymond Dart, the researcher who analyzed this fossil, observed several features that suggested that this child was a hominid.
           a. The foramen magnum was farther forward than in modern apes (although not as far forward as in modern humans).
           b. The slope of the forehead was not as receding as in apes.
           c. The milk canines were exceedingly small and the first molars were large, broad teeth.
       4. In all respects this fossil resembled a hominid rather than a pongid with the glaring exception of the very small brain.
       5. Dart named this species *Australopithecus africanus* and he believed it represented a "missing link" between apes and humans.
       6. Dart's interpretations were not well received.
   B. Further discoveries of South African hominids
       1. More australopithecine discoveries were made during the 1930's and 1940's.
       2. Additional sites included Sterkfontein, Kromdraai, Swartkrans, and Makapansgat.
       3. As the number of discoveries accumulated, it became increasingly difficult to insist that the australopithecines were simply aberrant apes.
       4. Among the fossils recovered were postcranial bones that indicated bipedalism in these hominids.
       5. The acceptance of the australopithecines as hominids required revision of human evolutionary theory.
           a. It had to be recognized that the greatest hominid brain expansion came after the earlier changes in teeth and locomotor anatomy.
           b. The mosaic nature of human evolution had to be recognized.
   C. Review of hominids from South Africa
       1. The Plio-Pleistocene hominid discoveries from South Africa are most significant.
           a. They were the first hominid discoveries in Africa and helped direct paleontologists to this continent and the later discoveries in East Africa.
           b. The presence of South African hominids provide another group with which to

compare the East African hominids.

    c. They are broadly similar in appearance, but with several distinctive features, when compared to East African forms.

    d. These differences argue for separation, at least at the species level.

2. New discoveries continue to be made at old sites such as Sterkfontein and at new sites as well.

    a. Drimolen, near Sterkfontein, has yielded up to 80 australopithecine specimens over the last decade.

3. There is a large assemblage of hominid fossils from South Africa, greatly adding to an understanding of our ancestors.

    a. Up to 1500 fossils have been recovered from at least 200 different individuals.

    b. Among the most meaningful remains are those of the pelvis, which indicates bipedalism, that most important of human characteristics.

D. "Robust" australopithecines

1. A robust species, *Australopithecus robustus*, is found in South Africa.

2. *A. robustus* is similar to the East African robust forms in their

    a. relatively small cranial capacities (the average is 530 cm^3).

    b. large, broad faces .

    c. very large premolars and molars (although not as massive as in the East African robust forms).

3. The South African robust forms differ from the East African robust forms in dental proportions and facial architecture.

    a. This justifies separate species status for *A. robustus* and its contemporary East African robust form, *A. boisei*.

    b. All members of the robust lineage appear to be specialized for a diet of hard food items, such as seeds and nuts.

    c. The (male?) robust australopithecines have a sagittal crest.

        i. The sagittal crest serves as additional attachment area for the large temporalis muscle, the primary muscle operating the massive jaw (see Fig. 10-22 in your text).

E. "Gracile" australopithecines

1. The gracile australopithecines are traditionally known from South Africa.

2. These hominids are also small-brained, but the teeth are not as large as those found in the robust varieties.

3. This is the species named by Dart, *Australopithecus africanus*.

4. Historically, it had been thought that there was significant differences in body size between the gracile and robust forms.

    a. It is now understood that there is not much difference in body size between the two forms.

    b. Most of the differences between the two types of australopithecines are found in the face and in the dentition .

5. The facial structure of the gracile australopithecine is lightly built and somewhat dish-shaped compared to the robust species.

6. The most distinctive difference between the gracile and robust australopithecines is in the dentition.

    a. The dental complex of the robust forms is extremely derived.

b. They exhibit deep jaws with greatly-enlarged back teeth, particularly the molars.
c. There is severe crowding of the front teeth (incisors and canines) and the canine is very reduced in size.
d. The first premolar is a much larger tooth than the small canine (about twice as large), whereas in the gracile specimens the premolar is only about 20 percent larger than the canine.

7. The differences in the relative proportions of teeth and jaws noted above best define a gracile, as compared to a robust australopithecine.
8. Most differences in skull shape can be attributed to contrasting jaw function in the two forms:
   a. The sagittal crest and the broad vertical face of the robust species are related to the muscles and biomechanical requirements of the extremely large-toothed chewing adaptation of this hominid.

F. Early *Homo* in South Africa.
   1. Early members of *Homo* have also been found in South Africa, apparently living at the same time as the australopithecines.
   2. The specimen Stw 53 is almost identical to the OH 24 *Homo habilis* specimen from Olduvai.
   3. There is disagreement whether South African *Homo* such as Stw 53 (and even the East African OH 24) should be included with *Homo habilis*, or deserve separate species designations.

G. Geology and dating problems in South Africa
   1. South African sites are geologically complex.
   2. The South African sites have a maze of limestone caves and fissures.
   3. It is likely that none of the South African australopithecine sites are primary hominid localities.
   4. At Swartkrans, Sterkfontein and Kromdraai the fossil bones were probably accumulated by carnivorous animals.
   5. So little is left of the Taung site that an accurate reconstruction is not possible.
   6. The best dating that can be done for South Africa is to correlate the faunal sequences from East Africa.
      a. Since no volcanoes were active in the region, chronometric methods such as potassium-argon are not available.
   7. All of the South African sites likely post-date *Australopithecus afarensis* from East Africa.

IX   INTERPRETATIONS: WHAT DOES IT ALL MEAN?
   A. Paleoanthropologists number fossil specimens in an attempt to keep designations neutral.
      1. Formal naming comes later.
      2. Using taxonomic nomenclature implies an interpretation of fossil relationships.
      3. The distinction between groups implies a basic difference in adaptive level.
   B. To interpret hominid evolutionary events, several steps are necessary:
      1. Select and survey a site.
      2. Excavate the site and recover fossil hominids.
      3. Designate fossils with specimen numbers for clear reference.
      4. Clean, prepare, study and describe the fossils.
      5. Compare individual fossils to others.

6. Compare fossil samples to other fossil samples and to modern, closely related species.

7. Assign formal, taxonomic names to the fossils.

C. Hominids that are interpreted to be on evolutionary side branches are thought to have become extinct.

X   CONTINUING UNCERTAINTIES--TAXONOMIC ISSUES

A. Researchers generally agree to a genus-level assignment for most Plio-Pleistocene hominids.

1. However, at the species-level very little consensus can be found.

2. Evolution is not a simple process.

3. Debate is at the heart of scientific research.

B. The following topics illustrate ongoing debates in paleoanthropology.

C. Are the earliest "hominids" really hominids?

1. The earliest "hominids" are not yet fully described (*Ardipithecus*) or very fragmentary (*Orrorin*).

2. Therefore their hominid status is still in question.

D. Are *A. anamensis* and *A. garhi* specifically distinct from *A. afarensis*?

1. Both of the former species are quite fragmentary.

2. The differences between *A. anamensis* and *A. afarensis* are not great.

3. Perhaps these new species should be viewed as tentative hypotheses that await further confirmation with the discovery of new fossil material.

E. How many genera of australopithecines?

1. In the 1960s and 1970s most researchers lumped all forms into the single genus *Australopithecus*.

2. In the last decade there has been an increasing tendency to split the robust group into a separate clade.

3. The robust forms have been generically termed *Paranthropus* whose species include *aethiopicus, boisei* and *robustus*.

4. This text continues to lump these closely related taxa into *Australopithecus* because it simplifies terminology.

F. How many species of early *Homo*?

1. The current debate will not likely be resolved soon.

2. The key issue is whether the variation we see is inter- or intra-specific.

3. One species implies extreme intraspecific variation.

4. The pattern of variation seen among early *Homo* does not fit the intraspecific pattern seen among extant primate species.

XI   PUTTING IT ALL TOGETHER

A. A diagram of evolutionary relationships is called a phylogeny.

B. Plio-Pleistocene hominid material can be divided into four broad groupings.

1. Set I dates to around 6.0-4.4 m.y.a. and includes basal hominids such as *Ardipithecus*.

2. Set II dates from 4.2-3.0 m.y.a. and includes the well-established primitive species of *Australopithecus afarensis* and the less well-established *Australopithecus anamensis*.

3. Set III dates from 2.5-1.4 m.y.a., includes remains from both South and East Africa, and have considerably larger molars than the hominids in Set II.

4. Set IV dates from 2.4-1.8 m.y.a. and includes early *Homo*.

XII   INTERPRETING THE INTERPRETATIONS
    A. All proposed phylogenies in the text postdate 1979.
       1.   Proposed phylogenies prior to this date did not include *Australopithecus afarensis*.
    B. The most difficult problems concern the phylogenetic placement of *A. aethiopicus* and *A. africanus*.
    C. Finally, the newest discoveries (e.g. *Orrorin, Ardipithecus, Kenyanthropus, A. anamensis* and *A. garhi*) need to be incorporated into newly proposed phylogenies.

KEY TERMS

Ardipithecus ramidus: a provisional species of the most primitive hominid yet discovered. It dates from 4.4 million years ago.

australopithecine: the common name for members of the genus *Australopithecus* . Originally this term was used as a subfamily designation. North American researchers no longer recognize this subfamily, but the term is well established in usage.

Australopithecus: a genus of Plio-Pleistocene hominids with at least five species. The genus is characterized by bipedalism, a relatively small brain, and large back teeth.

"black skull," the: a fossil cranium, designated WT 17 000, that was recovered from West Lake Turkana. This member of the robust group has been provisionally assigned to *Australopithecus aethiopicus* and lived about 2.5 million years ago.

breccia: a cement matrix comprised of sand, pebbles and soil.

endocast: a solid impression of the inside of the skull, showing the size, shape, and some details of the surface of the brain.

"First Family," the: a collection of the remains of at least 13 *Australopithecus afarensis* individuals who may have been contemporaries.

foramen magnum: the large opening at the base of the cranium through which the spinal cord passes and where the vertebral column joins the skull.

gracile australopithecine: the South African species, *Australopithecus africanus* , that is more lightly built than the stouter species inhabiting the same area.

habitual bipedalism: refers to the usual mode of locomotion of the organism. Used in reference to humans in the text, there are other habitual bipedal animals (e.g., large terrestrial flightless birds and kangaroos), although many hop rather than walk.

Homo habilis: a species of early *Homo*, well known in East Africa, but also perhaps from other regions.

"Lucy": a female Australopithecus afarensis for which 40 percent of the skeleton was recovered.

obligate bipedalism: refers to the fact that the organism cannot use another form of locomotion efficiently.

os coxa: the structure that consists of three bones (fused together in the adult) that, together with another ox coxa and the sacrum, constitutes the pelvis. It is also referred to as the coxal by some anatomists and as the innominate bone by an earlier generation of anatomists.

Osteodontokeratic: Presumed tools made from bone, tooth and horn (proposed by Raymond Dart).

phylogeny: a diagram depicting a family tree, usually in chronological order.

robust australopithecine: any of the three species of *Australopithecus* that are characterized by larger back teeth relative to front teeth, a more vertical face, and often a sagittal crest.

sagittal crest: a ridge of bone running along the midline (i.e., sagittal plane) of the cranium. The temporalis muscle, used in chewing, attaches to the sagittal crest in those mammals that possess this structure.

sectorial premolar: a premolar with a bladelike cutting edge that sections food by shearing against the cutting edge of the upper canine. The shearing action also sharpens both teeth.

INTERNET EXERCISES AND *INFOTRAC COLLEGE EDITION* EXERCISES

Check out "Becoming Human: Paleoanthropology, Evolution and Human Origins," a "broadband documentary experience" that lets you "journey through the story of human evolution" (http://becominghuman.org/). This very slick site is produced and maintained by The Institute of Human Origins of Arizona State University. You'll need Macromedia Flash Player 5, a high-speed internet connection and 64 MB RAM to run the documentary. Once you load it, however, the information and images are worth the effort.

The South African valley that is home to the famous australopithecine localities of Sterkfontein and Swartkrans has been designated as a "World Heritage Site" by the United Nations Educational, Scientific, and Cultural Organisation (UNESCO). Visit the very eye-catching and well-constructed "Cradle of Humankind" website published by the Department of Agriculture, Conservation, Environment and Land Affairs (DACEL) of the Gauteng Provincial Government, Republic of South Africa (http://www.cradleofhumankind.co.za/frontpage.htm#). This site displays the fossil finds and the geography of the discoveries in a very impressive cyber-package.

In *InfoTrac*, do keyword searches on "*garhi*", "*Ardipithecus*", "*Kenyanthropus*" and "*anamensis*" to read articles in the scholarly and popular press about the newest members of our family tree. Do the popular reviews of the scientific literature always agree about their interpretations of the new hominids phylogenetic placement?

CONCEPT APPLICATION

Fill in the "Hominid Matrix" with the "Choices" on the next page describing the early hominid species' geographical distribution, geological age, locomotion, dentition and cranial capacity. Some "Choices" can be used more than once and the "Choices" are listed randomly within columns.

Choices:

GEOGRAPHY	AGE (M.Y.A.)	LOCOMOTION	DENTITION	CRANIAL CAPACITY (CM^3)
A. Taung & Sterkfontein, South Africa	J. 3.5	T. Unknown	X. semisectorial 1st lower premolar	GG. Unknown
B. Laetoli, Tanzania & Hadar, Ethiopia	K. 3.9-3.0	U. Proposed biped	Y. huge premolars and molars	HH. 631 avg.
C. Allia Bay & Kanapoi, northern Kenya	L. 2.5	V. Likely biped	Z. thin enamel	II. 530
D. Koobi Fora and Olduvai Gorge	M. 6.0	W. Definite biped	AA. large canine and sectorial 1st premolar	JJ. 438 avg.
E. Swartkrans, South Africa	N. 4.4		BB. very large molars and premolars	KK. 410
F. Tugen Hills, Kenya	O. 1.9-1.0		CC. larger front teeth, narrow premolars	LL. 510-530
G. West Lake Turkana, Kenya	P. ~3.0-2.5		DD. fairly small molars	MM. ~400-500
H. Bouri, Ethiopia	Q. 4.2-3.9		EE. 1st premolar 20% bigger than canine	NN. 440
I. Aramis, Ethiopia	R. 2.4-1.6		FF. primitive and ape-like	
	S. ~2.0-1.5			

Hominid Matrix:

SPECIES	GEOGRAPHY	GEOLOGICAL AGE	LOCO-MOTION	DENTITION	CRANIAL CAPACITY
Orrorin					
Ardipithecus					
A. anamensis					
A. afarensis					
Kenyanthropus					
A. garhi					
A. aethiopicus					
A. africanus					
A. robustus					
A. boisei					
Homo habilis					

Now answer the True/False, Multiple Choice and Short Answer sample test questions. Following completion of the tests correct them with the answers and textbook page references at the end of this Study Guide chapter. Note the areas in which you are strong and weak to guide you in your studying. Finally, answer the sample Essay Questions.

TRUE/FALSE QUESTIONS

1. When compared to our quadrupedal relatives, the most dramatic changes arising from bipedalism are in the hominid pelvis.
   TRUE   FALSE

2. Unlike in apes, hominid feet are characterized by a non-divergent great toe and a longitudinal arch.
   TRUE   FALSE

3. Recently, the earliest possible hominids have been discovered in Brazil and the Czech Republic.
   TRUE   FALSE

4. Two of the most extraordinary discoveries of *Australopithecus afarensis* were the footprint trail at Laetoli and the "Lucy" skeleton from Hadar.
   TRUE   FALSE

5. "The black skull" is important because it documents the initial presence of "gracile" australopithecines in South Africa at 4.5 m.y.a.
   TRUE   FALSE

6. Early *Homo* from Olduvai Gorge and Koobi Fora are distinct from contemporary robust australopithecines in cranial size, cranial shape and tooth proportions.
   TRUE   FALSE

7. Raymond Dart's most important contribution to paleoanthropology was the announcement, description and interpretation of the Taung child as an early hominid ancestor that he named *Australopithecus africanus*.
   TRUE   FALSE

8. Important South African australopithecine sites include Koobi Fora, Olduvai Gorge and Hadar.
   TRUE   FALSE

9. *Ardipithecus* and *Orrorin* are universally agreed to be hominids among paleoanthropologists.
   TRUE   FALSE

10. A schematic representation showing ancestor-descendant relationships in known as a phylogeny.
    TRUE   FALSE

1. The gluteus maximus is the largest muscle in the human. Why?
   A. It provides a "cushion" for when we sit.
   B. It is a powerful muscle for throwing and was selected for in our spear-throwing ancestors.
   C. It is an important muscle in bipedal walking and is a powerful extensor of the upper leg.
   D. Its main purpose is energy storage in the form of fat. This would have been strongly selected for in our ancestors who lived through periods of food scarcity.

2. Which of the following is not a major feature of hominid bipedalism?
   A. Development of curves in the human vertebral column.
   B. The "straightening" of the human fingers from the curved condition found in the apes.
   C. The forward repositioning of the foramen magnum underneath the cranium.
   D. The modification of the pelvis into a basin-like shape.

3. Which of the following statements is true?
   A. The human vertebral column is fairly straight.
   B. The earliest definitive hominid, *A. afarensis*, was primarily a brachiator.
   C. All the major structural changes required for bipedalism are seen in the early hominids from East and South Africa.
   D. All of the above are true.

4. A foot that is highly capable of grasping and climbing is less capable as a stable platform during bipedal locomotion. This is because anatomical remodeling is limited by functional
   A. contingencies.
   B. constraints.
   C. paradoxes.
   D. drift.

5. One of the reasons that East Africa provides such an excellent window into our distant past is because
   A. the soil is acidic, making preservation of fossils more likely.
   B. it was once a sea and the fossilization of the shells of marine organisms provide for excellent stratigraphy.
   C. there is a great deal of commercial development occurring and these developers find fossil remains and alert paleoanthropologists.
   D. there is a great deal of geological activity, which not only churns up earlier sediments but also provides datable material.

6. Which of the following is **not** a hominid that was discovered in East Africa and given a new taxonomic name within the last decade?
    A. *Orrorin*
    B. *Ardipithecus*
    C. *Kenyanthropus*
    D. *Australopithecus afarensis*

7. Which of the following is **not** a characteristic of *Ardipithecus ramidus*?
    A. large canines
    B. a sectorial premolar
    C. the foramen magnum is positioned forward, consistent with bipedalism
    D. the pelvis is narrow with a long iliac blade

8. What hard evidence from Laetoli demonstrates that hominids were bipedal by 3.5 m.y.a.?
    A. a complete fossilized foot skeleton
    B. fossilized footprints imprinted in volcanic tuff
    C. the forward position of the foramen magnum on the Laetoli cranium
    D. a short and broad fossil hominid pelvis fragment

9. Which of the following sites have yielded fossil remains of *Australopithecus afarensis*?
    A. Hadar
    B. Laetoli
    C. Olduvai
    D. both A & B

10. Which of the following was **not** found at Hadar?
    A. "the black skull"
    B. "the First Family"
    C. "Lucy"
    D. All of the above were found at Hadar.

11. Which of the following is **not** a recently proposed species of *Australopithecus*?
    A. *A. africanus*
    B. *A. anamensis*
    C. *A. garhi*
    D. All of the above species have been proposed within the last five years.

12. Which of the following is **not** a characteristic of *Australopithecus afarensis*?
    A. small stature
    B. small brain, averaging around 420 cm^3
    C. upper limbs are longer, relative to lower limbs
    D. reduced canine size relative to the other teeth

13. The earliest species of robust australopithecine is
    A. *Australopithecus boisei.*
    B. *Australopithecus robustus.*
    C. *Australopithecus aethiopicus.*
    D. *Australopithecus africanus.*

14. WT 17000 ("the black skull") is an excellent example of mosaic evolution because is possesses
    A. a very small cranial capacity.
    B. a very broad face and a huge sagittal crest.
    C. a projecting upper face.
    D. All of the above

15. Early *Homo* is distinguished from the australopithecines largely by
    A. larger cranial capacity.
    B. shorter stature.
    C. larger back teeth.
    D. the presence of a chin.

16. By assigning certain specimens to *Homo habilis*, L. S. B. Leakey was
    A. stating that these hominids were more closely related to the South African australopithecines than to the East African australopithecines.
    B. arguing for at least two separate branches of hominid evolution in the Plio-Pleistocene.
    C. indicating that this was the toolmaking species at Olduvai.
    D. both B and C.

17. Which of the following australopithecine species is found in South Africa?
    A. *Australopithecus boisei*
    B. *Australopithecus afarensis*
    C. *Australopithecus robustus*
    D. *Australopithecus aethiopicus*

18. Raymond Dart's claim that *Australopithecus africanus* was a hominid was rejected by many of his contemporaries because they expected early members of the human family to have
    A. long faces, stabbing canines, and small brains.
    B. large brains.
    C. manufactured stone tools.
    D. apelike jaws and teeth, small brains.

19. The acceptance of the australopithecines as hominids by the scientific community required a complete revision of the thinking of the time, namely that
    A. large brains have always been part of the hominid line.
    B. the manufacture and use of stone tools and dental modifications occurred simultaneously.
    C. the brain expanded after modifications in the dental and locomotor systems.
    D. to be human requires a minimal cranial capacity of 750 cm³.

20. Pitting and scratches, revealed under electron microscopy, indicates that *A. robustus* was consuming a diet of
    A. hard food items, such as seeds and nuts.
    B. insects.
    C. meat.
    D. fruit.

21. Compared to *A. africanus*, *A. robustus*
    A. was larger, weighing up to 300 pounds (about the size of a gorilla).
    B. had smaller grinding teeth (molars).
    C. had a sagittal crest and larger back teeth.
    D. probably was more arboreal.

22. The sagittal crest present in the robust australopithecines functions as
    A. additional buttressing protecting the skull from heavy blows.
    B. a structure used in head-butting during competition for females.
    C. additional surface area for attachment of a large temporalis muscle.
    D. an area where brain expansion occurred.

23. The five South African early hominid sites were discovered
    A. by the same scientist.
    B. after tedious and lengthy excavation.
    C. by commercial quarrying activity.
    D. accidentally by local fishermen.

24. The best dating technique for the South African sites is
    A. paleomagnetism.
    B. biostratigraphy.
    C. carbon-14.
    D. dendrochronology.

25. The species-level distinctions of the African Plio-Pleistocene hominids
    A. are fairly clear.
    B. are the subject of ongoing disputes.
    C. are being resolved through dating.
    D. require immediate splitting.

26. *Australopithecus anamensis*
    A. is not very different than *A. afarensis* anatomically.
    B. is represented by two almost complete skeletons.
    C. requires further study and analysis before it can be confirmed as a separate species.
    D. A & C

27. The key issue with early *Homo* is
    A. dating.
    B. determining whether or not it was an obligate biped.
    C. evaluating its arboreal capabilities.
    D. interpreting the observed variation as being either intraspecific or interspecific.

28. A phylogeny is
    A. the formal naming of taxonomic groups.
    B. a diagram representing ancestor-descendant relationships.
    C. another name for the lumbar curve in the human spine.
    D. None of the above

29. Basal hominids may include
    A. *Ardipithecus ramidus* and *Orrorin*.
    B. *Australopithecus afarensis*.
    C. *Australopithecus africanus*.
    D. the robust australopithecines.

30. Consensus paleoanthropological opinions regarding the course of early human evolution
    A. should be arrived at soon.
    B. are premature since many fossils from East and South Africa are not fully described.
    C. are overdue since no new fossils have been found in recent years.
    D. are untrustworthy because human evolution is untestable.

SHORT ANSWER QUESTIONS (& PAGE REFERENCES)

1. How does a hominid's pelvis differ from an ape's? (pp. 243-244)

2. What are the features that define *A. afarensis* as a hominid? (pp. 255-257)

3. How does WT 17000 "the black skull" illustrate the concept of mosaic evolution? (pp. 259-260)

4. What were the contributions of Raymond Dart and Robert Broom to paleoanthropology? (pp. 263-265)

5. What are the geology and dating problems in South Africa? (pp. 269-271)

Essay Questions (& Page References)

1. Compare and contrast humans versus apes skeletons focusing on the differences that reflect bipedal versus quadrupedal locomotion (pp. 243-247)

2. Describe the anatomical changes that occurred during australopithecine evolution from *A. afarensis* through *A. africanus* to the "robusts." (pp. 253-260,266-268)

3. Discuss the controversy concerning early *Homo* from East Africa. (pp. 260-261)

4. Why are the taxonomic and phylogenetic status' of *Ardipithecus, Orrorin* and *A. anamensis* controversial? (pp. 275-277)

Answers, *Corrected Statement* if False & References To True/False Questions

1. TRUE, p. 243

2. TRUE, pp. 245-247

3. FALSE, pp. 249-250, Recently, the earliest possible hominids have been discovered in *Kenya* and *Ethiopia*.

4. TRUE, p. 254

5. FALSE, pp. 259-260, "The black skull" is important because it documents the initial presence of "*robust*" australopithecines in *East* Africa at *2.5 m.y.a.*

6. TRUE, p. 261

7. TRUE, pp. 263-264

8. FALSE, pp. 265-267, Important South African australopithecine sites include *Sterkfontein, Swartkrans and Kromdraai.*

9. FALSE, p. 276, *Ardipithecus* and *Orrorin* are *not* universally agreed to be hominids among paleoanthropologists.

10. TRUE, p. 277

ANSWERS AND REFERENCES TO MULTIPLE CHOICE QUESTIONS

1. C, p. 244
2. B, pp. 244-246
3. C, p. 245
4. B, p. 246
5. D, pp. 248-249
6. D, pp. 249-250,257
7. D, pp. 251-253
8. B, p. 254
9. D, pp. 255-257
10. A, pp. 254,259
11. A, pp. 253,257,263
12. D, pp. 255-257
13. C, pp. 259-260
14. D, pp. 259-260
15. A, p. 261

16. D, p. 261
17. C, p. 266
18. B, p. 264
19. C, p. 265
20. A, p. 266
21. C, p. 266
22. C, p. 260
23. C, p. 269
24. B, p. 271
25. B, p. 275
26. D, p. 276
27. D, p. 277
28. B, p. 277
29. A, pp. 277-278
30. B, p. 278

CONCEPT APPLICATION SOLUTION

Hominid Matrix:

Species (page numbers in text)	Geography	Geological Age	Loco-motion	Dentition	Cranial Capacity
Orrorin (p. 249)	F	M	U	FF	GG
Ardipithecus (pp. 251-253)	I	N	U	Z	GG
A. anamensis (p. 253)	C	Q	V	AA	GG
A. afarensis (pp. 253-257)	B	K	W	X	JJ
Kenyanthropus (p. 257)	G	J	T	DD	MM
A. garhi (pp. 257-258)	H	L	V	BB	GG
A. aethiopicus (pp. 259-260)	G	L	V	Y	KK
A. africanus (pp. 263-268)	A	P	W	EE	NN
A. robustus (pp. 263-268)	E	S	W	BB	II
A. boisei (pp. 259-260)	D	O	W	Y	LL
Homo habilis (pp. 260-261)	D	R	W	CC	HH

CHAPTER 11
HOMO ERECTUS AND CONTEMPORARIES

LEARNING OBJECTIVES
After reading this chapter you should be able to:
- Discuss the temporal and geographic distribution of *Homo erectus* (pp. 284-287).
- Briefly describe the time frame and glacial movements of the Pleistocene (p. 288).
- Describe the physical characteristics of *H. erectus* (pp. 288-290).
- Present an historical overview of *H. erectus* discoveries (pp. 291-293).
- Describe the fossil remains and related archeological evidence from Java, China and Africa (pp. 292-303).
- Compare African and Asian *H. erectus* fossils (pp. 300-302).
- Understand some of the disputes involving *H. erectus* fossils, particularly with regard to the European evidence (pp. 302-303).
- Understand the technological advances reflected in the tool kit of *H. erectus* (pp. 315-317).
- Explain how and why *H. erectus* was able to spread out of Africa and inhabit the Old World (pp. 305-306).

CHAPTER OUTLINE
Introduction

In the previous chapters we looked at early hominid evolution by examining fossils assigned to *Australopithecus* and early *Homo*. In this chapter we focus on *Homo erectus*, believed by most to be the ancestor of modern *Homo sapiens*. All aspects of this extinct hominid species are investigated, including its: geographic and temporal distribution, physical characteristics, history of discovery, variation exhibited by African and Asian forms and the technological advances made by this very significant hominid species over the approximately 1.5 million years of its existence.

I   INTRODUCTION
   A. Hominid evolution has been characterized by biocultural interaction.
   B. We need to look at the behavioral capacities of *H. erectus* in concert with morphological changes to understand its success as a hominid species.
II   HOMO ERECTUS – TERMINOLOGY AND GEOGRAPHICAL DISTRIBUTION
   A. The name first given for the Javanese fossils was *Pithecanthropus*.
   B. After World War II, the previous taxonomic splitting was abandoned in favor of classifying the fossils under the single species of *Homo erectus*.
   C. The earliest finds in East Africa have been chronometrically dated to 1.8 m.y.a.
      1. Evidence indicates that hominids may have left Africa around that time, between 1.5 and 2.0 m.y.a.
      2. A likely route that can be reconstructed for the *H. erectus* migration out of Africa would be through southwestern Asia.

3. One site supporting this route is Dmanisi, in the Republic of Georgia.
    a. A mandible and two crania were recently discovered there dating to possibly 1.7 m.y.a.
4. Fossil remains from the Gran Dolina site in Spain are approximately 780,000 years old.

III THE PLEISTOCENE (1.8 M.Y.A. – 10,000 Y.A.)
A. Also known as the "Age of Glaciers" or the "Ice Age."
B. The Northern Hemisphere was covered with ice.
C. New evidence indicates approximately 15 major cold periods and 50 minor glacial advances.
D. *Homo erectus* appeared and disappeared during the Pleistocene.

IV THE MORPHOLOGY OF *HOMO ERECTUS*
A. Brain size
    1. *Homo erectus* brain size ranges from 750 to 1250 cm^3.
        a. The mean for the species is about 900 cm^3.
    2. Brain size is related to overall body size.
    3. *H. erectus* was considerably less encephalized than later members of the genus *Homo*.
B. Body size
    1. *H. erectus* displays a dramatic increase in body size.
    2. Adults are estimated to have weighed well over 100 pounds.
    3. Average adult height is estimated at 5'6".
    4. *H. erectus* was quite sexually dimorphic as indicated by the East African specimens.
C. Cranial shape
    1. The cranium has a distinctive shape.
    2. Thick cranial bones are common, particularly among the Asian specimens.
    3. Supraorbital tori refer to large browridges.
    4. The forehead is receding with little development.
    5. The maximum breadth is low, below the ear opening.
D. Dentition
    1. Shovel-shaped incisors are a typical characteristic.
    2. Shovel-shaped incisors are typical in the Chinese specimens but are also present in the "Turkana Boy" (from Africa).

V HISTORICAL OVERVIEW OF *HOMO ERECTUS* DISCOVERIES
A. Java
    1. Eugene Dubois was the first laboratory scientist to search for fossils linking humans to apes.
    2. Incredibly he found them near Trinil in central Java in the early 1890s!
        a. The first fossils unearthed were a skullcap and a femur.
    3. Dubois named these fossils *Pithecanthropus erectus*.
    4. These fossils demonstrated that bipedalism evolved before the attainment of a fully human-sized brain.
B. *Homo erectus* from Java
    1. Six sites from central and eastern Java have yielded fossil hominids.
    2. Attaining reliable dates is a problem, in part, because of the complexity of Javanese geology.

       a. New dating techniques have revealed very ancient dates ranging from 1.8-1.6 m.y.a.

   3. At Sangiran, at least five individuals have been excavated.

       a. Their cranial capacities range from 813-1059 cm^3.

   4. At Ngandong 12 individuals were recovered.

       a. Dates published in the mid-1990s claim that these fossils are extremely young, between 50,000 and 25,000 years old.

   5. If the Ngandong dates are correct it would make *Homo erectus* contemporary with *Homo sapiens*.

   6. On Java, very few artifacts have been found that can be reliably associated with *Homo erectus*.

C. Peking (Beijing)

   1. "Dragon bones," ancient mammal fossils, were used as medicine and aphrodisiacs by the Chinese people.

   2. In a cave, near the village of Zhoukoudian, a remarkable fossil skull was found in 1929.

   3. Davidson Black, a Canadian anatomist, followed by Franz Weidenreich, a German anthropologist, directed excavations at Zhoukoudian through 1933.

   4. On the eve of the Japanese bombardment of Pearl Harbor in December 1941, the fossils from Zhoukoudian from were packed for shipment but were subsequently lost to science forever.

   5. Thankfully, Weidenreich brought meticulous descriptions, measurements, drawings and casts of the original fossils when he left China for the U.S. earlier that same year.

D. Zhoukoudian *Homo erectus*

   1. More than 40 *H. erectus* individuals (adult males, females and children) have been found.

   2. Cranial features include the supraorbital torus in front and the nuchal torus behind.

       a. The skull is keeled by a sagittal ridge.

       b. The face protrudes and the incisors are shoveled.

       c. The skull shows the greatest breadth near the bottom.

   3. Cultural Remains

       a. More than 100,000 artifacts have been unearthed.

       b. The site was inhabited intermittently for almost 250,000 years.

       c. Occupation has been divided into three cultural stages.

       d. Early tools are crude and shapeless.

       e. Materials used to make tools include stone, bone and horn.

       f. Food may have included hunted deer and horse, and gathered fruits, berries, eggs, seeds, herbs and tubers.

       g. It is unknown whether they used language.

   4. The life span of *Homo erectus* was not very long.

       a. 40% of the bones found were of individuals less than 14 years old.

       b. Only 2.6% of the bones found were of individuals in the 50-60 year range.

   5. Recent work has questioned whether or not *H. erectus* even lived in the Zhoukoudian cave.

       a. These researchers claim that most of the evidence suggests that giant hyenas were responsible for the bone accumulations.

b. Other researchers are also skeptical about the famous claims of fire-use by *H. erectus* in the cave.

E. Other Chinese sites
1. Chenjiawo and Gongwangling are two sites in close proximity often referred to together as "Lantian."
   a. At Chenjiawo a nearly complete mandible is provisionally dated at 650,000 y.a.
   b. At Gongwangling a crushed cranium is provisionally dated at 1.15 m.y.a..
2. Lontandong Cave is often referred to as "Hexian."
   a. In the Lontandong Cave a cranium was found exhibiting several advanced characteristics and is dated to 250,000 y.a.
3. In Yunxian County two relatively complete skulls were found dating to 350,000 y.a.
   a. The Yunxian County crania show a mid-facial morphology similar to that of modern Asians.

F. East Africa
1. Olduvai
   a. Louis Leakey unearthed OH 9 in 1960.
   b. OH 9 dates to 1.4 m.y.a. and has a cranial capacity is estimated at 1,067 cm^3.
   c. OH 9 has the largest cranial capacity of African *H. erectus* and the largest browridges of any fossil hominid yet discovered.
2. East Turkana
   a. ER 3733 is an almost complete skull that dates close to 1.8 m.y.a.
   b. Its cranial capacity is almost 850 cm^3.
   c. Not many stone tools have been found at *H. erectus* sites at East Turkana.
3. West Turkana
   a. WT 15000 was found at a site known as Nariokotome in August 1984.
   b. WT 15000 is the most complete *Homo erectus* skeleton ever found.
   c. WT 15000 dates to 1.6 m.y.a.
   d. WT 15000 was a boy about 12 years old.
   e. If WT 15000 had grown to his full height he would have been more than six feet tall.
   f. WT 15000's adult cranial capacity would have been over 900 cm^3.
4. Ethiopia
   a. An abundance of Acheulian stone tools were found at Konso-Gardula in 1991.
   b. A robust *H. erectus* mandible was found dating to 1.3 m.y.a.
5. Summary of East African *H. erectus*
   a. African *H. erectus* finds display several differences from the Javan and Chinese fossils.
   b. The crania of the East African specimens have thinner cranial bones than those found in the Asian representatives.
   c. Some scientists would argue that the African and Asian *H. erectus* finds should be classified as separate species.
      i. In support of this position, the newly published early dates from Java suggest that the African and Asian populations may have had a separate history for more than one million years.

       d. However, most paleoanthropologists consider *H. erectus* to have been a widespread single species that accommodated a considerable range of intraspecific variation.

   6. South Africa

       a. Disagreement exists concerning classification of a mandible (attributed by some to *H. erectus*) found at Swartkrans amongst faunal remains collected in the 1940s and 1950s.

   7. North Africa

       a. Remains are almost entirely made up of mandibles and mandibular fragments.

       b. The Ternifine (Algeria) mandibles are quite robust and date to 700,000 y.a.

       c. The Moroccan mandible, from the Thomas Quarry, is less robust than those from Ternifine and slightly younger at 500,000 y.a.

       d. At Salé in Morocco, a cranium with a capacity of 900 cm^3 dating to approximately 400,000 y.a. was discovered.

   8. Europe

       a. Recent discoveries are pushing back initial hominid occupation of this continent to nearly the origins of *H. erectus*.

       b. Dmanisi in the republic of Georgia has yielded a mandible and two crania that date, perhaps, to 1.8-1.7 m.y.a.

          i. The skulls are similar to east African *H. erectus* and are relatively small in their cranial capacities: 650 cm^3 and 775 cm^3.

       c. Elsewhere in Europe, all of the fossil hominid evidence is at least one million years younger than Dmanisi.

          i. Hominid fossils dating to roughly 700,000 y.a. have been found in Spain (Gran Dolina) and Italy (Ceprano).

       d. After 400,000 y.a. the European fossil hominid record becomes much more abundant.

          i. Taxonomic assessment of these fossils remains controversial.

VI   TECHNOLOGICAL AND POPULATION TRENDS IN THE MIDDLE PLEISTOCENE

  A. Technological trends

   1. Debate exists over the physical and cultural changes of that occurred during the evolutionary lifespan of *H. erectus*.

       a. Some suggest that the species was static, others support a position that the species underwent significant long-term changes.

       b. The text endorses a moderate position of some brain size increase and reduction in body robusticity when comparing late versus early *H. erectus*.

   2. Technological changes also occurred during the development of *H. erectus*.

       a. A core stone tool that was worked on both sides is called a biface.

       b. These tools are commonly called hand axes and cleavers.

   3. The Acheulian hand axe was an all-purpose tool for more than a million years.

       a. It has been found in Africa, parts of Asia and later in Europe.

       b. Recently, reports of Acheulian bifaces found in China dating to 800,000 y.a. have expanded the geographic range of this stone tool tradition.

   4. Early toolmakers used a hammer made of stone to chip their bifaces.

   5. Later toolmakers began using wood and bone which gave them more control.

   6. Widespread evidence for butchering exists.

a. Thousands of Acheulian hand axes have been found in association with remains of large animals.
7. *Homo erectus* can be interpreted as a potential hunter and scavenger.
B. Population trends
1. It appears that *Homo erectus* had a penchant for travel.
2. Hunters-scavengers and gatherers are nomadic.
a. As populations grew, small groups budded-off and made their way elsewhere on their own.
3. Of course, *H. erectus* eventually made it to far-off lands such as Java
a. Stone tools found on the island of Flores, 375 miles east of Java, suggest that erectus may have had the capability of constructing sea-going vessels!
4. *Homo erectus* was the first hominid species to embrace culture as a strategy of adaptation.
5. Therefore, it is with this species that we can begin to talk of human (rather than just hominid) evolution.

KEY TERMS

Acheulian: a tool technology from the lower and middle Pleistocene characterized by bifacial tools usually made of stone.
artifacts: objects or materials made or modified for use by hominids
biface: a stone tool consisting of a core stone worked on both sides; commonly referred to as hand axes and cleavers. Associated with *H. erectus* in Africa, W. Asia and W. Europe.
biocultural: An approach to the study of human evolution taking into account the interaction between morphological evolution and cultural changes.
contemporaneous: living at the same time
encephalization: the relationship between brain size and overall body size
mandible: lower jaw
morphology: refers to the form or shape of anatomical structures or an entire organism
Nariokotome: also known as WT 15000. Refers to an almost complete skeleton of a 12 year old boy from West Lake Turkana in Kenya classified as *H. erectus*.
nuchal torus: large bony buttress at the rear of the skull
Pleistocene: the epoch of the Cenozoic dating from 1.8 m.y.a. to 10,000 y.a. characterized by continental glaciations of the northern latitudes. Frequently referred to as the "Age of Glaciers" or the "Ice Age."
postcranial: refers to the skeleton. Anything except the skull (cranium).
sagittal ridge: a ridge of bone running along the center of the skull (like parting the hair down the middle) where chewing muscles attach.
supraorbital torus: heavy browridge
taxonomy: the science of classifying organisms based on evolutionary relationship
temporal: refers to either time or a cranial bone.
Zhoukoudian: A village near Peking famous for a cave that has yielded rich fossil remains of *H. erectus*.

If working on Chinese *Homo erectus* sites such as Zhoukoudian is exciting to you (and you have over $6000 in disposable income), then check out the field school hosted by George Washington University in cooperation with the Chinese Institute of Vertebrate Paleontology and Paleoanthropology (http://www.gwu.edu/~anth/fieldschool.html#china).

A wonderfully informative website on Chinese paleoanthropology has been created and maintained by Dr. Dennis A. Etler, titled "The Fossil Evidence for Human Evolution in China" (http://www.chineseprehistory.org//index.htm). The site includes a picture gallery of fossils ranging from late Miocene hominoids, through Chinese *H. erectus*, to the first modern humans from China (http://www.chineseprehistory.org//pics1.htm).

In *InfoTrac* do a keyword search on "*Homo erectus* Pickrell" to read a *Science News* article written by J. Pickrell on the very recent discovery of a new *H. erectus* skull from Ethiopia dating to one million years ago. After reading the article, what are your opinions on whether or not *H. erectus* should be split into two different species: one from Africa called *H. ergaster* and the traditionally-named *H. erectus* from Asia?

Now answer the True/False, Multiple Choice and Short Answer sample test questions. Following completion of the tests correct them with the answers and textbook page references at the end of this Study Guide chapter. Note the areas in which you are strong and weak to guide you in your studying. Finally, answer the sample Essay Questions.

TRUE/FALSE QUESTIONS

1. Current interpretations view the first hominid migrations out of Africa taking place between 500,000-250,000 years ago.
    TRUE   FALSE

2. The Pliocene Epoch is also known as the "Age of Glaciers" or the "Ice Age."
    TRUE   FALSE

3. Brain size in *H. erectus* ranges from 750-1250 cm^3 with an average of around 900 cm^3.
    TRUE   FALSE

4. Eugene Dubois discovered the first *H. erectus* fossils in Java in the early 1890s.
    TRUE   FALSE

5. Zhoukoudian, a very important *H. erectus* site, is a cave located outside of Hanoi, Vietnam.
    TRUE   FALSE

6. WT 15000 is significant because it is the most complete *H. erectus* skeleton yet discovered.
    TRUE   FALSE

7. The site of Dmanisi, in the Republic of Georgia, is important because the hominid fossils found there are the youngest of all *H. erectus* finds, dating to 200,000 y.a.
   TRUE   FALSE

8. The Acheulian cultural tradition is characterized by bifacially worked core tools, such as hand axes and cleavers.
   TRUE   FALSE

9. Evidence for butchering is lacking in all *H. erectus* sites.
   TRUE   FALSE

10. The first hominid species to wholeheartedly embrace culture as an adaptive strategy was *H. erectus*.
    TRUE   FALSE

MULTIPLE CHOICE QUESTIONS

1. New dates from two sites in Java indicate that
   A. *H. erectus* may have originated in Australia.
   B. the Java finds are as old as the East African finds.
   C. *H. erectus* arrived in Java one million years later than previously thought.
   D. All of the above

2. Currently, it is believed that hominids first left Africa
   A. between 1.5 and 2 m.y.a.
   B. due to a geologic catastrophe.
   C. around 500,000 y.a.
   D. and went directly to North and South America.

3. At the Ubeidiya site in Israel, what have been dated to 1.4-1.3 m.y.a?
   A. Stone tools
   B. Crania
   C. Floral remains
   D. Fauna remains

4. *H. erectus* crania and a mandible found in the Republic of Georgia are dated from 1.8 to 1.6 m.y.a. If these dates are confirmed it would demonstrate that *H. erectus*
   A. originated in southwestern Asia.
   B. left Africa quite early in its evolution.
   C. evolved from a European robust australopithecine.
   D. None of the above

5. Fossil remains from the Atapuerca region of northern Spain
   A. may be the oldest hominids in Western Europe.
   B. are agreed by all paleoanthropologists to represent *H. erectus*.
   C. are the oldest fossils of *H. sapiens*.
   D. are evidence of *H. habilis* in Europe.

6. The dispersal of *H. erectus* from Africa was **not** influenced by which of the following?
   A. Continental drift
   B. Climate
   C. Water boundaries
   D. Food

7. Oscillations of cold and warm temperatures during the Pleistocene affected
   A. hominid evolution.
   B. plant distribution.
   C. animal speciation and extinction.
   D. All of the above

8. The Pleistocene lasted
   A. approximately 100,000 years.
   B. longer than the Miocene.
   C. more than 1.75 million years.
   D. until 3.5 million years ago.

9. Compared to earlier hominids, *H. erectus* was
   A. dramatically larger-bodied.
   B. somewhat shorter.
   C. more or less the same body size.
   D. less skeletally robust.

10. Compared to australopithecines, *H. erectus*
    A. was smaller-brained.
    B. was larger-brained.
    C. had more or less the same brain size.
    D. was much less encephalized.

11. If the Nariokotome "boy" had survived to adulthood he would have
    A. been obese.
    B. a leader of his clan.
    C. been over 6 feet tall.
    D. had relatively long arms compared to his legs (like australopithecines).

12. What characteristic(s) distinguish(es) *H. erectus* cranial shape?
    A. Long and low skull vault
    B. Little or no forehead development with large browridges
    C. Wide cranial base with maximum breadth beneath the ear opening
    D. All of the above

13. Shovel-shaped incisors are
    A. found among Chinese *H. erectus* specimens.
    B. a primitive feature of *H. erectus*.
    C. present on the Nariokotome specimen.
    D. All of the above

14. Eugene Dubois was the first scientist to
    A. understand the significance of cranial size.
    B. design a research plan to take him out of his lab and into the field to deliberately look for hominid fossils.
    C. dissect specimens.
    D. apply chronometric dating techniques to fossils.

15. In 1894 Dubois published a paper based on his discoveries in Java. This paper was
    A. embraced by the scientific community.
    B. strongly criticized by the scientific community.
    C. was completely ignored by the scientific community.
    D. withdrawn by Dubois after he realized his interpretations were in error.

16. With regard to his analysis of the skullcap from Java, Dubois was eventually shown to be
    A. correct in identifying it as a previously undescribed hominid species.
    B. completely wrong in his interpretation of "*Pithecanthropus*" as a "missing link."
    C. correct in his classification of the fossils as a new species of *Australopithecus*.
    D. wrong in his cranial capacity estimate. The skull's capacity was only 450 cm^3.

17. Which of the following is **not** true of *Homo erectus* from Java?
    A. Six sites in eastern Java have yielded *H. erectus* fossils.
    B. Dating is difficult due to the island's complex geology.
    C. Most of the fossils are older than 2.0 million years.
    D. Very few artifacts have been found in association with Javan *H. erectus*

18. If the date range of 50,000 to 25,000 years ago for the Ngandong hominids from Java is confirmed, it would show that *H. erectus*
    A. lived contemporaneously with *H. sapiens*.
    B. had art.
    C. went extinct one million years before the appearance of modern *H. sapiens*.
    D. exhibited complex tool use.

19. Which of the following individuals were **not** involved in the excavations at Zhoukoudian?
    A. Davidson Black
    B. Franz Weidenreich
    C. Eugene Dubois
    D. Pei Wenshong

20. The cultural remains at Zhoukoudian Cave
    A. are nonexistent.
    B. are limited to well-constructed fireplaces.
    C. consist of over 100,000 artifacts.
    D. enable archaeologists to easily reconstruct a day in the life of *H. erectus*.

21. Which of the following have been conclusively demonstrated for *H. erectus* at Zhoukoudian?
    A. They made and controlled fire.
    B. They were proficient hunters of deer and horses.
    C. They lived in the cave.
    D. None of the above (recent research has cast doubt on all three propositions).

22. OH 9 found in 1960 by Louis Leakey at Olduvai Gorge
    A. is dated at 1.4 m.y.a.
    B. has a cranial capacity of 1067 cm^3.
    C. has the largest browridges of any hominid yet discovered.
    D. All of the above

23. Which of the following is **not** true about WT 15000 from Nariokotome?
    A. It is the most complete *H. erectus* skeleton ever found.
    B. It dates to 1.6 m.y.a.
    C. It is the first *H. erectus* specimen from Egypt.
    D. He was about 12 years old when he died.

24. An important lesson taught to us by WT 15000 is
    A. that hominids were already fishing during the Lower Pleistocene.
    B. that *H. erectus* had already attained modern human height by 1.5 million years ago.
    C. that *H. erectus* had already attained a fully human language.
    D. All of the above

25. Which of the following North African countries have **not** yielded remains of *H. erectus*?
    A. Algeria
    B. Egypt
    C. Morocco
    D. Ternifine

26. European hominid finds that are at least 700,000 years old have been claimed in
    A. the Republic of Georgia.
    B. Italy.
    C. Spain.
    D. All of the above

27. The Acheulian stone biface, the standard tool for *H. erectus* for over a million years,
    A. served to cut, pound, scrape and dig.
    B. was widely distributed over Africa, parts of Asia and Europe.
    C. was recently found in archaeological assemblages in southern China.
    D. All of the above

28. The use of wood and bone "soft-hammers" allowed later Acheulian toolmakers
    A. exert more control over the flaking of their tools.
    B. to make more asymmetric hand axes.
    C. to create flatter edges so they would not cut themselves by mistake.
    D. All of the above

29. *H. erectus* sites around the Old World display extensive evidence of
    A. butchering.
    B. cave art.
    C. projectile hunting technology (e.g. spear throwers and bows and arrows).
    D. primitive horticulture.

30. *H. erectus* was
    A. nomadic.
    B. sedentary.
    C. igneous.
    D. metamorphic.

SHORT ANSWER QUESTIONS (& PAGE REFERENCES)

1. Where are the earliest *H. erectus* fossils found and how old are they? (pp. 284-285)

2. What was the significance of Eugene Dubois' discoveries in Java in the early 1890s? (pp. 291-292)

3. What are the most important *H. erectus* finds made at East Turkana, West Turkana and Olduvai Gorge? (pp. 299-300)

4. What is the difference in producing Acheulian tools with "hard-hammer" versus "soft-hammer" percussion? (p. 305)

5. What are some criticisms of *H. erectus* as a hunter? (pp. 305-306)

Essay Questions (& Page References)

1. Describe the brain size, body size, cranial shape, and dentition of *H. erectus*. How do these features differ from earlier hominids? (pp. 288-290)

2. What is the importance of Zhoukoudian in the history of discovery and interpretations of *H. erectus*? How has recent research at Zhoukoudian challenged ideas about the lifeways of *H. erectus*? (pp. 292-297)

3. What is the importance of WT 15000, the "boy" from Nariokotome? What can this spectacular discovery tell us about the biology and lifeways of *H. erectus*? (pp. 300-301)

4. How does the Acheulian stone tool culture differ from the Oldowan? (pp. 303-305)

Answers, *Corrected Statement* if False & References To True/False Questions

1. FALSE, p. 285, Current interpretations view the first hominid migrations out of Africa taking place between *1.5 and 2.0 m.y.a.*

2. FALSE, p. 288, The *Pleistocene* Epoch is also known as the "Age of Glaciers" or the "Ice Age."

3. TRUE, p. 288

4. TRUE, p. 291

5. FALSE, p. 292, Zhoukoudian, a very important *H. erectus* site, is a cave located outside of *Beijing, China.*

6. TRUE, p. 300

7. FALSE, pp. 302-303, The site of Dmanisi, in the Republic of Georgia, is important because the hominid fossils found there *among the oldest* of all *H. erectus* finds, dating to *1.7-1.8 m.y.a.*

8. TRUE, pp. 303-305

9. FALSE, p. 305, Evidence for butchering is *widespread* in all *H. erectus* sites.

10. TRUE, p. 306

ANSWERS AND REFERENCES TO MULTIPLE CHOICE QUESTIONS

1. B, pp. 284-285
2. A, p. 285
3. A, p. 285
4. B, p. 285
5. A, p. 285
6. A, p. 285
7. D, p. 288
8. C, p. 288
9. A, p. 289
10. B, pp. 288-289
11. C, p. 289
12. D, p. 289
13. D, pp. 289-290
14. B, p. 291
15. B, p. 291
16. A, p. 291
17. C, p. 292
18. A, p. 292
19. C, pp. 292-293
20. C, pp. 294-297
21. D, pp. 296-297
22. D, p. 299
23. C, pp. 300-301
24. B, pp. 300-301
25. B, p. 302
26. D, pp. 302-303
27. D, pp. 304-305
28. A, p. 305
29. A, p. 305
30. A, p. 306

CHAPTER 12
NEANDERTALS AND OTHER ARCHAIC *HOMO SAPIENS*

LEARNING OBJECTIVES

After reading this chapter you should be able to:

- Understand the morphological changes that occurred in the transition from *Homo erectus* to archaic *Homo sapiens* (pp. 313-319).
- Know the geographic distribution of archaic *H. sapiens*. (pp. 314-319).
- Describe specific fossils of archaic *H. sapiens* and note their distinguishing characteristics (pp. 314-319).
- Compare the tool technology of archaic *H. sapiens* to that of *H. erectus* and early modern *H. sapiens* (pp. 320-322).
- Discuss the physical characteristics of classic Neandertals (pp. 323-326).
- Discuss specific Neandertal finds and their distinguishing characteristics (pp. 326-332).
- Describe Neandertal technology, shelters, subsistence and burials (pp. 332-336).
- Understand the genetic evidence that bears on the relationships and fate of the Neandertals (pp. 336-337).
- Be familiar with the three major transitions in the evolution of *H. sapiens*. (pp. 337-338).
- Understand the debates regarding classification of non-modern *Homo* fossil material (pp. 338-339).

CHAPTER OUTLINE

Introduction

In the previous chapter we examined *Homo erectus*, believed by most to be the ancestor of modern *Homo sapiens*. In this chapter we take a look at archaic *H. sapiens* from Europe, Africa, China and Java who display both *H. erectus* and *H. sapiens* characteristics. We then take a look at Neandertals including their physical characteristics, culture, technology, settlements, subsistence patterns and burials. We conclude with discussions on the debates surrounding Neandertal origins as well as their disappearance.

I   INTRODUCTION
   A. Some fossils from Europe, Africa, China and Java display both *Homo erectus* and *Homo sapiens* characteristics.
   B. They are referred to as "archaic *Homo sapiens*" because they exhibit certain derived traits in comparison to *H. erectus*.
   C. Some populations of *H. erectus* continued to evolve and emerge as transitional forms between *H. erectus* and anatomically modern *H. sapiens* (humans that are basically indistinguishable from you or me).
II   EARLY ARCHAIC *H. SAPIENS*
   A. These humans exhibit derived characteristics like brain expansion.
   B. It is difficult to taxonomically classify the Middle Pleistocene material.

C. Archaic *H. sapiens* have been found on three Old World continents including Africa, Asia and Europe.
D. The most well-known are the Neandertals from Europe and western Asia.
E. Africa
   1. The best known archaic *H. sapiens* fossil from Africa is from Broken Hill (Kabwe), in Zambia, dating from 150,000-125,000 y.a.
   2. The Broken Hill cranium has a very heavy browridge, reminiscent of *H. erectus*.
   3. However, it is advanced in its cranial shape when compared to *H. erectus*.
   4. In Africa, the archaic *H. sapiens* fossils are all morphologically similar which may signify a close genetic relationship among these hominids.
F. Asia
   1. China
      a. Certain *H. erectus* features can be found in modern Chinese such as a sagittal ridge and flattened nasal bones.
      b. This indicates to some Chinese scholars that modern Chinese evolved from a separate *H. erectus* lineage in China.
      c. Dali, the most complete Chinese archaic *H. sapiens* skull, has a relatively small cranial capacity of 1120 cm^3.
   2. India
      a. A partial skull was discovered in the Narmada Valley, in central India, in 1982.
      b. It was associated with various stone tools and its cranial capacity has been estimated between 1155-1421 cm^3.
G. Europe
   1. Early archaic *H. sapiens* from Europe show *H. erectus* characteristics like a robust mandible.
   2. Later archaics from Europe show derived characteristics like a rounded occipital area and reduced tooth size.
   3. The later group of European archaics may have given rise to Neandertals.
   4. The largest sample of European archaic *H. sapiens* comes from a site called Sima de los Huesos in northern Spain.
      a. This site dates to approximately 300,000 y.a.
      b. It has yielded the remains of at least 32 individuals.

III   A REVIEW OF MIDDLE PLEISTOCENE EVOLUTION (CIRCA 400,000-125,000 Y.A.)
A. Fossils from Europe, Africa and China exhibit a mosaic of traits from both *H. erectus* and *H. sapiens*.
B. The earlier European forms are more robust possessing more commonalities with *H. erectus*.
C. The later European forms are more like Neandertals.
D. African and Asian forms exhibit more modern human similarities.

IV   MIDDLE PLEISTOCENE CULTURE
A. Acheulian tools are commonly associated with many archaic *H. sapiens* sites.
B. African and European archaics invented the Levallois technique for controlling flake size and shape.
   1. This highly-complex technique indicates an increased cognitive ability.
C. During this period different tool traditions co-existed in some areas.
D. Archaic *H. sapiens* lived in caves and open-air sites.

E. Chinese archaeologists insist that these early humans did control fire, although not all authorities share that view.

F. The Lazaret Cave shelter, near Nice in southern France, had a framework of poles covered by hides that was supported by rocks and large bones.
   1. Inside were two hearths.
   2. Archaeology suggests that the inhabitants likely exploited a wide range of food sources.

G. At Terra Amata, also on the southern coast of France, evidence of short-term, seasonal (possible) hunting camps have been found.

H. At La Cotte de Saint-Brelade, on the Channel Island of Jersey, strong evidence for hunting large Pleistocene mammals (such as wooly mammoths and wooly rhinoceros) by driving them off cliffs has been reported.

I. In Schöningen, Germany, three well preserved wooden throwing spears were found in 1995.
   1. These implements are provisionally dated to 380,000-400,000 y.a.
   2. These weapons were found in association with horse fossils suggesting that archaic *H. sapiens* were in fact proficient hunters.

V NEANDERTALS: LATE ARCHAIC HOMO SAPIENS (130,000-35,000 Y.A.)

A. Neandertals are like us yet not like us, they are difficult to classify and interpret.

B. Neandertals lived in Europe and Western Asia for around 100,000 years.

C. "Classic" Neandertals date from around 75,000 y.a. to 35,000 y.a. and are primarily from western Europe.

D. While modern *H. sapiens* brain size averages between 1300-1400 cm^3, Neandertal brain size averaged 1520 cm^3.
   1. Large brain size in Neandertals may be associated with greater metabolic efficiency in cold weather.
   2. It may also be associated with the need for large brains to run relatively large bodies.

E. The Neandertal cranium is large, long, low and bulges at the sides.
   1. The forehead rises more vertically than in earlier archaic hominids.
   2. Over the orbits are arched browridges instead of a bar-like supraorbital torus.

F. Postcranially, Neandertals are very robust.
   1. They were barrel-chested and heavily muscled.

G. France and Spain
   1. At La Chapelle-aux-Saints, in southwestern France, a nearly complete Neandertal burial was found in 1908.
   2. The skeleton was sent to Marcellin Boule, a well-known French paleontologist, for analysis.
      a. He depicted this find as a brutish, bent-kneed, not-fully-erect biped.
      b. This resulted in a general misunderstanding that Neandertals were very primitive.
      c. In fact, the skeleton was of an older male suffering from spinal osteoarthritis.
      d. The pathologies were misinterpreted by Boule as representing normal anatomy for Neandertals.
      e. This has led to today's caricature of Neandertals as "ape-like, cavemen."
   3. However, at the Moula-Guercy cave site in southern France, recent work has uncovered the best evidence to date for a particularly gruesome Neandertal behavior: cannibalism.

a. Neandertal bones found here were broken and cut just like the animal bones at the site, suggesting to the researchers that the Neandertals were processed for food.

4. Some of the most late-surviving Neandertals come from France and Spain.
    a. St. Césaire in southwestern France dates to 35,000 y.a.
    b. Zafarraya Cave in southern Spain dates to 29,000 y.a.
    c. If the date for Zafarraya is correct it would make this the most recent of Neandertal fossils.

5. It appears that Neandertals and modern *H. sapiens* may have lived in close proximity for several thousand years.
    a. An Upper Paleolithic culture called the Chatelperronian is associated with some late-surviving Neandertals such as St. Césaire.
    b. Some researchers see this as evidence of Neandertal cultural "borrowing" from the tool-kits of modern humans.

H. Central Europe
  1. Krapina, Croatia
     a. Remains of up to 70 Neandertal individuals were recovered from this site dating to the last interglacial (130,000-110,000 y.a.).
     b. Over 1,000 stone tools and flakes were found.
     c. Krapina has one of the oldest intentional burials on record.
  2. Vindija, Croatia
     a. About 30 miles from Krapina, this site documents much later Neandertal occupation.
     b. Dating from 42,000-28,000 y.a., 35 Neandertal specimens have been recovered.
     c. The later forms are less robust than "Classic" Neandertals leading some researchers to conclude that the Vindija hominids document some continuity between Neandertals and modern humans in the region.

I. Western Asia
  1. Israel
     a. Tabun
        i.   This site yielded a female skeleton dated to about 120,000-110,000 y.a.
        ii. If the dating is correct it indicates that Neandertals and modern humans lived contemporaneously in the Middle East.
     b. Kebara
        i.   This site dates to 60,000 y.a.
        ii. Although the skeleton is incomplete (it is missing the skull), it boasts the most complete Neandertal pelvis yet found.
        iii. The skeleton also yielded the first ever hyoid bone, which is very important in reconstructing speech capabilities.
  2. Iraq
     a. Shanidar yielded the remains of nine individuals, four of whom were deliberately buried.
     b. Shanidar 1 was a 35 to 40 year old male whose stature is estimated at 5'7".
     c. He survived extreme injuries (e.g. a crushing blow to his head, loss of the use of his right arm) suggesting to researchers that his survival was only possible if he was helped by others in his group.

J. Central Asia
    1. Uzbekistan
        a. Teshik-Tash cave, 1600 miles from Shanidar, is the easternmost Neandertal discovery.
        b. A nine-year-old Neandertal boy was buried there.
    2. This site extends the Neandertal range to 4000 miles, from France to central Asia.

VI   CULTURE OF NEANDERTALS
  A. The stone tool industry associated with Neandertals is the Mousterian.
    1. These cultural remains are found in Europe, North Africa, the former Soviet Union, Israel, Iran, Uzbekistan and perhaps even into China.
  B. Technology
    1. Neandertals improved on the previous prepared-core (e.g. Levallois) techniques.
    2. There are indications of the development of specialized tools.
        a. These were used for skin and meat preparation, hunting, woodworking and hafting (making composite tools such as stone-tipped spears).
  C. Settlements
    1. Neandertals lived in open sites, caves and rock shelters.
    2. On the tundra there is some evidence of the building of structures.
        a. At the site of Moldova, Ukraine, archeologists found traces of an oval ring of mammoth bones.
        b. Inside the ring they found traces of a number of hearths.
    3. Fire was in general use by this time for cooking, warmth, light and to ward off predators.
  D. Subsistence
    1. Neandertals were successful hunters, although unlike later Upper Paleolithic hunters, Neandertals likely had to get "up close and personal" with their prey.
        a. After the beginning of the Upper Paleolithic (around 40,000 y.a.) the spearthrower, or atlatl, was invented.
        b. This allowed Upper Paleolithic hunters to ply their trade from a (much-safer) distance.
        c. The pattern of trauma found among Neandertals is similar to modern day rodeo riders, demonstrating how dangerous was their way of life .
    2. Besides meat, Neandertals likely also ate berries, nuts and other plants, when they were available.
    3. Since it was so cold we assume that Neandertals must have worn crude, but warm, clothing, such as an animal skin poncho.
  E. Symbolic behavior
    1. The general scientific consensus is that Neandertals were capable of speech.
    2. Many archaeologists, however, interpret the record as indicating significant cognitive deficits in Neandertals compared to the modern humans who followed them in Europe.
    3. These researchers view Neandertals as evolutionary dead-ends.
  F. Burials
    1. Some form of deliberate and consistent disposal of the dead dates back at least to 300,000 y.a. (at the Sima de los Huesos site, Atapuerca, Spain).

2. Burial is seen in Western Europe long before it appears in either Africa or eastern Asia.
3. In many Neandertal burials, the bodies were deliberately placed in a flexed position.
4. In some Neandertal burials, grave goods (e.g. stone tools, animal bones, flowers) were intentionally interred with the deceased.

VII GENETIC EVIDENCE
A. Mitochondrial DNA has been isolated from two Neandertals (at this writing):
  1. the original Neandertal specimen, discovered in 1856, whose DNA sequence was published in 1997.
  2. a new Neandertal child from Mezmaiskaya Cave, in the Caucasus region of Russia, whose sequence was published in 2000.
B. These studies have shown that Neandertal mtDNA is about three times as different from modern human mtDNA as modern humans are when compared to one another.
  1. The researchers used these data to estimate the divergence times between Neandertals and modern humans at 690,000-550,000 y.a. and suggest that Neandertals went extinct, having little to do with modern human origins.
C. Not all researchers agree with these interpretations, although the genetic evidence is very promising in providing potential answers concerning the fate of the Neandertals.

VIII EVOLUTIONARY TRENDS IN THE GENUS *HOMO*
A. At least three major transitions have taken place over the last two million years.
  1. The first transition was from early *Homo* to *H. erectus*.
    a. This transition was limited to Africa and occurred quite rapidly (perhaps 200,000 years or less).
  2. The second transition was very complex and involved *H. erectus* grading into early *H. sapiens*.
    a. Unlike the first transition, it was not geographically limited and it occurred slowly and unevenly.
    b. Many hominid populations during this time period could have been small and isolated.
    c. The differing effects of natural selection, genetic drift and gene flow on these widely-dispersed hominid populations contributes to the ambiguity researchers face in trying to explain this transition.
  3. The third transition was from archaic *H. sapiens* to modern *H. sapiens*.
    a. It was apparently faster than the second transition.
    b. This is the focus of the next chapter.
B. Taxonomic issues
  1. In this text, fossils attributed to *Homo* have been classified into three species.
    a. This is a conservative interpretation.
    b. Other researchers interpret the evolutionary history of *Homo* as much more complex, involving up to seven different species within our genus.
  2. Three major issues have been raised concerning interpretations and the taxonomy of archaic *H. sapiens*.
    a. The classification of "archaic *H. sapiens*" is viewed by some researchers as taxonomically imprecise.

b. Several early archaic specimens from Africa and Europe show derived characteristics that differ from *H. sapiens*.
   i. These fossils have been classified as *H. heidelbergensis*.
c. Neandertals are also viewed by numerous researchers as representing a distinct species (*H. neanderthalensis*) reflecting the view that Neandertals were not part of our species, but were rather a failed experiment in hominid evolution.

KEY TERMS

anatomically modern *Homo sapiens*: all modern humans and some fossil forms, defined by a set of derived characteristics including skull shape and a general reduction in skeletal robustness.

archaic *Homo sapiens*:: earlier forms of *H. sapiens*, including but not limited to Neandertals, that succeeded *H. erectus* but preceded modern humans.

Chatelperronian: a tool industry created by Neandertals modifying technology perhaps borrowed from anatomically modern humans.

flexed: the position in which bodies were found in Neandertal burials. The arms and legs are drawn up to the chest.

hearth: floor of a fireplace.

Levallois: a technique for the manufacture of tools by striking flakes from a flat flint nodule.

Mousterian: the stone tool technology associated with Neandertals and some modern *H. sapiens* groups.

Neandertal: a group of archaic *H. sapiens* that flourished in glacial Europe between 75,000 and 35,000 y.a.

occipital bun: a mounding of bone typically found on the back of Neandertal skulls.

transitional forms: fossils that have both primitive and derived characteristics. They are not fully one form but rather exhibit traits from two different species, i.e., *H. erectus/H. sapiens* or Neandertal/moderns.

Upper Paleolithic: a culture period usually associated with early modern humans in Europe that is characterized by blade tools and the use of horn, antler and ivory.

INTERNET EXERCISES AND *INFOTRAC COLLEGE EDITION* EXERCISES

The Atapuerca sites, in northern Spain, have yielded the largest collection of archaic *Homo sapiens* fossils from anywhere in the world. This collection of localities has recently been designated a "World Heritage Site" by UNESCO. Researchers from the "Human Paleontology Group" of the Universidad Complutense in Madrid have designed an excellent set of web pages that take you throughout the sites and display the fossils in virtual 3D (requiring a VRML plug-in) or in more traditional photo format (http://www.ucm.es/info/paleo/ata/english/main.htm).

Two very well-done Neandertal websites deserve a visit. The first is a wonderful digest of Neandertal research by Scott J. Brown titled "Neanderthals and Modern Humans: A Regional Guide." (http://www.neanderthal-modern.com/). It is very up-to-date and the resources and links are quite extensive. The second is hosted by the "Neanderthal Museum," which was opened in 1996 in the Neander Valley of Germany, commemorating the recovery of the first Neandertal specimen 140 years earlier. Take a virtual tour at http://www.neanderthal.de/e_thal/fs_1.htm.

In *InfoTrac* do a keyword search on "Neandertals." As you can see, our ancient cousins still spark a lot of interest many millennia after their disappearance. Read some of the short articles in *Science News* on Neandertals and compare that information to that presented in your text. Are the perspectives similar or different between the authors?

CONCEPT APPLICATION

Mystery Fossils

From the hints given below, try to determine what archaic *H. sapiens* or Neandertal fossil is being described. Give yourself 5 points if you can figure it out with only the first clue ("a"), 3 points if you need both clue "a" and "b," and 1 point if you need all three clues ("a, b & c").

1. Mystery fossil #1
    a. Found in a gravel pit in Germany.
    b. It is a nearly complete skull, but lacks the mandible.
    c. Its cranial capacity is 1100 cm^3 and it had a rounded occipital.

2. Mystery fossil #2
    a. Dates to 35,000 y.a. in southwestern France.
    b. Found in association with Chatelperronian tools.
    c. "Classic" Neandertal facial and cranial morphology.

3. Mystery fossil #3
    a. Found in cave deposits near Kabwe, Zambia.
    b. Has a massive browridge, a low vault and a prominent occipital torus.
    c. Its cranial capacity is 1280 cm^3.

4. Mystery fossil #4
    a. Found in Shaanxi Province, north China.
    b. It is the most complete skull of an archaic *H. sapiens* from China.
    c. It has a relatively small cranial capacity of 1120 cm^3.

5. Mystery fossil #5
    a. A Neandertal burial discovered in Israel in 1983.
    b. It has the most complete Neandertal pelvis yet found.
    c. It has the only Neandertal hyoid bone ever discovered.

6. Mystery site #6
    a. At least 32 individuals were recovered from this archaic *H. sapiens* site.
    b. It is a cave in the northern hills of Spain.
    c. It dates to around 300,000 y.a.

7. Mystery fossil #7
    a. A 30-45 year old Neandertal male recovered from a cave site in Iraq.
    b. He survived extreme trauma including a crushing blow to the side of his skull.
    c. He was 5'7" tall and had a cranial capacity of 1600 cm^3.

8. Mystery site #8
    a. At least 70 individuals were recovered from this Neandertal site.
    b. It is located in Croatia, in central Europe.
    c. It is relatively ancient for Neandertals, dating to 130,000-110,000 y.a.

9. Mystery fossil #9
    a. Marcelin Boule's description of this fossil is partially responsible for today's caricature of Neandertals as "brutish cavemen."
    b. Discovered in a cave in southwestern France in 1908.
    c. He was an old individual afflicted with arthritis and other pathologies.

10. Mystery fossil #10
    a. The easternmost Neandertal fossil, found in a cave in Uzbekistan.
    b. A nine-year-old child's burial.
    c. He was perhaps buried with five pairs of wild goat horns.

Now answer the True/False, Multiple Choice and Short Answer sample test questions. Following completion of the tests correct them with the answers and textbook page references at the end of this Study Guide chapter. Note the areas in which you are strong and weak to guide you in your studying. Finally, answer the sample Essay Questions.

TRUE/FALSE QUESTIONS

1. Temporally, archaic *Homo sapiens* are placed in between *H. erectus* and modern *H. sapiens*.
   TRUE   FALSE

2. Archaic *H. sapiens* are known from all seven continents.
   TRUE   FALSE

3. Archaic *H. sapiens* in Africa and Europe invented the Levallois technique for controlling stone tool flake size and shape.
   TRUE   FALSE

4. The earliest evidence of bows and arrows were discovered at the German site of Schöningen, dating to 380,000-400,000 y.a.
   TRUE   FALSE

5. Neandertal brain size averaged 1100 cm^3, much less than the modern human average of 1350 cm^3.
   TRUE   FALSE

6. The first Neandertal fossils were discovered in Africa during the 1960s.
   TRUE   FALSE

7. Neandertal facial anatomy and their stocky bodies have been interpreted as adaptations to the challenges of living in glacial climates.
   TRUE   FALSE

8. Some of the latest-surviving Neandertals are from St. Césaire, in southwestern France, and Zafarraya Cave, in southern Spain.
   TRUE   FALSE

9. Neandertals improved and elaborated upon the toolmaking techniques of their predecessors.
   TRUE   FALSE

10. Modern humans were the first people to bury their dead with grave goods (such as stone tools, animal bones and flowers).
    TRUE   FALSE

MULTIPLE CHOICE QUESTIONS

1. Which of the following is **not** an archaic *H. sapiens* specimen?
   A. Nariokotome
   B. Broken Hill
   C. Dali
   D. Petralona

2. Which of the following is **not** a derived morphological change found in archaic *H. sapiens*?
   A. Brain expansion
   B. Increase in molar size
   C. Increased parietal breadth
   D. Decreased robusticity

3. The archaic *H. sapiens* finds from South and East Africa
   A. are very similar to one another, suggesting a fairly close genetic relationship.
   B. evolved from different gracile australopithecines ancestors.
   C. indicate that Neandertals evolved in southern Africa.
   D. suggest that these hominids went extinct by 25,000 y.a.

4. Neandertals are found in
   A. Kenya.
   B. Cambodia.
   C. Australia.
   D. None of the above

5. Modern Chinese populations retain certain archaic *H. sapiens* traits including
   A. extreme post orbital constriction and sagittal crests.
   B. projecting canines and diastemata.
   C. sagittal ridges and flattened nasal bones.
   D. All of the above

6. Earlier European archaic *H. sapiens* fossils
   A. retain some *H. erectus* features such as thick cranial bones and heavy browridges.
   B. display some derived features including larger cranial capacity and reduced tooth size.
   C. share some traits with later Neandertals, indicating an evolutionary relationship between earlier and later European hominids.
   D. All of the above

7. Narmada is an archaic *H. sapiens* site from
   A. China.
   B. Tanzania.
   C. India.
   D. Croatia.

8. The site of Sima de los Huesos is important because it
   A. yielded the largest sample of archaic *H. sapiens* from anywhere in the world.
   B. documents the appearance of archaic *H. sapiens* in Mexico.
   C. is where Neandertal toolmakers first discovered the Levallois technique.
   D. All of the above

9. The Levallois technique for tool manufacturing
   A. arose both in Africa and in Europe.
   B. enabled the toolmaker to control flake size and shape.
   C. required coordinated steps.
   D. All of the above

10. The stone tool tradition referred to as Acheulian
    A. exhibits considerable intra-regional diversity.
    B. is restricted to eastern Asia.
    C. is uniform throughout Europe and Africa.
    D. is associated with modern humans.

11. Which of the following was **not** found in the Lazaret Cave shelter in southern France?
    A. three archaic *H. sapiens* burials
    B. rock and large bone supports for the base of the shelter
    C. two hearths
    D. evidence of a framework of poles

12. Which of the following is **not** true of the throwing spears found in Schöningen, Germany?
    A. They were found embedded in the ribs of extinct mammoths.
    B. They were each about 6 feet long.
    C. They were made out of hard spruce wood.
    D. They were expertly balanced.

13. The evidence from the site of La Cotte de Saint-Brelade, on the Channel Island of Jersey, suggests that
    A. Neandertals learned the technique of slash and burn horticulture.
    B. archaic *H. sapiens* hunters drove large mammal prey (including wooly mammoths) off of a nearby cliff.
    C. early modern humans evolved there first.
    D. the last surviving population of *H. erectus* survived there until 25,000 y.a.

14. Neandertals take their name from a valley in
    A. Israel.
    B. France.
    C. Germany.
    D. Belgium.

15. Average brain size among Neandertals
    A. is larger than among modern humans.
    B. may be related to metabolic efficiency in cold climates.
    C. is close to that of modern Inuit (Eskimo) brain size.
    D. All of the above

16. Which of the following is **not** typical of Neandertal crania?
    A. The skull is long and low.
    B. The browridges are arched over the orbits and do not form a bar-like supraorbital torus.
    C. The occipital bone is sharply angled.
    D. The forehead begins to appear and rises more vertically.

17. The La Chapelle-aux-Saints Neandertal was buried with
    A. flint tools.
    B. broken animal bones.
    C. a bison leg.
    D. All of the above

18. The Neandertal skeleton from La Chapelle-aux-Saints
    A. was a gracile, adult female.
    B. was an arthritic, older male.
    C. was a typical Neandertal in every way.
    D. died in his early teen-age years from a massive head injury.

19. Zafarraya Cave, in southern Spain, is significant because it
    A. may document a very late-surviving Neandertal occupation.
    B. provides the first evidence of fire use among archaic *H. sapiens*.
    C. provides the best evidence of interbreeding between Neandertals and early modern humans.
    D. documents the final extermination of Neandertals by archaic *H. sapiens*.

20. St. Césaire, in southwestern France, has produced a Neandertal in association with tools of what industry?
    A. Oldowan
    B. Acheulian
    C. Mousterian
    D. Chatelperronian

21. The Krapina, Croatia, Neandertal finds
    A. include fragments representing up to 70 individuals.
    B. date to around 30,000 y.a.
    C. have very few stone tools associated with them.
    D. All of the above

22. The Tabun and Kebara Neandertal discoveries are from which country?
    A. Iceland
    B. Israel
    C. Iran
    D. Indonesia

23. The Kebara skeleton is the first Neandertal fossil to preserve which bone?
    A. patella
    B. calcaneus
    C. hyoid
    D. vomer

24. The Shanidar 1 male
    A. lived to be approximately 30-45 years old.
    B. was 5'7" tall.
    C. survived extreme trauma.
    D. All of the above

25. The tool industry that is generally associated with Neandertals is the
    A. Upper Paleolithic.
    B. Developed Oldowan.
    C. Acheulean.
    D. Mousterian.

26. Neandertal hunting
    A. utilized bows and arrows.
    B. probably required close contact with their prey.
    C. was probably rare and generally unsuccessful.
    D. was learned by copying from early modern human hunters.

27. Deliberate burial of the dead
    A. was characteristic of the Neandertals.
    B. is first observed in the archaeological record among *H. habilis*.
    C. is only a modern human behavior.
    D. was infrequent among European Neandertals.

28. What amazing technological breakthrough was published during the summer of 1997?
    A. The ability to use a new kind of carbon-14 dating to obtain an absolute age from ancient hominid bone that is over 100,000 years old.
    B. The use of a new kind of ground-penetrating radar to search for ancient, buried hominid skeletons.
    C. The extraction and sequencing of mtDNA from the original 50,000-year-old Neandertal fossil.
    D. The completion of the human genome project that conclusively demonstrated that Neandertals could not possibly be our ancestors.

29. The evolution of the genus *Homo* over the last two million years
    A. can be divided into at least three major transitions.
    B. has been fairly steady.
    C. has been uniform over the different geographic regions.
    D. can be easily and clearly interpreted.

30. Which of the following have been proposed as additional species names within genus *Homo*?
    A. *H. ergaster*
    B. *H. heidelbergensis*
    C. *H. neanderthalensis*
    D. All of the above

SHORT ANSWER QUESTIONS (& PAGE REFERENCES)

1. What is the difference between archaic and anatomically modern *Homo sapiens*? (p. 313)

2. What was the importance of the Levallois technique? (pp. 320-321)

3. What is the significance of the Chatelperronian stone tool culture? (pp. 326-327)

4. Does Shanidar 1 represent an example of Neandertal compassion for the disabled? (p. 305)

5. Why is the extraction and sequencing of mtDNA from the original Neandertal fossil so exciting and significant? (pp. 336-337)

Essay Questions (& Page References)

1. Describe the Middle Pleistocene culture of archaic *H. sapiens*. What archaeological evidence has been recovered that informs us about their tool use, shelter and subsistence? (pp. 320-322)

2. What is distinctive about the Neandertals? Discuss their brain size, skull shape, dentition, body size, robusticity and proportions in this context. (pp. 323-326)

3. What is the evidence for symbolic behavior and intentional burial among the Neandertals? (pp. 334-336)

4. Discuss the three major transitions that have occurred over the two-million-year evolution of the genus *Homo*. (pp. 337-338)

Answers, *Corrected Statement* if False & References To True/False Questions

1. TRUE, p. 313

2. FALSE, pp. 314-319, Archaic *H. sapiens* are known from *Africa, Asia and Europe.*

3. TRUE, p. 320

4. FALSE, p. 322, The earliest evidence of *throwing spears* were discovered at the German site of Schöningen, dating to 380,000-400,000 y.a.

5. FALSE, p. 323, Neandertal brain size averaged *1520* cm^3, *more* than the modern human average of 1350 cm^3.

6. FALSE, pp. 323-324, The first Neandertal fossils were discovered in *western Europe more than a century ago.*

7. TRUE, p. 323

8. TRUE, pp. 326-327

9. TRUE, p. 332.

10. FALSE, pp. 335-336, *Neandertals* were the first people to bury their dead with grave goods (such as stone tools, animal bones and flowers).

ANSWERS AND REFERENCES TO MULTIPLE CHOICE QUESTIONS

1. A, pp. 314-319
2. B, p. 313
3. A, p. 314
4. D, pp. 323,328-329
5. C, p. 314
6. D, p. 318
7. C, p. 315
8. A, p. 318
9. D, pp. 320-321
10. A, p. 321
11. A, p. 321
12. A, p. 323
13. B, p. 322
14. C, p. 324
15. D, p. 323

16. C, p. 323
17. D, p. 326
18. B, p. 326
19. A, pp. 326-327
20. D, pp. 326-327
21. A, p. 330
22. B, pp. 330-331
23. C, p. 331
24. D, pp. 331-332
25. D, p. 332
26. B, p. 333
27. A, pp. 335-336
28. C, p. 336
29. A, p. 337
30. D, p. 339

CONCEPT APPLICATION SOLUTION

Mystery Fossils (and page number references)
1. Steinheim (Table 12-2, p. 319)
2. St. Césaire (p. 326)
3. Broken Hill (Table 12-1, p. 315)
4. Dali (p. 314, Table 12-1, p. 315)
5. Kebara (p. 331)
6. Sima de los Huesos, Atapuerca (p. 318, Table 12-2, p. 319)
7. Shanidar 1 (p. 331)
8. Krapina (p. 330)
9. La Chapelle-aux-Saints (p. 326)
10. Teshik-Tash (p. 332)

CHAPTER 13
HOMO SAPIENS SAPIENS

LEARNING OBJECTIVES

After reading this chapter you should be able to:

- Compare the three basic hypotheses for the origin and dispersal of anatomically modern humans (pp. 343-346).
- Discuss the earliest evidence of modern *Homo sapiens sapiens* including geographic distribution, technology and art (pp. 347-363).
- Distinguish between the cultural periods of the Upper Paleolithic (pp. 355-363)
- Describe early art from Europe and Africa (pp. 357-363).
- Evaluate the various hypotheses attempting to interpret Upper Paleolithic art (pp. 357-363).

CHAPTER OUTLINE

Introduction

In the previous chapter we looked at archaic *Homo sapiens* including Neandertals. In this chapter we investigate the origins of anatomically modern humans. We discuss the problems in trying to determine when, where and how modern *H. sapiens* first appeared and look at the competing hypotheses that attempt to answer these questions. We then examine early modern *H. sapiens* fossils, technological artifacts and art in a wide range of geographic locations.

I   INTRODUCTION
   A. It is difficult to say when modern *H. sapiens* first appeared due to ongoing ambiguities in dating.
   B. It appears, however, that the dispersal of modern humans in the Old World was rapid.

II   THE ORIGIN AND DISPERSAL OF *HOMO SAPIENS SAPIENS* (ANATOMICALLY MODERN HUMAN BEINGS)
   A. The Complete Replacement Model (Recent African Evolution)
      1. This hypothesis was developed by Stringer and Andrews in 1988.
      2. According to this theory, modern humans originated in Africa within the last 200,000 years.
      3. Moderns then migrated out of Africa and into Europe and Asia, where they replaced existing populations of archaic hominids.
      4. This theory does not accept a transition from archaic to modern *H. sapiens* anywhere except Africa.
      5. A cornerstone of this model is that the appearance of modern humans is interpreted as a biological speciation event.
         a. This means that no admixture could have occurred between the migrating moderns and any of the local archaic populations that they replaced.
         b. Taxonomically, this implies that all of the replaced archaic hominids represented different species from modern humans.

      c.   For example, modern humans (*H. sapiens*) replaced Neandertals (*H. neanderthalensis*).

   6. An important source of evidence used to support this theory comes from genetic data obtained from living peoples, specifically mitochondrial DNA (mtDNA).

   7. Using mtDNA, scientists at U.C. Berkeley constructed evolutionary "trees" and concluded that the world's population descended from a single African lineage.

      a.   However, other scientists using the same mtDNA data, have constructed different "trees" and found that some of them have no African roots.

   8. There is great deal of controversy surrounding the applicability of mtDNA and other genetic evidence to resolving the pattern and timing of the presumed modern human replacement of archaic hominid populations.

B. The Partial Replacement Model

   1. This theory was proposed by Günter Bräuer from University of Hamburg.

   2. Modern *H. sapiens* populations first evolved in Africa over 100,000 y.a. and their initial dispersal out of Africa was a gradual process.

   3. Moderns then moved into Eurasia where there was limited hybridization with local archaic *H. sapiens* populations.

   4. Eventually modern humans established themselves as the only hominid species through a gradual and complex interaction of hybridization and replacement.

C. The Regional Continuity Model (Multiregional Evolution)

   1. This model was proposed by Milford Wolpoff and colleagues.

   2. This theory contends that archaic hominid populations in Europe, Asia and Africa contributed, at least in part, to the evolution of their local, modern successors.

   3. A key distinction between the Replacement and Multiregional Evolution models is that the latter does not invoke a speciation event for the origin of modern humans.

      a.   Therefore, for example, modern humans (*H. sapiens sapiens*) are seen as only sub-specifically distinct from Neandertals (*H. sapiens neanderthalensis*).

   4. Local selective forces and genetic drift are invoked by this model to explain the maintenance of regional differentiation.

   5. Most importantly, gene flow between regions was the most important evolutionary force that prevented speciation amongst archaic hominids.

   6. The interaction of these forces resulted in the evolution of the single, regionally-diverse (i.e. polytypic) human species that occupies the planet today.

III   THE EARLIEST HOMO SAPIENS SAPIENS DISCOVERIES

A. Africa

   1. Fully anatomically modern human fossils dating from about 120,000-80,000 y.a. have been claimed from the following sites:

      a.   Klasies River Mouth, South Africa.

      b.   Border Cave, South Africa.

      c.   Omo Kibish, Ethiopia.

   2. However, at all three sites problems exist with either dating, provenience or the presumed modernity of the fossil evidence.

B. Near East

   1. In Israel at least 10 individuals have been found in the Skhūl Cave at Mt. Carmel.

      a.   This site is close, both in geography and time, to the Neandertal site of Tabun.

      b.   It has been dated to about 115,000 y.a.

2. The Qafzeh Cave in Israel has yielded the remains of at least 20 individuals.
   a. It has been dated at around 100,000 y.a.
3. Both the Skhūl and Qafzeh hominids display some Neandertal-like features, suggesting to some researchers that there may have been inter-breeding between the "moderns" and Neandertals in the Near East.

C. Central Europe
   1. At many sites, fossils display both Neandertal and modern human features.
      a. This supports the Multiregional Evolution hypothesis.
   2. From Mlade, in the Czech Republic, human fossils have been found that date to 33,000 y.a.
      a. The sample exhibits a great deal of variation.
      b. Although modern, all but one cranium exhibits a prominent supraorbital torus, reminiscent of Neandertals.

D. Western Europe
   1. Because archaeology and paleoanthropology have their scholarly roots in western Europe, initial theories of human evolution were based almost exclusively on western European material.
   2. The best known western European modern human fossils are from the Cro-Magnon rock shelter, discovered in 1868 outside of the village of Les Eyzies in southern France.
      a. The Upper Paleolithic tool industry associated with the Cro-Magnon fossils is called the Aurignacian.
      b. Cro-Magnon dates to 30,000 y.a., making it the earliest modern human fossil site in France.
   3. A very important find was announced in 1998 from the site of Lagar Velho, Portugal.
      a. Dating to 24,500 y.a., the child's skeleton recovered from this burial has been interpreted as representing millennia of admixture between modern human and Neandertal populations.
      b. The burial itself was typical of Upper Paleolithic interments of its time and many of the features of the child were typical of modern humans.
      c. Atypically, some aspects of the child's anatomy (lack of a chin, limb thickness and proportions) were very Neandertal-like.
      d. Not all researchers, however, are convinced of modern human-Neandertal hybridization by the evidence from this single specimen.

E. Asia
   1. There are at least six early modern human sites in China.
   2. Ordos (from Dagouwan, Inner Mongolia) is probably the oldest anatomically modern find from China dating to perhaps 50,000 y.a.
   3. The Upper Cave at Zhoukoudian has yielded modern human crania dating between 18,000-10,000 y.a.
   4. The skeleton from Jinniushan, dating to perhaps 200,000 y.a. has been suggested to display some modern features.
   5. Chinese paleoanthropologists see a continuous evolution in their region from *H. erectus*, through archaic *H. sapiens*, to anatomically modern humans.

F. Australia
   1. Sahul refers to the area including New Guinea and Australia.

       a.   Even during the height of glaciations, there were always significant water gaps between Sahul and southeast Asia, including Java.

       b.   Therefore some kind of water craft (e.g. crude bamboo rafts) was necessary for humans to occupy Australia.

  2. Nevertheless, human arrival in Australia may have been quite early since some archeological sites there may date to 55,000 y.a.

  3. Dating of the human fossils has been problematic.

       a.   For example, the Lake Mungo remains from southeastern Australia have been dated by some to 60,000 y.a., by others to 30,000-25,000 y.a.

  4. The Kow Swamp people date between 14,000-9000 y.a. and exhibit certain archaic traits such as heavy browridges and thick bones, suggesting to some researchers regional continuity between modern Australians and ancient Javans.

IV   TECHNOLOGY AND ART IN THE UPPER PALEOLITHIC

  A. Europe

    1. The Upper Paleolithic began approximately 40,000 y.a. in western Europe.

       a.   It has been divided into five cultural periods based on stone tool technologies.

    2. A warming trend lasting several thousand years began around 30,000 y.a.

       a.   This resulted in the growth of flowering plants and other kinds of vegetation.

       b.   Herbivorous animals lived thrived from the new vegetation and predatory animals exploited the browsers and grazers.

       c.   Europe became a hunter's paradise.

       d.   In addition, humans also began to regularly eat fish and fowl at this time.

    3. Evidence of sewn clothing first dates to this period.

       a.   From Sungir, near Moscow, remnants of a cap, shirt, trousers and moccasins were found among grave goods dating to 22,000 y.a.

    4. Climatic pulses were common during the last glacial.

       a.   Around 20,000 y.a. the weather became noticeably colder in Europe and Asia.

       b.   At the same time in Africa, it became significantly wetter.

    5. Humans had an advantage to changing conditions due to their technology.

       a.   Humans began inventing new and specialized tools.

       b.   Solutrean lance heads were among the finest, most expertly-knapped stone tools ever produced.

       c.   These toolmakers displayed a finely-honed aesthetic sensibility.

    6. The Magdalenian was the last stage of the Upper Paleolithic.

       a.   It was characterized by still more advances in technology.

       b.   Spear-throwers (atlatls), the barbed harpoon and perhaps the bow and arrow all make their first appearances during this culture period.

       c.   Burins, chisel-like stone tools used to engrave and punch holes, were common.

    7. These technological advances may have influenced human biological evolution as well.

       a.   At this time there are reductions in anterior tooth size probably owing to more efficient food processing.

       b.   This led to the lower face of moderns becoming less prognathic compared to archaics.

       c.   A distinctive characteristic of modern humans, the chin, also becomes more common.

8. "Symbolic representation" in the form of art is widespread during the Upper Paleolithic.
   a. For 25,000 years this kind of art was present in Europe, Siberia, northern and southern Africa and Australia.
   b. The carving and engraving of bone and ivory was improved with the use of specialized tools.
   c. "Venus figurines," female effigies, are found from France to Siberia.
   d. Small animal figures produced from fired clay at two sites in the Czech Republic date to 27,000 y.a., documenting the earliest use of ceramic technology in the archaeological record.
9. The most spectacular Upper Paleolithic art is found on cave walls in western Europe dating to the Magdalenian period.
   a. The majority of cave art comes from southwestern France and northern Spain.
   b. Two of the most famous sites are Lascaux Cave in southern France and Spain's Altamira Cave.
      i. Altamira was the first of Europe's painted caves to be discovered in 1879.
   c. In 1994 the amazing images from Chauvet Cave in France were broadcast to the world.
      i. This cave art is surprisingly ancient, having been provisionally dated to the Aurignacian period, possibly more than 30,000 y.a.
      ii. It contains images of panther, hyena and owl which have never been seen in cave art before.
      iii. On the floor there are footprints of bears and humans.
   d. A common motif in cave art is the depiction of human hands.
10. The partial sculpting of a rock face is termed bas-relief and this technique is always found in areas near the living sites within the caves
    a. This differs from the painted wall art which is generally found much deeper in caves.
    b. The subjects of bas-relief typically include animals, although one human figure has been depicted in this fashion.
11. Themes differ when comparing portable to wall art.
    a. Portable art representations are generally horses, reindeer and stylized humans, with bison very rarely depicted.
    b. In caves, horses and bison are the rule, but rarely reindeer.
12. Archaeologists have struggled for years to explain the meaning(s) of Paleolithic art.
    a. The association of ritual, magic and hunting is considered by some to be important in this context.
    b. Others argue that a single explanation for these artistic activities is likely to prove inadequate.
    c. A recent hypothesis suggest that a very cold snap in the last glacial (ca. 20,000-18,000 y.a.) may have influenced groups to come together to share hunting techniques and knowledge.
    d. Thus, paintings and engravings could have been used to encode this knowledge which would have been passed down generationally.
B. Africa
   1. Rock art is found in southern Africa dating to between 28,000-19,000 y.a.

2. Personal adornment dates back to 38,000 y.a. in the form of beads made from ostrich eggshells.
3. In central Africa bone and antler were used to make tools.
4. Harpoons from Katanda, in eastern Zaire, were made from the ribs or long bone splinters of large mammals.
   a. They were probably used to spear giant catfish weighing up to 150 pounds!
5. The Katanda harpoons are significant because they have been claimed to date between 180,000-75,000 y.a., much older than similar cultural implements from Europe.
6. If these dates are accurate, this would imply that modern human behavior was attained earlier in Africa than elsewhere, supporting an African Replacement model.
7. However, there is not professional consensus concerning the reliability of these dates.

V SUMMARY OF UPPER PALEOLITHIC CULTURE
A. For most of the Pleistocene cultural change was very slow.
B. In the late Pleistocene of Europe and central Africa, however, cultural innovations were attained in a dramatically shorter time span.
C. These included more effective big game hunting, enabled by new weapons, body ornamentation, tailored clothing and burials with elaborate grave goods.
D. However, this big-game hunting and gathering way of life was radically altered by the retreat of the continental glaciers.
E. With the major environmental change, prey species became much less abundant and the stage was set for the development of plant domestication, a more sedentary lifestyle and much more complex social organizations.

KEY TERMS

atlatl: spear-thrower developed during the later Upper Paleolithic.
Aurignacian: an Upper Paleolithic stone tool assemblage dating to around 30,000 y.a. and associated with early modern Europeans.
burin: small, chisel-like stone tool thought to engrave bone, antler, ivory and/or wood.
Ĉhatelperronian: an Upper Paleolithic stone tool assemblage dating to around 35,000 y.a. and associated with Neandertals. It appears that Neandertals modified technology borrowed from anatomically modern humans thus creating a new tool technology.
Cro-Magnon: A term commonly used when referring to early modern humans from Europe. The term derives from the rock shelter in southern France which dates to around 30,000 y.a. where eight skeletons were found in 1868. The skeletons included three adult males, one adult female and four young children.
Gravettian: An Upper Paleolithic culture period dating to around 27,000 y.a.
Magdalenian: The final stage of the Upper Paleolithic dating to around 17,000 y.a.
Solutrean: An Upper Paleolithic stone culture period dating to around 21,000 y.a. Considered to be the most highly developed stone tool industry.
Upper Paleolithic: refers to a cultural period of early modern humans distinguished by innovative stone tool technologies. Dates from around 40,000 to 10,000 y.a. It is further divided into five different cultural periods associated with stone tool technology. These five cultural periods (from the oldest to the most recent) are Chatelperronian, Aurignacian, Gravettian, Solutrean and Magdalenian.

INTERNET EXERCISES AND *INFOTRAC COLLEGE EDITION* EXERCISES

Visit "Peter Brown's Australian and Asian Paleoanthropology" site to view images and learn about the Australian early modern human fossil evidence. Each important fossil is pictured and thoroughly discussed by Dr. Brown, Associate Professor of Archaeology and Paleoanthropology at the University of New England, Australia. Peter Brown's colleague at the University of New England, Associate Professor Mike Morwood, has also put together a very useful website titled: "Contemporary Approaches to World Rock Art" that is thoroughly illustrated and annotated. Brown's site: http://www-personal.une.edu.au/~pbrown3/palaeo.html
Morwood's site: http://www.une.edu.au/Arch/ROCKART/MMRockArt.html

A useful site that brings together "under one roof" various resources, images and links concerning the appearance of our species is C. David Kreger's "A Look at Modern Human Origins." Kreger's purpose for the site is to help "students of paleoanthropology in the process of research, and to provide a source of information for any layperson who may or may not have access to the requisite background or general information needed to come to a fuller understanding of human evolution." (http://www.modernhumanorigins.com/)

In *InfoTrac* do a keyword search on "modern human origins" and read a few of the shorter articles or reviews that are displayed. How do these authors' opinions on the debate reflect or diverge from the perspectives offered in your text?

CONCEPT APPLICATION

Mystery sites
From the hints given below, try to determine what modern human paleoanthropological and/or archaeological site is being described. Give yourself 5 points if you can figure it out with only the first clue ("a"), 3 points if you need both clue "a" and "b," and 1 point if you need all three clues ("a, b & c").

1. Mystery site #1
    a. Dated to 14,000-9000 y.a. in Australia.
    b. Crania preserve certain archaic traits, such as heavy browridges.
    c. Skeletons are robust, with thick bones.

2. Mystery site #2
    a. May date between 180,000-75,000 y.a. in central Africa.
    b. Twelve intricately fashioned bone tools found there.
    c. The bone tools are most similar to Upper Paleolithic "harpoons."

3. Mystery site #3
    a. Dates to 30,000 y.a. in the Dordogne region of southern France.
    b. Eight individuals were discovered in a rock shelter there in 1868.
    c. The fossils are associated with an Aurignacian tool assemblage.

4. Mystery site #4
    a. Dates to about 100,000 y.a. in Israel.
    b. Remains of at least 20 individuals found there.
    c. Some specimens show certain archaic, Neandertal-like features.

5. Mystery site #5
    a. The first example of advanced cave art recorded in Europe.
    b. Discovered in Spain in 1879.
    c. Filled with spectacular bison painted in red and black.

6. Mystery site #6
    a. Dates to about 33,000 in the Czech Republic.
    b. The crania display a great deal of variation, perhaps due, in part, to sexual dimorphism.
    c. Each of the crania (save one) are marked by a prominent supraorbital torus.

7. Mystery site #7
    a. A spectacular cave art site discovered in 1994.
    b. Dates relatively early at perhaps more than 30,000 y.a.
    c. Unlike other cave art sites, painters depicted panthers, owls, and hyenas.

8. Mystery site #8
    a. *H. erectus* and early modern humans found in this cave complex.
    b. Dates to 18,000-10,000 y.a. in China.
    c. The modern human fossil crania are reported to have a number of regional (i.e. Chinese) features.

9. Mystery site #9
    a. May date from anywhere between 25,000 to 60,000 y.a.
    b. Site is in southeastern Australia.
    c. Reports have been published claiming that mtDNA has been isolated and sequenced from one of these fossils.

10. Mystery site #10
    a. Dates to 24,500 y.a. from Portugal.
    b. A four-year-old child's burial.
    c. Skeleton displays both modern human and Neandertal features.

Now answer the True/False, Multiple Choice and Short Answer sample test questions. Following completion of the tests correct them with the answers and textbook page references at the end of this Study Guide chapter. Note the areas in which you are strong and weak to guide you in your studying. Finally, answer the sample Essay Questions.

TRUE/FALSE QUESTIONS

1. The complete replacement model requires a biological speciation event for the origin of modern humans.
   TRUE   FALSE

2. The multiregional evolution model requires gene flow to prevent speciation between regional archaic populations of humans.
   TRUE   FALSE

3. Border Cave, Klasies River Mouth and Omo Kibish are three early modern human sites in southeast Asia.
   TRUE   FALSE

4. Cro-Magnon is the earliest modern human site from western Europe.
   TRUE   FALSE

5. Lake Mungo and Kow Swamp are early modern human sites from Australia.
   TRUE   FALSE

6. The Magdalenian is earlier in time than the Aurignacian.
   TRUE   FALSE

7. The atlatl, barbed harpoon and bow and arrow are cultural innovations of the later Mousterian.
   TRUE   FALSE

8. "Venus figurines" were depictions of planetary motions.
   TRUE   FALSE

9. Chauvet Cave is significant because it is relatively early in the Upper Paleolithic and it depicts some animals not seen in other cave art.
   TRUE   FALSE

10. Rock art in Africa may be as old as that from Europe.
    TRUE   FALSE

MULTIPLE CHOICE QUESTIONS

1. The dispersal of anatomically modern *H. sapiens*
   A. was a relatively rapid event.
   B. was a relatively slow event.
   C. is agreed upon by scientists to have occurred around the world 175,000 y.a.
   D. is agreed upon by scientists to have occurred from Europe into Africa.

2. Regarding the origin of anatomically modern humans, scientists
    A. agree that it involved a speciation event in Africa.
    B. agree that it first occurred in China.
    C. do not agree concerning the timing and geography of our origins.
    D. do not agree that there is only one modern human species on the planet today.

3. Which of the following is **not** a model of modern human origins?
    A. The Partial Replacement Model
    B. The Multiregional Evolution Model
    C. The Regional Replacement Model
    D. The Complete Replacement Model

4. The model also known as "Recent African Evolution" is based on the origin of modern humans
    A. in Africa and their interbreeding with local African populations.
    B. in Africa and their replacement of local populations in Europe and Asia.
    C. in China and their relatively recent evolution in Africa.
    D. simultaneously in Africa and China.

5. According to the partial replacement model
    A. modern humans evolved in Africa and Europe at the same time.
    B. archaic *H. sapiens* first evolved into modern *H. sapiens* in southern Africa.
    C. the dispersal of modern humans was relatively rapid.
    D. moderns never interbred with archaics in Eurasia.

6. According to the multiregional evolution model
    A. anatomically modern *H. sapiens* originated exclusively in Africa.
    B. modern *H. sapiens* are a separate species from Neandertals.
    C. some local populations of archaic *H. sapiens* in Europe, Asia and Africa contributed to the evolution of modern *H. sapiens* in those regions.
    D. All of the above

7. Although there is no consensus, current evidence indicates that modern *H. sapiens*
    A. evolved simultaneously in Africa, Europe and Asia.
    B. arose exclusively from Neandertals.
    C. originated in southeast Asia.
    D. fossils may appear earliest in Africa.

8. Which of the following is **not** an additional technique for dating Middle Pleistocene sites?
    A. carbon-14
    B. uranium series
    C. thermoluminescence
    D. electron spin resonance

9. The Skhūl Cave at Mt. Carmel, Israel has yielded
    A. more than 30 individuals.
    B. a single Neandertal mandible.
    C. a sample of individuals who are modern in every respect.
    D. a sample whose overall configuration is modern, but some individuals retain archaic
    (i.e. Neandertal-like) features.

10. The Mlade site in the Czech Republic
    A. dates to about 33,000 y.a.
    B. displays a great deal of cranial variation.
    C. suggests some continuity with Neandertals.
    D. All of the above

11. The area of the world that has produced the most evidence of early modern *H. sapiens* is
    A. Australia.
    B. southeast Asia.
    C. China.
    D. western Europe.

12. Cro-Magnon is
    A. typical of the European races of early modern *H. sapiens*.
    B. a site from southern Germany.
    C. an early human site that yielded eight individuals and is dated to 30,000 y.a.
    D. a mythical bird figure that is a recurrent theme in Upper Paleolithic cave art.

13. Aurignacian refers to
    A. a tool assemblage associated with France's earliest anatomically modern humans.
    B. a site in western Spain that yielded 10 skeletons.
    C. an archeologist who uncovered a rich site in northern Belgium.
    D. a tool tradition associated with archaic *H. sapiens* in western Asia.

14. A four-year-old child, dating to 24,500 y.a., that displays both modern human and Neandertal
    characteristics was recently discovered at
    A. Vindija, Croatia.
    B. Lagar Velho, Portugal.
    C. Cro-Magnon, France.
    D. Qafzeh, Israel.

15. The Upper Cave at Zhoukoudian
    A. dates to between 18,000 and 10,000 y.a.
    B. has yielded fossils that exhibit both modern and Neandertal characteristics.
    C. may be the oldest anatomically modern find.
    D. All of the above

16. The oldest anatomically modern find in Asia may be from
    A. Niah Cave, Borneo.
    B. Zhoukoudian, China.
    C. Ordos, Inner Mongolia.
    D. Batadomba, Sri Lanka.

17. In Australia, the oldest archaeological sites date to
    A. 55,000 y.a.
    B. 25,000 y.a.
    C. 200,000 y.a.
    D. 125,000 y.a.

18. The earliest human site in Australia is
    A. Kow Swamp.
    B. Lake Mungo.
    C. Cooperville.
    D. Adcockton.

19. The Kow Swamp people
    A. date to 14,000 to 9,000 y.a.
    B. are robust, displaying thick bones.
    C. exhibit archaic cranial traits such as heavy supraorbital tori.
    D. All of the above

20. Which of the following is **not** a cultural period of the European Upper Paleolithic?
    A. Magdalenian
    B. Solutrean
    C. Mousterian
    D. Aurignacian

21. Magdalenian refers to
    A. the first evidence of religion.
    B. a geographic region in western Asia.
    C. the final phase of the stone tool tradition in the Upper Paleolithic in Europe.
    D. a type of facial structure found among early moderns.

22. In which of the following regions has Paleolithic art **not** been found?
    A. Australia
    B. Siberia
    C. North America
    D. South Africa

23. Dolni Vestonice and Predmosti from the Czech Republic yielded the first documented use of
    A. ceramics.
    B. metals.
    C. controlled fire.
    D. sewn on buttons.

24. Solutrean tools
    A. are excellent examples of Upper Paleolithic skill and aesthetics.
    B. are among the finest examples of Paleolithic flintknapping known.
    C. include beautiful parallel-flaked lance heads that can be considered works of art.
    D. All of the above

25. The partial sculpting of a rock face is called
    A. knapping.
    B. pressure-engraving.
    C. the punch technique.
    D. bas-relief.

26. In Africa, we find very early evidence (38,000 y.a.) of
    A. hunting weapons such as the bow and arrow.
    B. portable personal adornment in the form of beads made from ostrich eggshells.
    C. the use of fire.
    D. cave paintings.

27. In Paleolithic cave art, women are
    A. always depicted alone.
    B. always depicted in groups.
    C. usually depicted with animals.
    D. never represented.

28. During the Magdalenian
    A. European prehistoric art reached its climax.
    B. humans first started cooking their meat.
    C. the European climate was warm and temperate.
    D. All of the above

29. Which of the following is **not** an Upper Paleolithic cave art site?
    A. Cro-Magnon, France
    B. Chauvet, France
    C. Lascaux, France
    D. Altamira, Spain

30. The Sungir site, not far from Moscow, is significant because
    A. it documents the efficiency of Upper Paleolithic reindeer hunters.
    B. there, for the first time, is evidence that humans buried their dead.
    C. it preserves evidence of sewn clothing dating to 22,000 y.a.
    D. the first Paleolithic solar visors derive from that site.

SHORT ANSWER QUESTIONS (& PAGE REFERENCES)

1. How do the Complete and Partial Replacement models differ? (pp. 344-346)

2. Why was the Upper Paleolithic a time of relative affluence? (p. 355)

3. What were burins used for by Upper Paleolithic people? (pp. 357)

4. Describe the punch blade technique. (p. 358, Fig. 13-12)

5. How does the cave art at Grotte Chauvet differ from other famous cave art sites? (p. 360)

ESSAY QUESTIONS (& PAGE REFERENCES)

1. Compare and contrast the Complete Replacement to the Multiregional Evolution models of modern human origins. How do these models differ in their interpretations of Neandertal taxonomy and fate? (pp. 343-346)

2. Summarize the technological advancements of the Upper Paleolithic. (pp. 355-357)

3. What interpretations have been offered to explain Upper Paleolithic art? (pp. 357-363)

ANSWERS, *CORRECTED STATEMENT* IF FALSE & REFERENCES TO TRUE/FALSE QUESTIONS

1. TRUE, p. 344

2. TRUE, p. 346

3. FALSE, p. 347, Border Cave, Klasies River Mouth and Omo Kibish are three early modern human sites in *Africa*.

4. TRUE, p. 352

5. TRUE, pp. 354-355

6. FALSE, p. 355, The *Aurignacian* is earlier in time than the *Magdalenian*.

7. FALSE, p. 357, The atlatl, barbed harpoon and bow and arrow are cultural innovations of the later *Upper Paleolithic*.

8. FALSE, p. 359, "Venus figurines" were depictions of *human females*.

9. TRUE, p. 360

10. TRUE, p. 363

ANSWERS AND REFERENCES TO MULTIPLE CHOICE QUESTIONS

1. A, p. 343	16. C, p. 354
2. C, pp. 343-346	17. A, p. 354
3. C, pp. 344-346	18. B, pp. 354-355
4. B, pp. 344-346	19. D, p. 355
5. B, p. 346	20. C, p. 355, Fig. 13-8
6. C, p. 346	21. C, p. 357
7. D, p. 347	22. C, pp. 357-363
8. A, p. 347, Table 13-1	23. A, p. 359
9. D, pp. 347-349	24. D, p. 357
10. D, p. 351	25. D, p. 360
11. D, p. 352	26. B, p. 363
12. C, pp. 352-353	27. B, p. 363
13. A, p. 352	28. A, p. 359
14. B, p. 353	29. A, pp. 359-360
15. A, p. 354	30. C, p. 355

CONCEPT APPLICATION SOLUTION

Mystery sites (and page number references)
1. Kow Swamp (p. 355)
2. Katanda (pp. 363-364)
3. Cro-Magnon (pp. 352-353)
4. Qafzeh (pp. 347-348)
5. Altamira (p. 359)
6. Mlade (p. 351)
7. Grotte Chauvet (p. 360)
8. Upper Cave, Zhoukoudian (p. 354)
9. Lake Mungo (p. 354)
10. Lagar Velho (p. 353)

CHAPTER 14
MICROEVOLUTION IN MODERN HUMAN POPULATIONS

LEARNING OBJECTIVES
After reading this chapter you should be able to
- explain what a population is and the evolutionary dynamics that occur within these entities (pp. 370-371, 375-376).
- name the assumptions of the Hardy-Weinberg theory of genetic equilibrium (p. 371).
- calculate a simple Hardy-Weinberg example (pp. 372-374).
- discuss the different polymorphisms and understand why they are studied (pp. 376-385).
- discuss how human cultural activities have influenced human evolution (pp. 385-388).
- cite at least two instances of human biocultural evolution (pp. 385-388).

CHAPTER OUTLINE
Introduction
    In the preceding chapters we looked at human macroevolution. However, our species continues to evolve and in this chapter we look at the minute changes that occur within our species. This is called microevolution and, unlike macroevolution, does not result in the evolution of new species. In chapters three and four we learned about the genetic basis of life. We now continue to look at how these genetic principles lie at the very foundation of the evolutionary process and how these processes interact to produce evolutionary change in living human populations. We also look at another aspect of human evolution: biocultural influences. Humans are unusual in the natural world because cultural activities have greatly influenced our evolution.

I   HUMAN POPULATIONS
    A. A population is a group of interbreeding individuals.
        1. Populations contain a degree of relatedness and, thus, share a gene pool.
        2. The largest population of *Homo sapiens* that could be described is the entire species.
            a. All members of a species are potentially capable of interbreeding, but are incapable of fertile interbreeding with members of other species.
            b. A species such as ours is a genetically closed system.
    B. Breeding isolation
        1. Geography, by isolating populations through barriers such as bodies of water or mountains, causes the formation of breeding isolates.
        2. However, cultural rules can also play a role by prescribing who is most appropriate among those potentially available.
            a. Human populations tend to mate within their own group; this is called endogamy.
            b. However, human populations are not completely closed and individuals may choose mates from outside of their group; this is called exogamy.
II   POPULATION GENETICS
    A. The Hardy-Weinberg theory of genetic equilibrium is a mathematical model that helps researchers to determine if evolution is occurring at any particular genetic locus.
    B. The Hardy Weinberg equilibrium postulates a set of conditions in an idealized, hypothetical population in which no evolution is occurring.

1. The Hardy Weinberg equilibrium makes the following assumptions:
   a. The population is infinitely large. This eliminates genetic drift as a factor.
   b. There is no mutation; therefore, no new variation is added at the molecular level.
   c. There is no gene flow, i.e., there are no new alleles coming into the population from another population.
   d. Natural selection is not operating. Specific alleles confer no advantage over others that might influence reproductive success.
   e. Mating is random. Each adult member of one sex has an equal chance of mating with any adult member of the opposite sex.
2. If the above conditions are met, allele frequencies will not change from one generation to the next, i.e., no evolution will take place.
3. By setting the conditions that would exist if no evolution were occurring, the Hardy-Weinberg equilibrium can be used to predict the allele and genotype frequencies for the next generation.
   a. Expected (predicted) genetic frequencies can be compared to observed genetic frequencies.
   b. This makes the Hardy-Weinberg equilibrium testable.
   c. The null hypothesis is that no evolution is occurring.
   d. If observable frequencies differ significantly from expected frequencies the null hypothesis is rejected.
   e. This would mean that evolution has occurred at the locus in question.
4. For a simple Mendelian trait with two alleles, the first Hardy-Weinberg equation is: $p + q = 1$
   a. where p = the frequency of the first allele, and
   b. q = the frequency of the second allele.
   c. Frequencies are simply defined as percentages of a whole, so p and q must always sum to one.
5. Given the allele frequencies of p and q, the second Hardy-Weinberg equation is used to predict the expected genotype frequencies in that population: $p^2 + 2pq + q^2 = 1$
   a. where p^2 = the expected frequency of the first homozygote,
   b. 2pq = the expected frequency of the heterozygote, and
   c. q^2 = the expected frequency of the second homozygote.
   d. Again, the frequencies have to sum to one.

C. Calculating allele frequencies
   1. The simplest example would be to analyze a trait coded for by only two, codominant alleles at one locus.
      a. In this situation, the two alleles would produce three genotypes that directly correspond to three recognizable phenotypes.
      b. In contrast, when one allele is dominant to another, these two alleles would still produce three genotypes, but only two phenotypes, since the dominant homozygote's phenotype would be indistinguishable from that of the heterozygote.
   2. In a two-allele, codominant system, you can simply count the individuals displaying each phenotype.
   3. From these data, you can calculate the numbers of each allele in the population and determine their frequencies, which become p and q.
      a. Check your work by seeing if the two allele frequencies add up to one.

4. Once allele frequencies are calculated, the next step is to plug those numbers into the second Hardy-Weinberg equation to determine the expected genotype frequencies.
   a. Again, check your work to make sure that $p^2 + 2pq + q^2 = 1$.
5. Finally, compare your expected genotype frequencies to those observed in the population.
6. If the expected frequencies significantly differ from the observed frequencies (that is determined statistically), then
   a. you can conclude that the population is not in equilibrium, and
   b. that at least one of the above assumptions has been violated.
   c. In short, you may conclude that evolution (at that locus) has occurred.
7. Refer to the examples in your text (pp. 372-374, including Box 14-1) and the Concept Application in this chapter of the Study Guide.

III   EVOLUTION IN ACTION: MODERN HUMAN POPULATIONS
   A. A number of factors initiate changes in allele frequencies.
      1. In addition to such factors that appear to work in a random fashion, nonrandom factors must also be taken into account.
   B. Nonrandom mating
      1. Any consistent bias in mating patterns can alter the genotypic proportions.
      2. There are different types of nonrandom mating.
         a. Assortative mating occurs when individuals who are phenotypically alike (positive), or phenotypically different (negative) from themselves mate with each other more often than expected.
            i. Neither positive nor negative assortative mating appear to have much influence in the vast majority of human populations
         b. Inbreeding occurs when relatives mates among themselves more often than expected.
            i.   This results in an increase in homozygosity and a decrease in variability.
            ii. Almost all societies have taboos against incest (matings between parent and child, and brother and sister).
            iii. In some societies however, mating between close relations such as cousins is encouraged or even unavoidable.
            iv. However, most human groups work hard at maintaining exogamy.

IV   HUMAN POLYMORPHISMS
   A. Simple polymorphisms
      1. Polymorphic traits are governed by a locus with more than one allele and found at frequencies greater than accounted for by mutation.
         a. Simple Mendelian traits, linked to one locus, are polymorphic traits.
         b. Simple Mendelian polymorphic traits are much more straight forward than the polygenic traits (traits governed by more than one locus) usually associated with human variation.
      2. Polymorphic traits are useful in studying the genetic differences between different populations.
         a. Genetic differences between human populations demand evolutionary explanations.
         b. By comparing allele frequencies evolutionary events can be reconstructed.

B. ABO blood system
   1. The ABO system is a polymorphic trait with three different alleles, A, B, and O.
   2. The phenotypes associated with this system are expressed by antigens (proteins) found on red blood cells.
   3. The frequencies of the three alleles vary tremendously, with most human groups being polymorphic for all three alleles.
      a. One exception is blood type O among South American Indians, where the allele frequency for O is 100%. This is referred to as being fixed in the population.
      b. The B allele is the rarest of the three alleles.
      c. The A allele has two peaks.
         i. The highest frequencies of A in the world are found among the North American Blackfeet who are over 50%.
         ii. A also occurs in high frequencies in central Australia.
      d. These two peaks illustrates the point that the distribution of alleles for a single trait do not conclusively demonstrate genetic relationships between populations; to understand patterns of population relationships the allele frequencies for several traits must be considered simultaneously.
   4. The distribution of the alleles in the ABO system around the world illustrates the concept of cline.
      a. A cline is a gradual change in frequency of genotypes and phenotypes over geographical space, often maintained by natural selection.
C. Rh system
   1. The Rh system is another group of antigens found on red blood cells.
   2. The two phenotypes are Rh positive (antigen present) and Rh negative (antigen absent).
      a. The phenotypes are accounted for by three genotypes: DD, Dd, dd.
      b. The actual genetics is more complicated and several loci appear to be involved that act as large genes.
   3. The distribution of Rh allele combinations varies considerably among human populations.
   4. Clinically, the Rh factor can lead to serious complications, especially maternal-fetal incompatibility.
D. Other red blood cell antigen systems
   1. MN blood group
      a. The MN blood system is a preferred research tool because the pattern of inheritance is very straightforward.
      b. All three genotypes, MM, MN, and NN are observable through the use of antisera.
      c. Almost all human groups are polymorphic for the MN system, although the allele frequencies vary tremendously.
E. Polymorphisms in white blood cells
   1. The HLA (human lymphocyte antigen) system is an antigen system found on white blood cells (lymphocytes).
      a. The HLA system is very complex and there is a potential of at least 30 million genotypes.
      b. This system is composed of a number of loci on chromosome 6 which act as a "supergene."
      c. Some of these loci control for other factors in the immune response.

d. Together this whole system is called the major histocompatibility complex (MHC).
e. The geographical distribution of HLA is not yet well known; however, because HLA is involved with the immune response, there is some suggestion that infectious diseases may be major factors that play a role in the distribution of HLA alleles.

F. Miscellaneous polymorphisms
1. PTC tasting
a. PTC is a bitter chemical which individuals can either taste, or not taste.
b. The ability, or the lack thereof, to taste PTC is inherited by a simple Mendelian transmission.
c. As with other polymorphic traits in this chapter, the distribution of phenotypes and alleles varies between populations.
d. The ability to taste PTC by humans may have resulted from selection to taste bitter (and toxic) plants.
2. Earwax (cerumen)
a. The two phenotypes are yellow and sticky, and gray and dry.
b. This trait is also inherited as a simple Mendelian transmission.

G. Polymorphisms at the DNA level
1. Recent advances in technology has permitted the study of polymorphisms at the DNA level.
2. mtDNA
a. Mitochondria (organelles involved with energy production for the cell) have their own DNA (called mtDNA).
b. mtDNA is considerably shorter than nuclear DNA.
c. The smaller length of mtDNA has enabled researchers to work out the mtDNA genome.
d. Variation of the mtDNA genome in humans is much less pronounced than is the case for other species.
e. The small degree of variation in the human mtDNA genome suggests to some researchers that all modern humans have a recent origin from a restricted ancestral population base.
3. Nuclear DNA
a. By using restriction enzymes considerable insight has been gained regarding human variation directly at the DNA level.
i. Researchers have observed great variation in the length of the DNA fragments at numerous DNA sites.
ii. These genetic differences are called restriction fragment length polymorphisms (RFLPs).
b. Microsatellites are sites scattered throughout the genome where DNA segments are repeated, ranging from a few up to hundreds of times.
i. These microsatellites are extremely variable from person to person.
ii. Therefore they are very useful in providing "genetic fingerprints" and can be used to identify a wide range of individuals from victims of mass disasters (such as those that perished on 9/11) to criminal suspects.
c. SNPs (single nucleotide polymorphisms, pronounced "Snips") reflect patterns of variation at single nucleotide sites.

      i. Like microsatellites, SNPs are very variable from individual to individual.

      ii. Already, more than a million SNPs have been mapped throughout the human genome.

  d. Population geneticists have begun to utilize these new techniques to address genetic patterning between and within populations around the world.

  e. Researchers are also hopeful that these new methods will be soon be able to isolate particular gene variants that contribute to polygenic traits such as skin color, stature and other complex features.

V   HUMAN BIOCULTURAL EVOLUTION

  A. Culture is the human strategy of adaptation.

  B. Culture, evolution, and malaria

    1. Before the advent of agriculture humans rarely lived near mosquito breeding areas.

    2. About 2,000 years ago slash-and-burn agriculturists penetrated and cleared forested areas in Africa.

    3. A result of deforestation was the creation of stagnant pools of water which served as prime breeding areas for mosquitoes, the vectors for malaria.

  C. Malaria has served as a powerful selective force.

    1. Sickle-cell trait is a biological adaptation to malaria.

    2. There is an advantage for carriers of sickle-cell, but only in malarial environments.

    3. After WWII extensive spraying of DDT eliminated large numbers of mosquito breeding grounds.

    4. Malaria declined, as did the sickle-cell allele.

    5. During the intervening years, mosquitoes, also subject to natural selection, have developed DDT-resistant strains with the result that malaria is again on the rise.

  D. Sickle-cell trait, in which the heterozygote has an advantage in a specific environment, is an example of natural selection in humans.

    1. The precise evolutionary mechanism in sickle-cell is called a balanced polymorphism.

    2. As defined earlier, a polymorphism is a trait with more than one allele in appreciable frequencies.

    3. For example, in some parts of Central Africa, sickle-cell allele is found at a frequency of 10 percent, which can not be accounted for by mutation alone.

    4. A fuller evolutionary explanation is needed, and that explanation is natural selection.

      a. "Balanced" refers to the interaction of selective pressures to maintain both alleles in appreciable frequencies.

      b. This is due to the selective advantage of the heterozygotes who pass on both alleles.

  E. Two other traits that may be influenced by malaria as a selective agent are G-6-PD deficiency and thalassemias.

  F. Lactose intolerance

    1. Lactose is a sugar found in milk which is broken down by the enzyme lactase.

    2. In adult mammals the gene coding for lactase is "switched off."

    3. In most adult mammals (including humans and cats) lactose in milk that is ingested is not broken down and ferments in the large intestine.

      a. This results in diarrhea and gastrointestinal distress.

    4. Many African and Asia populations, most of the world's population, are intolerant of milk as adults.

    5. This inability to digest milk is called lactose intolerance.

6. Why can the majority of adults in some populations tolerate milk?
    a. Peoples whose ancestors were pastoralists (such as modern Europeans and African peoples like the Tutsi and Fulani) probably drank large quantities of milk.
    b. In a cultural environment where milk was consumed, strong selection pressures would act to shift allele frequencies in the direction of more lactose tolerance.
    c. Some populations rely on dairying, but consume milk products as fermented dairy products such as cheese and yogurt.
        i. These populations have not developed a tolerance for lactose.
7. This interaction of human cultural environments and changes in lactose tolerance is another example of biocultural evolution.

KEY TERMS

ABO blood group system: a polymorphism based on the presence (or absence) of two antigens found in the cell membrane of red blood cells.

balanced polymorphism: the maintenance of two or more alleles in a population due to the selective advantage of the heterozygote.

breeding isolates: a population that is distinctly isolated geographically and/or socially from other breeding groups.

cline: a gradient of genotypes (usually measured as allele frequencies) over geographical space, often maintained by natural selection.

endogamy: mating with individuals from the same group.

exogamy: mating with individuals from other groups.

gene pool: the total complement of alleles shared by the reproductive members of a population.

Hardy-Weinberg theory of genetic equilibrium: the mathematical relationship expressing, under ideal conditions, the predicted distribution of genes in populations; the central theorem of population genetics.

Human Lymphocyte Antigen (HLA): antigens found on the surface of an individual's cell surfaces which provides a way for the immune system to identify "self." "Non-self" antigens are attacked. HLA is a very complex genetic system and provides a rich ground for anthropologists to study human genetic relationships.

inbreeding: a type of nonrandom mating in which relatives mate more often than predicted under random mating conditions.

incest taboo: the rule found in almost every human society that prohibits sexual relationships between parents with offspring and siblings with each other.

lactose intolerance: the inability to digest fresh milk products; caused by the discontinued production of lactase, the enzyme that breaks down lactose or milk sugar.

microsatellites: sites scattered throughout the genome where DNA segments are repeated, ranging from a few up to hundreds of times.

mitochondrial DNA (mtDNA): circular DNA found in the mitochondria and inherited through the maternal line.

MN blood group system: a blood polymorphism based upon the presence of the two alleles, which are codominant.

negative assortative mating: a type of nonrandom mating in which individuals of different phenotypes mate more often than predicted under random mating conditions.

non-random mating: patterns of mating in a population in which individuals choose mates preferentially.

polymorphism: genetic trait governed by a locus with more than one allele in appreciable frequencies.

population: a group of individuals of the same species that regularly interbreed with one another.

positive assortative mating: a type of nonrandom mating in which individuals of like phenotype mate more often than predicted under random mating conditions.

PTC Tasting: refers to the ability to taste, or not to taste, the chemical phenylthiocarbamide (PTC).

racial: in biology, pertaining to populations of a species that differ from other populations of the same species with regard to some aspects of outwardly expressed phenotype. Such phenotypic variation within a species is usually associated with differences in geographical location.

restriction fragment length polymorphisms (RFLPs): variation among individuals in the length of DNA fragments produced by enzymes that break the DNA at specific sites.

Rh system: a blood polymorphism with two phenotypes, Rh^+ and Rh^-. This system is clinically important because of its involvement with hemolytic disease of the newborn.

slash-and-burn agriculture: a traditional land-clearing practice whereby trees and vegetation are cut and burned. In many areas, fields are abandoned after a few years and clearing occurs elsewhere.

sickle-cell anemia: a severe inherited disease that results from a double dose of a mutant allele, which in turn results from a single base substitution at the DNA level.

SNPs (single nucleotide polymorphisms): reflect patterns of variation at single nucleotide sites, pronounced "Snips."

INTERNET EXERCISES AND *INFOTRAC COLLEGE EDITION* EXERCISES

Browse through the "Evolution and Population Genetics" section of the "Biology Web Site References for Students and Teachers." (http://www.hoflink.com/~house/evolution.html) Click on "Population Genetics, Microevolution" in the Table of Contents to be taken to a series of links on numerous relevant topics including, for example: 3 sites on gene frequencies, 2 sites on gene pools, 6 sites on Hardy-Weinberg and 2 sites on heterozygote advantage. Use these sites to better understand the concepts and processes discussed in your text.

In *InfoTrac* do a keyword search on "human RFLPs" and read a few of the abstracts from the scholarly articles that are retrieved. What are some of the anthropological questions being asked by today's researchers that are using modern technological advances such as RFLP analysis? What answers have they proposed?

In *InfoTrac* do a keyword search on "sickle cell malaria" and read a few of the abstracts and articles that are retrieved. What are some of the advances in knowledge that are being reported concerning the relationship of the sickle cell trait and malaria?

Hardy-Weinberg Walk-Through Fill-Ins

Solve the following Hardy-Weinberg problems by filling in the blanks.

Problem #1. You are a geneticist working on a breeding population of 100 individuals on an island. Your research question is to find out whether or not this population is at _____ at the MN locus. First, you draw the 100 individuals' _____ and determine their MN blood types by observing reactions with specially prepared _____. You then record the populational distribution of MN blood types:

People with Type M blood	People with Type MN blood	People with Type N blood
24	52	24

You know that because the MN system is _____, each of the three MN blood types (their _____) correspond to a specific MN _____. "Type M blood" individuals are genotype MM, "Type MN blood" individuals are _____ (genotype MN) and the "Type N blood" individuals are the other _____, genotype NN. Your next step is to determine allele _____ for M and N in this population. You know that each individual has ___ alleles at the MN locus, so that there are ___ total M and N alleles in this population (2 times the number of people in the breeding population). You also know that each person with Type M blood has two M alleles because their genotype is MM. Similarly, each Type N individual carries ___ N alleles since their genotype is NN. Finally, each Type MN person is a heterozygote and carries ___ of each allele, an ___ and an ___. So now you can calculate the frequencies of the M and N alleles using the following formulae:

f(M) = # of M alleles in the population / total # of M & N alleles in the population
f(N) = # of N _____ in the population / total # of M & N alleles in the _____

The table below summarizes the numbers so far:

MN blood type:	Type M blood	Type MN blood	Type N blood
# of individuals:	24	52	24
genotype:	MM	___	NN
# of M alleles:	24 X 2 = 48	52	0
# of N alleles:	___	___	___

so f(M) = (48 + 52) / (2 X 100) = 100/200 = .50, and since we know that the allele frequencies have to add up to ___, the f(N) also has to equal .50, but you'll check to make sure anyway:
f(N) = (52 + 48) / (2 X 100) = 100/200 = .50

Now, you start to plug those _____ frequencies into the Hardy-Weinberg formulae to determine if the population is in equilibrium. First you set the frequency of the M allele equal to __ and the frequency of the N allele to __, so f(M) = .50 = p and f(N) = .50 = q therefore p + q = 1

Next you calculate the expected genotype frequencies by plugging the values of p and q into the second _____ formula: $p^2 + 2pq + q^2 = 1$, so
the expected frequency of MM genotypes is $f(MM_{exp}) = p^2 = (.\_\_)^2 = .\_\_$, and
the expected frequency of MM genotypes is $f(MN_{exp}) = 2pq = 2(.\_\_)(.\_\_) = 2(.\_\_) = .\_\_$, and
the expected frequency of NN genotypes is $f(NN_{exp}) = q^2 = (.\_\_)^2 = .\_\_$

Next you check your math: does $p^2 + 2pq + q^2 = \_\_$? Since $.\_\_ + .\_\_ + .\_\_ = \_\_$, you move on to the next step: do the expected genotype frequencies that you just calculated match the observed _____ frequencies in the population? The observed _____ frequencies are simply calculated by counting the number of people with each MN blood type (remembering that there is a one-to-one match with blood types and _____ in this codominant system) and dividing that number by the total number of people in the population (in this case __).
The observed frequency of MM genotypes is $f(MM_{obs}) = 24$ Type M people / 100 people = .24
The observed frequency of MM genotypes is $f(MN_{obs}) = \_\_$ Type MN people / ___ people = $.\_\_$
The observed frequency of MM genotypes is $f(NN_{obs}) = \_\_$ Type N people / ___ people = $.\_\_$

Finally, you compare the observed to the expected frequencies:

MN blood type:	Type M blood	Type MN blood	Type N blood
# of individuals:	24	52	24
Observed frequencies	24/100 = .24	__/__ = .__	__/__ = .__
Expected frequencies	$p^2 = (.5)^2 = .25$	$2pq = 2(.\_)(.\_) = .\_\_$	$q^2 = (.\_\_)^2 = .\_\_$

From these comparisons, you conclude that this population is likely at _____ for the MN locus because the _____ and _____ frequencies are very _____. You attribute the _____ differences between the observed and expected values to the _____ size of the population. Therefore, this population is ___ evolving at this _____.

Problem #2. You, the geneticist, return to the same island 25 years later and discover that the next generation's breeding population has doubled to 200 individuals. You intend to investigate whether or not this population is still at _____ at the MN _____. You again draw the populations' blood and determine their MN _____ by observing reactions with specially prepared antisera. You record the following populational distribution of MN blood types:

People with Type M blood	People with Type MN blood	People with Type N blood
40	40	120

You know that because the MN system is codominant, each of the _____ MN blood types (their phenotypes) correspond to a specific MN genotype. "Type M blood" individuals are genotype

__, "Type MN blood" individuals are heterozygotes (genotype __) and the "Type N blood" individuals are the other homozygote, genotype __. Your next step is to determine allele frequencies for M and N in this population. You know that each individual has two alleles at the __ locus, so that there are ___ total M and N alleles in this population (2 times the number of people in the breeding population). You also know that each person with Type M blood has two M alleles because their genotype is MM. Similarly, each Type N individual carries two N alleles since their genotype is NN. Finally, each Type MN person is a _____ and carries one of each allele, an M and an N. So now you can calculate the frequencies of the M and N alleles using the following formulae:

$f(M)$ = # of M alleles in the _____ / total # of M & N alleles in the population
$f(N)$ = # of N alleles in the population / total # of M & N _____ in the population

The table below summarizes the numbers so far:

MN blood type:	Type M blood	Type MN blood	Type N blood
# of individuals:	40	40	120
genotype:	__	MN	__
# of M alleles:	_____	__	__
# of N alleles:	0	40	120 X 2 = 240

so $f(M)$ = (__ + __) / (2 X ___) = ___/___ = __/__ = _/__ = .__, and since we know that the allele frequencies have to add up to 1.0, then $f(N)$ has to equal .__, but you'll check to make sure anyway:
$f(N)$ = (40 + 240) / (2 X 200) = 280/400 = 28/40 = 7/10 = .__

Now, you start to plug those allele frequencies into the Hardy-Weinberg formulae to determine if the population is in equilibrium. First you set the frequency of the M allele equal to p and the frequency of the N allele to q, so $f(M)$ = .__ = p and $f(N)$ = .__ = q therefore p + q = 1

Next you calculate the expected genotype frequencies by plugging the values of p and q into the second Hardy-Weinberg formula: $p^2 + 2pq + q^2 = 1$, so
the expected frequency of MM genotypes is $f(MM_{exp}) = p^2 = (.\_)^2 = .\_\_$, and
the expected frequency of MM genotypes is $f(MN_{exp}) = 2pq = 2(.\_)(.\_) = 2(.\_\_) = .\_\_$, and
the expected frequency of NN genotypes is $f(NN_{exp}) = q^2 = (.\_)^2 = .\_\_$

Next you check your math: does $p^2 + 2pq + q^2 = 1$? Since .__ + .__ + .__ = 1, you move on to the next step: do the expected genotype frequencies that you just calculated match the _____ genotype frequencies in the population? The _____ genotype frequencies are simply calculated by counting the number of people with each MN blood type (remembering that there is a one-to-one match with _____ and genotypes in this codominant system) and dividing that number by the total number of people in the population (in this case ___).
The observed frequency of MM genotypes is $f(MM_{obs})$ = __ Type M people / ___ people = .__
The observed frequency of MM genotypes is $f(MN_{obs})$ = __ Type MN people / ___ people = .__
The observed frequency of MM genotypes is $f(NN_{obs})$ = 120 Type N people / 200 people = .60

Finally, you compare the observed to the expected frequencies:

MN blood type:	Type M blood	Type MN blood	Type N blood
# of individuals:	__	__	60
Observed frequencies	__ / __ = __	__ / __ = __	120/200 = .60
Expected frequencies	$p^2 = (.\_)^2 = .\_\_$	$2pq = 2(.\_)(.\_) = .\_\_$	$q^2 = (.7)^2 = .49$

From these comparisons, you conclude that this population is likely ___ at equilibrium for the MN locus because the observed and expected _____ are very _____. You note that there are less than half of the _____ that are expected and that both _____ are more frequent that you would expect given the observed _____ frequencies of M and N in this population. Therefore, you conclude that this population has _____ at this locus.

Now answer the True/False, Multiple Choice and Short Answer sample test questions. Following completion of the tests correct them with the answers and textbook page references at the end of this Study Guide chapter. Note the areas in which you are strong and weak to guide you in your studying. Finally, answer the sample Essay Questions.

TRUE/FALSE QUESTIONS

1. A mating pattern whereby individuals obtain mates from groups other than their own is called endogamy.
   TRUE   FALSE

2. The Hardy-Weinberg theory of genetic equilibrium is a minor theorem of population genetics.
   TRUE   FALSE

3. According to the Hardy-Weinberg theory of genetic equilibrium, the two equations p + q and $p^2 + 2pq + q^2$ must each sum to 1.
   TRUE   FALSE

4. Inbreeding will increase the amount of homozygosity, since relatives share more alleles than strangers.
   TRUE   FALSE

5. Polymorphism is a genetic trait governed by a locus with a single allele.
   TRUE   FALSE

6. Generally, the O allele is the rarest of the three in the ABO system.
   TRUE   FALSE

7. Clinically, the Rh factor can lead to serious complications, especially maternal-fetal incompatibility.

   TRUE   FALSE

8. MN is a red blood cell antigen system while HLA is a polymorphism on some white blood cells (lymphocytes).

   TRUE   FALSE

9. The ability to taste PTC and the consistency of ear wax are both examples of complex, polygenic inheritance.

   TRUE   FALSE

10. The maintenance of a single allele in a population due to the selective advantage of the recessive homozygote results in a balanced polymorphism.

    TRUE   FALSE

MULTIPLE CHOICE QUESTIONS

1. The total complement of genes shared by reproductive members of a population, is that population's
   A. gene flow.
   B. gene drift.
   C. gene pool.
   D. bottleneck effect.

2. Which of the following is **not** a factor that influences mate choice?
   A. geography
   B. ecology
   C. social
   D. genetic diversity

3. Which of the following is **not** an assumption of the Hardy-Weinberg theory of genetic equilibrium?
   A. the population is infinitely large.
   B. mating is non-random
   C. no mutation is occurring
   D. there is no natural selection occurring

4. Random mating means
   A. every adult individual of one sex has an equal opportunity to mate with any other mature individual of the opposite sex.
   B. every individual of one sex can mate with any individual of the opposite sex, except close family members.
   C. that people may have as many spouses of the opposite sex as they please.
   D. that adults may mate only with those individuals from the same social standing as they are.

5. You have taken blood samples from 100 individuals. You want to know what the allele frequencies for the MN blood group is in this population. You find that 70 individuals have type M blood, 20 have type MN blood, and 10 have type N blood. What are the allele frequencies for blood types M and N?
    A. M = .7, N = .3
    B. M = .7, N = .2
    C. M = .8, N = .2
    D. M = .9, N = .1

6. You find in a population, while taking blood samples and looking at the MN blood group, that the M allele is present at a frequency of 0.7. Using the Hardy-Weinberg theorem predict the genotypic frequencies for the next generation.
    A. .64(MM) + .32(NN) + .04(NN).
    B. .36(MM) + .48(MN) + .16(NN).
    C. .49(MM) + .42(NN) + .09(NN).
    D. .25(MM) + .5 (MN) + .25(NN) .

7. If significant deviations are shown from Hardy-Weinberg expectations, this may suggest
    A. equilibrium.
    B. evolution.
    C. the locus in this population is not evolving.
    D. a balanced polymorphism.

8. When allele frequencies do not change between generations and it appears that our population is in equilibrium conditions, what does it mean?
    A. Evolution is occurring for the trait in question.
    B. Evolution does not appear to be occurring for this trait.
    C. We can reject the null hypothesis.
    D. All of the above.

9. Patterns of mating in a population in which individuals choose mates preferentially is known as
    A. nonrandom mating.
    B. a balanced polymorphism.
    C. the null hypothesis.
    D. a cline.

10. The common result of positive assortative mating and inbreeding is to
    A. increase homozygosity.
    B. decrease homozygosity.
    C. increase heterozygosity.
    D. increase gene flow.

11. Mating with relatives more often than would be expected by chance is called
   A. nonrandom mating.
   B. negative assortative mating.
   C. inbreeding.
   D. incest avoidance.

12. When closely related humans, such as first cousins, produce offspring there is an elevated danger of
   A. gene flow.
   B. congenital disorders.
   C. mutations occurring.
   D. All of the above.

13. Most human populations are polymorphic for the ABO system, but one notable exception is the fixed O allele among
   A. Australian Aborigines.
   B. the peoples of central Asia.
   C. South American Indians.
   D. Blackfeet Indians.

14. The rarest allele in the ABO system is
   A. A.
   B. B.
   C. O.
   D. AB.

15. The highest frequencies of type A blood are found among
   A. the Inuit of Alaska.
   B. the peoples of central Asia.
   C. South African Kung San.
   D. Blackfeet Indians.

16. Which of the following is a true statement?
   A. Polygenic traits are usually more straightforward than polymorphic traits.
   B. Comparing allele frequencies between populations can tell us nothing about evolutionary events.
   C. Distributions of alleles for a single genetic trait do not conclusively demonstrate genetic relationships between populations.
   D. The best way to understand patterns of population relationships is to follow a single polymorphic trait.

17. It has been suggested that type O individuals are more likely to be bitten by mosquitoes. If this is true, which of the following would be an important selective factor against individuals with type O blood?
    A. infectious diseases
    B. cancers
    C. diabetes
    D. heart disease

18. Which of the following is **not** a clinically important genetic trait?
    A. ABO blood type
    B. HLA system
    C. Rh factor
    D. MN blood type

19. The most genetically complex blood polymorphism yet discovered is the
    A. ABO blood group.
    B. HLA system.
    C. MN blood system.
    D. Rh system.

20. It has been observed that higher rates of PTC tasters are found among peoples who gather a great deal of vegetable matter. Among people who eat mostly meat or cook their food the percentage of PTC tasters is low. This suggests PTC tasting is adaptive for peoples
    A. consuming large amounts of meat.
    B. eating uncooked vegetables which may contain toxins.
    C. who cook vegetables in which the toxins are leeched out.
    D. that are strictly carnivorous.

21. Which of the following is not a blood polymorphism?
    A. ABO
    B. Rh factor
    C. MN
    D. cerumen

22. One of the results of mitochondrial DNA research has been
    A. that the variation of mtDNA within *Homo sapiens* is much less than found in other species.
    B. that the variation of mtDNA within *Homo sapiens* is much more than found in other species.
    C. chimpanzees have much less variation in their mtDNA than humans do.
    D. the length of the mtDNA is as long as nuclear DNA, about 3 billion nucleotides.

23. The surprising results of mtDNA analysis (refer to question 22) may be explained if
    A. the common ancestor of humans and chimps separated 3 million years ago.
    B. the last common ancestor of modern humans was in east Africa about 2 million years ago.
    C. all modern humans have a fairly recent common ancestor.
    D. mtDNA mutates much more slowly than nuclear DNA.

24. DNA can actually be "cut" at particular points by
    A. lipids.
    B. restriction enzymes.
    C. phospholipids.
    D. nanosaws.

25. A new molecular technique that is very valuable in obtaining "genetic fingerprints" uses
    A. Rh factors.
    B. microsatellites.
    C. PTC tasting strips.
    D. ABO antigens.

26. SNPs are
    A. Semi-Networked Polygenes.
    B. Solid Nodal Pods.
    C. Stringy Nano-Polypeptides.
    D. Single Nucleotide Polymorphisms.

27. The sickle cell allele is maintained at relatively high frequencies in some populations by
    A. the selective advantage of the heterozygote in malarial areas.
    B. mutation.
    C. positive assortative mating.
    D. the susceptibility of the heterozygote to malarial infection.

28. Which of the following is **not** a trait that has been influenced by the selective agent of malaria?
    A. sickle-cell trait
    B. G-6-PD deficiency
    C. thalassemia
    D. lactose deficiency

29. Many individuals have difficulty digesting milk because
    A. they have an Rh antigen producing an immune response to milk.
    B. they do not have enough lactose in their cardiovascular system.
    C. they cannot process the lipoproteins in the milk.
    D. as adults, they have ceased the production of the lactase enzyme.

30. Some European, Middle Eastern and African populations do not have problems digesting milk as adults because
    A. their recent ancestors had a pastoral (cow or goat herding) subsistence which selected for the continued production of lactase.
    B. their recent ancestors were rice farmers, not pastoralists.
    C. they do not have any dairy products in their diet.
    D. their diets are rich in cholesterol which chemically transforms into lactase in the small intestine.

SHORT ANSWER QUESTIONS (& PAGE REFERENCES)

1. What are breeding isolates? (p. 370)

2. Why are polymorphisms of greatest use in contemporary studies of human genetic variation? (p. 376)

3. Briefly describe the world-wide distribution of the A allele. (pp. 377, 379)

4. What is the importance of the HLA system? (pp. 382-383)

5. What are RFLPs and why are they useful in genetic studies? (p. 384)

ESSAY QUESTIONS (& PAGE REFERENCES)

1. What is the Hardy-Weinberg theory of genetic equilibrium? What assumptions have to be met if a population is concluded to be in genetic equilibrium for a particular locus? (pp. 371-372)

2. What are the factors that can cause allele frequency change within populations? In particular, discuss the role of nonrandom mating in this regard. (pp. 375-376)

3. How does the relationship of sickle-cell trait to malaria illustrate the concepts of biocultural evolution and balanced polymorphism? (pp. 387-387)

ANSWERS, *CORRECTED STATEMENT* IF FALSE & REFERENCES TO TRUE/FALSE QUESTIONS

1. FALSE, p. 370, A mating pattern whereby individuals obtain mates from groups other than their own is called *exogamy*.

2. FALSE, p. 371, The Hardy-Weinberg theory of genetic equilibrium is *the central* theorem of population genetics.

3. TRUE, pp. 372-373

4. TRUE, p. 375

5. FALSE, p. 376, Polymorphism is a genetic trait governed by a locus with *more than one* allele.

6. FALSE, p. 377, Generally, the *B* allele is the rarest of the three in the ABO system.

7. TRUE, pp. 380-381

8. TRUE, p. 382

9. FALSE, p. 383, The ability to taste PTC and the consistency of ear wax are both examples of *simple, Mendelian* inheritance.

10. FALSE, p. 386, The maintenance of *two or more* allele*s* in a population due to the selective advantage of the *heterozygote* results in a balanced polymorphism.

ANSWERS AND REFERENCES TO MULTIPLE CHOICE QUESTIONS

1. C, p. 370	16. C, p. 379
2. D, p. 370	17. A, p. 379
3. B, p. 371	18. B, p. 382
4. A, p. 371	19. B, p. 382
5. C, pp. 373-374	20. B, p. 383
6. C, pp. 373-374	21. D, p. 383
7. B, pp. 373-374	22. A, p. 384
8. B, pp. 373-374	23. C, p. 384
9. A, p. 375	24. B, p. 384
10. A, p. 375	25. B, p. 384
11. C, p. 375	26. D, p. 385
12. B, p. 376	27. A, p. 386
13. C, p. 377	28. D, pp. 386-387
14. B, p. 377	29. D, p. 388
15. D, pp. 377,379	30. A, p. 388

CONCEPT APPLICATION SOLUTIONS

Blanks are filled-in with **bolded italics**. Refer to pages 372-374, including Box 14-1, in your text for more examples.

Problem #1. You are a geneticist working on a breeding population of 100 individuals on an island. Your research question is to find out whether or not this population is at **equilibrium** at the MN locus. First, you draw the 100 individuals' **blood** and determine their MN blood types by observing reactions with specially prepared **antisera**. You then record the populational distribution of MN blood types:

People with Type M blood	People with Type MN blood	People with Type N blood
24	52	24

You know that because the MN system is **codominant**, each of the three MN blood types (their **phenotypes**) correspond to a specific MN **genotype**. "Type M blood" individuals are genotype MM, "Type MN blood" individuals are **heterozygotes** (genotype MN) and the "Type N blood" individuals are the other **homozygote**, genotype NN. Your next step is to determine allele **frequencies** for M and N in this population. You know that each individual has **two** alleles at the MN locus, so that there are **200** total M and N alleles in this population (2 times the number of people in the breeding population). You also know that each person with Type M blood has two M alleles because their genotype is MM. Similarly, each Type N individual carries **two** N alleles since their genotype is NN. Finally, each Type MN person is a heterozygote and carries **one** of each allele, an **M** and an **N**. So now you can calculate the frequencies of the M and N alleles using the following formulae:

f(M) = # of M alleles in the population / total # of M & N alleles in the population
f(N) = # of N **alleles** in the population / total # of M & N alleles in the **population**

The table below summarizes the numbers so far:

MN blood type:	Type M blood	Type MN blood	Type N blood
# of individuals:	24	52	24
genotype:	MM	MN	NN
# of M alleles:	24 X 2 = 48	*52*	0
# of N alleles:	*0*	52	*24 X 2 = 48*

so f(M) = (48 + 52) / (2 X 100) = 100/200 = .50, and since we know that the allele frequencies have to add up to **1.0**, the f(N) also has to equal .50, but you'll check to make sure anyway:
f(N) = (52 + 48) / (2 X 100) = 100/200 = .50

Now, you start to plug those *allele* frequencies into the Hardy-Weinberg formulae to determine if the population is in equilibrium. First you set the frequency of the M allele equal to *p* and the frequency of the N allele to *q*, so f(M) = .50 = p and f(N) = .50 = q therefore p + q = 1

Next you calculate the expected genotype frequencies by plugging the values of p and q into the second *Hardy-Weinberg* formula: $p^2 + 2pq + q^2 = 1$, so
the expected frequency of MM genotypes is $f(MM_{exp}) = p^2 = (.5)^2 = .25$, and
the expected frequency of MM genotypes is $f(MN_{exp}) = 2pq = 2(.5)(.5) = 2(.25) = .50$, and
the expected frequency of NN genotypes is $f(NN_{exp}) = q^2 = (.5)^2 = .25$

Next you check your math: does $p^2 + 2pq + q^2 = 1$? Since *.25 + .50 + .25 = 1*, you move on to the next step: do the expected genotype frequencies that you just calculated match the observed *genotype* frequencies in the population? The observed *genotype* frequencies are simply calculated by counting the number of people with each MN blood type (remembering that there is a one-to-one match with blood types and *genotypes* in this codominant system) and dividing that number by the total number of people in the population (in this case *100*).
The observed frequency of MM genotypes is $f(MM_{obs})$ = 24 Type M people / 100 people = .24
The observed frequency of MM genotypes is $f(MN_{obs})$ = *52* Type MN people / *100* people = *.52*
The observed frequency of MM genotypes is $f(NN_{obs})$ = *24* Type N people / *100* people = *.24*

Finally, you compare the observed to the expected frequencies:

MN blood type:	Type M blood	Type MN blood	Type N blood
# of individuals:	24	52	24
Observed frequencies	24/100 = .24	*52/100 = .52*	*24/100 = .24*
Expected frequencies	$p^2 = (.5)^2 = .25$	$2pq = 2(.5)(.5) = .50$	$q^2 = (.5)^2 = .25$

From these comparisons, you conclude that this population is likely at *equilibrium* for the MN locus because the *observed* and *expected* frequencies are very *similar*. You attribute the *insignificant* differences between the observed and expected values to the *small* size of the population. Therefore, this population is *not* evolving at this *locus*.

Problem #2. You, the geneticist, return to the same island 25 years later and discover that the next generation's breeding population has doubled to 200 individuals. You intend to investigate whether or not this population is still at *equilibrium* at the MN *locus*. You again draw the populations' blood and determine their MN *blood types* by observing reactions with specially prepared antisera. You record the following populational distribution of MN blood types:

People with Type M blood	People with Type MN blood	People with Type N blood
40	40	120

You know that because the MN system is codominant, each of the *three* MN blood types (their phenotypes) correspond to a specific MN genotype. "Type M blood" individuals are genotype *MM*, "Type MN blood" individuals are heterozygotes (genotype *MN*) and the "Type N blood" individuals are the other homozygote, genotype *NN*. Your next step is to determine allele frequencies for M and N in this population. You know that each individual has two alleles at the *MN* locus, so that there are *400* total M and N alleles in this population (2 times the number of people in the breeding population). You also know that each person with Type M blood has two M alleles because their genotype is MM. Similarly, each Type N individual carries two N alleles since their genotype is NN. Finally, each Type MN person is a *heterozygote* and carries one of each allele, an M and an N. So now you can calculate the frequencies of the M and N alleles using the following formulae:

f(M) = # of M alleles in the *population* / total # of M & N alleles in the population
f(N) = # of N alleles in the population / total # of M & N *alleles* in the population

The table below summarizes the numbers so far:

MN blood type:	Type M blood	Type MN blood	Type N blood
# of individuals:	40	40	120
genotype:	*MM*	MN	*NN*
# of M alleles:	*40 X 2 = 80*	*40*	*0*
# of N alleles:	0	40	120 X 2 = 240

so f(M) = *(80 + 40)* / (2 X *200*) = *120/400 = 12/40 = 3/10* = *.30*, and since we know that the allele frequencies have to add up to 1.0, then f(N) has to equal *.70*, but you'll check to make sure anyway:
f(N) = (40 + 240) / (2 X 200) = 280/400 = 28/40 = 7/10 = *.70*

Now, you start to plug those allele frequencies into the Hardy-Weinberg formulae to determine if the population is in equilibrium. First you set the frequency of the M allele equal to p and the frequency of the N allele to q, so f(M) = *.30* = p and f(N) = *.70* = q therefore p + q = 1

Next you calculate the expected genotype frequencies by plugging the values of p and q into the second Hardy-Weinberg formula: $p^2 + 2pq + q^2 = 1$, so
the expected frequency of MM genotypes is $f(MM_{exp}) = p^2 = (.3)^2 = $ *.09*, and
the expected frequency of MM genotypes is $f(MN_{exp}) = 2pq = 2(.3)(.7) = 2(.21) = $ *.42*, and
the expected frequency of NN genotypes is $f(NN_{exp}) = q^2 = (.7)^2 = .49$

Next you check your math: does $p^2 + 2pq + q^2 = 1$? Since *.09 + .42 + .49* = 1, you move on to the next step: do the expected genotype frequencies that you just calculated match the *observed* genotype frequencies in the population? The *observed* genotype frequencies are simply calculated by counting the number of people with each MN blood type (remembering that there is a one-to-one match with *blood types* and genotypes in this codominant system) and dividing that number by the total number of people in the population (in this case *200*).
The observed frequency of MM genotypes is $f(MM_{obs}) = 40$ Type M people / 200 people = .20
The observed frequency of MM genotypes is $f(MN_{obs}) = 40$ Type MN people / 200 people = .20
The observed frequency of MM genotypes is $f(NN_{obs}) = 120$ Type N people / 200 people = .60
Finally, you compare the observed to the expected frequencies:

MN blood type:	Type M blood	Type MN blood	Type N blood
# of individuals:	*40*	*40*	60
Observed frequencies	*40/100 = .20*	*40/200 = .20*	120/200 = .60
Expected frequencies	$p^2 = (.3)^2 = .09$	$2pq = 2(.3)(.7) = .42$	$q^2 = (.7)^2 = .49$

From these comparisons, you conclude that this population is likely *not* at equilibrium for the MN locus because the observed and expected *frequencies* are very *dissimilar*. You note that there are less than half of the *heterozygotes* that are expected and that both *homozygotes* are more frequent that you would expect given the observed *allele* frequencies of M and N in this population. Therefore, you conclude that this population has *evolved* at this locus.

CHAPTER 15
HUMAN VARIATION AND ADAPTATION

LEARNING OBJECTIVES

After reading this chapter you should be able to:
- understand the history of how human racial categories were established (pp. 392-394).
- describe the concept behind biological determinism and associated philosophies (p. 394).
- understand the difference between "race" and "ethnicity" and the problems with using these terms (pp. 395-397).
- distinguish between the clinal approach to human variation and the racial approach (pp. 397-398).
- discuss the significance of Lewontin's multivariate study of 17 polymorphic traits (pp. 397-398).
- understand scientific racism and its applications to intelligence studies (pp. 399-400).
- describe the adaptive significance of human variation (pp. 400-401).
- describe the relationship between solar radiation and skin color (pp. 401-403).
- list how humans respond to the thermal environment (pp. 404-406).
- list the ways that humans respond to high altitude stress (pp. 406-408).
- understand how infectious disease has affected human evolution (pp. 408-410).
- discuss current culturally mediated factors that may contribute to the spread of infectious disease (pp. 411-413).

CHAPTER OUTLINE

Introduction.

In previous chapters we have focused on the patterns of inheritance from one generation to the next and the physical mechanisms (DNA) for inheritance. We also learned how evolution works and saw how Mendelian traits have been used to study evolutionary factors in human populations. In this chapter, our focus shifts to polygenic traits, or traits that express *continuous* variation. We will see how these traits have been used as a basis for traditional racial classification and we look at some of the issues that currently surround the topic of race in physical anthropology. After reviewing the traditional ideas of human biological diversity we look at more recent explanations of certain polygenic traits; instead of emphasizing their historical uses as "racial" markers, we will focus on their adaptive value for human populations living in specific environments. We will also examine how populations and individuals differ in their adaptive responses to the environment. Finally, we consider the role of infectious disease in human evolution and adaptation.

I   HISTORICAL VIEWS OF HUMAN VARIATION.
   A. When humans first came into contact with other human groups they categorized them.
      1. Skin color was one of the more noticeable traits that was used to classify people and there were attempts to explain skin color.
      2. During the European "Age of Discovery," there was an increased awareness of human biological diversity.
      3. Two schools of thought developed to explain human variation.

B. Monogenism
   1. Monogenists believed that all humans were descended from a single pair of humans (Adam and Eve).
      a. According to monogenists, the reason modern humans exhibited a great deal of biological diversity was due to plasticity of the human phenotype in response to local environmental conditions.
      b. Human races were the result of modification to the original form.
   2. Monogenism was attractive because it did not contradict Genesis.
C. Polygenism
   1. Polygenists believed that all humans were descended from a number of different pairs of humans (i.e., different "Adams and Eves").
   2. Polygenists believed that, in addition to physical differences, there were differences between races in intelligence and morality.
   3. Polygenists did not accept the idea that the environment could modify a phenotype.
D. Racial classification.
   1. Throughout the eighteenth and nineteenth centuries the primary focus regarding human variation was on description and classification.
   2. Linnaeus' classification of life also included humans.
      a. In addition to the physical features used to classify other life forms, Linnaeus used cultural attributes to classify humans.
      b. Linnaeus ranked humans with the least complimentary traits being assigned to sub-Saharan (black) Africans.
      c. Europeans were ranked highest and reflected the Euro-centric view that they were superior.
   3. Johann F. Blumenbach (1752-1840)
      a. Blumenbach classified humans into five races: Caucasoid, Mongoloid, American, Ethiopian, and Malayan.
      b. Blumenbach emphasized that racial divisions based on skin color were arbitrary.
      c. Blumenbach recognized that many traits, including skin color, were not discrete phenomena.
         i. Individuals within a group that expressed traits that were intermediate would be difficult to classify.
         ii. Furthermore, many traits showed overlapping expression between groups.
   4. It was thought that racial taxonomies should be based on characteristics unique to particular groups and uniformly expressed within them.
      a. Such traits were believed to be stable and not influenced by the environment.
      b. These nonadaptive traits should exhibit only minimal within group variation.
   5. In an attempt to find unique traits, Anders Retzius developed the cephalic index to describe head shape.
      a. The cephalic index, a ratio of head breadth to length, was calculated by dividing maximum head breadth by maximum length and multiplying that quotient by 100.
      b. Peoples, such as northern Europeans, with a long narrow head and a cephalic index under 75 were termed dolichocephalic.
      c. Populations with broad heads, such as southern Europeans, had a cephalic index over 80 and were termed brachycephalic.
      d. Mesocephalic were people that were intermediate, with cephalic indices between 75 and 80.

6. In the end, racial classification resulted in ranked human groups, with (northern) Europeans being at the top of the racial hierarchy.
E. Biological determinism
1. The idea that there is a cause and effect association between physical characteristics and behavioral characteristics is called biological determinism; i.e., cultural variations are inherited.
   a. It follows from this logic that there are inherent behavioral and cognitive differences between groups. This is called racism.
   b. It also follows from this logic that there are inherent behavioral and cognitive differences between the sexes. This is called sexism.
2. When biological determinism is accepted as a reasonable explanation, it is easy to justify the persecution and enslavement of other peoples.
3. Eugenics was a scientific discipline which was grounded in biological determinism.
   a. Eugenics promoted the idea of "race improvement" and suggested that the government should be involved in this endeavor.
   b. By the end of WWI some scientists began turning away from racial typologies in favor of a more evolutionary approach.

II THE CONCEPT OF RACE
A. All modern humans belong to the same polytypic species, *Homo sapiens*.
1. A polytypic species consists of local populations that differ from one another in the expression of one or more traits.
2. Most species are polytypic, thus there is no species "type" to which all members conform.
B. The traditional concept of race
1. In the past people were clumped together by various combinations of attributes and placed into categories associated with particular geographical areas.
2. The term race is often misused and has developed various definitions.
   a. Race has been used synonymously with species.
   b. Since the 1600s race has been used to refer to various culturally defined groups.
   c. The perception that there is an association between physical traits and many cultural attributes is still widespread.
   d. "Racial traits" are not the only phenotypic expressions that contribute to social identity: sex and age are also critically important.
3. In the 1950s the use of the term "race" was challenged and it was proposed that the term "ethnicity" replace it.
C. The biological use of the word "race"
1. "Race" refers to geographical phenotypic variation within a species.
2. Even within modern biology there are no established criteria by which races of plants and animals are to be assessed, so classifications of non-human organisms into races are subjective biological decisions.
3. Prior to WWII, most studies of human variation focused on phenotypic variation between large geographically defined populations.
D. Modern studies of human variation focus on the examination of allele frequencies within and between populations.
1. Specifically we want to know the adaptive significance of phenotypic and genotypic variation.

2. Application of evolutionary principles to human variation has replaced the older view that was based solely on observed phenotypes.
3. Races are no longer viewed as fixed biological entities, composed of individuals fitting a particular type, which do not change.
4. While human variability is recognized between geographic areas, the following questions must be asked regarding this phenotypic difference.
   a. What is the adaptive significance attached to the observed phenotypic variation?
   b. What is the degree of underlying genetic variation that influences the observed variation?
   c. How important is the underlying genetic variation?
E. Controversies and debates about human variation
1. Attempts to reach a consensus regarding "race" in humans have failed.
2. However, no modern scholar subscribes to the pre-modern synthesis concept of races as fixed biological units.
3. Many who continue to use broad racial categories do not view them as important.
4. Forensic anthropologists find the phenotypic criteria associated with race to have practical applications.
   a. These anthropologists assist in identification of human skeletal remains.
   b. Metrical analysis assists forensic anthropologists in identifying the sex, age, stature and "racial" or "ethnic" background of skeletal remains up to about 80% accuracy.
5. Other modern anthropologists see race as a meaningless concept when applied to humans.
F. Objections to racial taxonomies
1. Such classificatory schemes are typological.
   a. The categories are discrete and based on stereotypes that comprise a specific set of traits.
   b. Such typologies do not account for individuals who do not conform to the particular type for the group.
2. Many of the characteristics used to define races are polygenic.
   a. Polygenic traits exhibit a continuous range of variation.
   b. Using polygenic traits to define a group makes it difficult, if not impossible, to draw discrete boundaries between populations.
III   CONTEMPORARY INTERPRETATIONS OF HUMAN POPULATION DIVERSITY
A. By the 1960s the study of clinal distributions of individual polymorphic traits had become an alternative to the study of race.
1. A cline is a gradual change in the frequency of a single trait in populations dispersed over space.
2. Clinal distributions are believed to reflect microevolutionary influences of natural selection and/or gene flow.
3. Utilizing single traits has limitations when we try to sort out population relationships.
B. Multivariate approaches consider several traits simultaneously.
1. Harvard geneticist, Richard D. Lewontin analyzed human diversity using a multivariate approach in 1972.
   a. Lewontin considered 17 polymorphic traits for seven geographical areas ("races").
   b. He showed that only 6.3% of genetic variation could be explained by differences between these seven major continental groupings of people (i.e. "races").

248

      c. After partitioning his seven geographical groups into subgroups, Lewontin could only account for about 15% of human genetic diversity as being due to geographic and local "races."

      d. Most human genetic diversity appears to be explained in terms of differences from one village to another, one family to another, and even between one individual to another (even within the same family!).

      e. Superficially, obvious visible traits suggest that human races exist.

      f. However, those traits used to form races may produce a highly biased sample and not give an accurate picture of the actual pattern of genetic variation.

      g. Lewontin's final conclusion is that human racial classification, shown to have no genetic or taxonomic significance, should be discontinued.

  2. Other geneticists have conducted multivariate studies and produced similar results to Lewontin's ground-breaking work.

      a. For example, a 1993 study of genetic variation in 59 different groups (representing over 12,000 people) demonstrated that 98.5% of this variation was present within each of these groups.

  3. These nuclear DNA studies suggest that the vast majority of variation occurs within populations at the individual level.

IV   RACISM

  A. The most detrimental outcome of biological determinism is racism.

    1. Racism is based on the false belief that intellect and various cultural factors are inherited along with physical characteristics.

    2. According to this view culturally defined variables typify all members of particular populations.

    3. Such beliefs commonly rest on the assumption that one's own group is superior to other groups.

  B. Racism is a cultural, not a biological, phenomenon, and it is found worldwide.

  C. To summarize the modern anthropological perspective on "race":

    1. What we really observe when we see biological variations between populations are the traces of our evolutionary past.

    2. These variations represent adaptations to the different environments that our ancestors moved into while increasing the geographical range of humans.

    3. Our variations are a preserved record of how natural selection shaped our species to meet different environments.

    4. Instead of using our differences as a basis for prejudice, we should praise them.

V   INTELLIGENCE

  A. Whether or not there is an association between "race" and intelligence has been widely debated in scientific, social and political circles.

  B. Both genetic and environmental factors contribute to intelligence.

    1. It is not possible to measure accurately the percentage each factor contributes to intelligence.

    2. IQ scores are often confused with intelligence; IQ scores and intelligence are not the same thing.

      a. Many psychologists say that IQ scores measure life experience.

      b. IQ scores can change within an individual's lifetime.

    3. Complex cognitive abilities, no matter how they are measured, are influenced by multiple loci and are strikingly polygenic.

4. Individual abilities result from complex interactions between genetic and environmental factors.
   a. One product of this interaction is learning.
   b. Elucidating what proportion of the variation in test scores is due to biological factors is probably not possible.
C. Innate differences in abilities reflect individual variation within populations, not inherent differences between groups.
D. There is no convincing evidence that populations vary with regard to cognitive abilities.

VI   THE ADAPTIVE SIGNIFICANCE OF HUMAN VARIATION
A. Physical anthropologists view human variation as the result of adaptations to environmental conditions, both past and present.
   1. Environmental conditions can place stress on humans.
      a. Stress in this context is defined as any environmental factor that disrupts homeostasis.
      b. Homeostasis is the condition of balance, or stability, within a biological system (such as a human body).
      c. Therefore we can think of adaptation as an individual's attempt to maintain or regain homeostasis.
B. Physiological response to environmental change is under genetic control and operates at two levels.
   1. Long-term (i.e. genetic) evolutionary changes characterize all individuals within a population or species.
   2. Short-term physiological response to environmental change is called acclimatization; such physiological change is temporary.
C. Solar radiation and skin color
   1. Before 1500, skin color in populations followed a particular geographical distribution, particularly in the Old World.
      a. Populations with the greatest amount of pigmentation are found in the topics.
      b. Populations with lighter skin color are associated with more northern latitudes.
   2. Skin color is influenced by three substances.
      a. Hemoglobin when it is carrying oxygen, gives a reddish tinge to the skin.
      b. Carotene is a plant pigment, which the body synthesizes into vitamin A, and it provides a yellowish cast.
      c. Melanin is the most important contributor to skin color.
   3. Melanin has the ability to absorb ultraviolet (UV) radiation, preventing damage to DNA
      a. UV radiation can produce mutations in skin cell DNA and ultimately cause skin cancer.
      b. Melanin is produced by specialized cells in the epidermis called melanocytes.
      c. All humans appear to have about the same number of melanocytes.
      d. Exposure to sunlight triggers a protective mechanism which temporarily increases melanin production (i.e., a tan).
   4. Natural selection appears to have favored dark skin in areas nearest the equator where the most intense UV radiation is found.
      a. In considering skin color from an evolutionary perspective, three points should be kept in mind:
         i. Early hominids lived mostly in the tropics.

  ii. Most earlier hominids spent the majority of time outdoors.

  iii. Early hominids did not wear clothing that would have provided some protection against UV radiation.

 b. In addition to the selective benefits of dark skin preventing skin cancers in the tropics, it has been recently suggested that melanin also prevents the destruction of folate, an important B vitamin.

  i. Folate is critical for normal neural development in fetuses.

  ii. Loss of folate can lead to spina bifida and other neural tube defects.

 c. As hominids migrated to the northern latitudes, selective pressures changed.

  i. Europe had cloudy skies, a winter with fewer hours of daylight, and with the sun to the south, solar radiation was indirect.

  ii. The use of clothing prevented exposure of the skin to sunlight.

  iii. Selection favoring dark skin was relaxed, but there also had to be a selective pressure favoring lighter skin.

 5. Vitamin D plays a vital role in mineralization and normal bone growth during infancy and childhood.

  a. While vitamin D is available in some foods, the body's primary source comes from its own ability to synthesize vitamin D through the interaction of UV light and a cholesterol-like substance found in the subcutaneous layer of the skin.

  b. Insufficient amounts of vitamin D during childhood results in rickets, which leads to bone deformities.

 D. The vitamin D hypothesis

  1. Reduced exposure to sunlight would have been detrimental to darker-skinned individuals in northern latitudes who would have been deficient in vitamin D.

   a. The higher melanin content of their skin would have filtered out much of the UV radiation available.

   b. Additionally, if the diet did not provide adequate amounts of vitamin D, selective pressures would have shifted over time to favor less pigmented skin.

  2. There is substantial evidence to support this vitamin D hypothesis.

   a. For example, blacks in northern U.S. cities have historically suffered higher incidences of rickets than northern whites.

   b. Rickets can be a powerful selective force because it can produce pelvic deformities that would be death sentences to pregnant mothers and their offspring before the advent of the C-section.

  3. Perhaps more social importance has been attached to variations in skin color than any other single human biological trait.

   a. However, skin color is of no particular biological importance except in terms of its adaptive significance.

VII THE THERMAL ENVIRONMENT

 A. Mammals and birds have evolved homeothermy, a physiological mechanism which enables an organism to maintain a constant body temperature.

  1. Humans are found in a wide variety of thermal environments, ranging from 120° F to -60° F.

B. Human response to heat
   1. Humans and many other mammalian species have sweat glands widely distributed throughout the skin.
      a. Sweat on the body surface removes heat through evaporative cooling.
      b. This is a mechanism that has evolved to a high degree in humans.
   2. The capacity to dissipate heat by sweating is a feature found in all human populations almost equally.
      a. However, there is variation in that people not generally exposed to hot conditions need a period of acclimatization to warmer temperatures.
      b. A negative side-effect to heat reduction through sweating is that critical amounts of water and minerals can be lost.
   3. Another mechanism for radiating body heat is vasodilation.
      a. Vasodilation refers to a widening (dilation) of the capillaries.
      b. Vasodilation of the capillaries near the skin's surface permit "hot" blood from the body's core to dissipate heat to the surrounding air.
   4. Body size also plays a role in temperature regulation.
      a. There is a general relationship between climate and body size and shape in homeothermic species (although, as always in biology, there are exceptions).
      b. Two biological rules apply to body size, body proportions, and temperature.
      c. Bergmann's rule states that body size tends to be greater in populations that live in cold environments.
         i. This is because surface area decreases relative to mass as an object increases in size. For example, for every three-fold increase in the mass of a globular animal, there is only a two-fold increase of surface area.
         ii. Because heat is lost from the surface, increased mass allows for greater heat retention and reduced heat loss.
      d. Allen's rule states that in colder climates, populations should have shorter appendages (arms, legs, and sometimes noses) to increase mass-to-surface ratios preventing heat loss.
         i. In warmer climates, populations should have longer appendages with increased surface area relative to mass which promotes heat loss.
      e. According to both Bergmann's and Allen's rules:
         i. In warmer environments body shape should be linear with long arms and legs, such as that found today among East African pastoralists.
         ii. In cold environments people should have stocky bodies with shorter arms and legs as is found among the Inuit.
      f. There is much human variability regarding body proportions and not all populations conform to Bergmann's and Allen's rules.
C. Human response to cold
   1. Humans can respond to cold by increasing heat production or in ways that enhance heat retention
      a. Heat retention is more efficient because it requires less energy.
   2. Short-term human responses to cold include:
      a. Increased metabolic rate uses energy to produces body heat.
         i. People living in chronic cold generally have higher metabolic rates than people living in warmer environments.

ii. High metabolic rates can be maintained by larger consumptions of animal protein and fat such as is seen among the Inuit.
   3. Shivering uses energy to produce body heat.
   4. Vasoconstriction is a narrowing of the blood vessels which reduces blood flow to the skin.
      a. Vasoconstriction restricts heat loss.
      b. A small amount of energy is used to constrict blood vessels, but more energy is saved by retaining heat and avoiding the use of more energetically expensive responses.
   5. Behavioral modifications include:
      a. Increased physical activity to produce heat from contracting muscles.
      b. Increased food consumption, which provides more calories from which to produce more energy.
      c. Bringing all body parts into a center, such as a curled-up position, in order to reduce the amount of surface area exposed to the cold.
   6. Long-term human responses to cold vary among human groups.
VIII HIGH ALTITUDE
   A. Multiple factors produce stress on the human body at higher altitudes, including:
      1. more intense solar radiation,
      2. cold,
      3. low humidity,
      4. wind (which amplifies cold stress, hence the wind chill factor in winter weather reports), and most importantly
      5. hypoxia.
   B. Hypoxia refers to a reduction in the available oxygen.
      1. It can mean reduced oxygen in the atmosphere, due to a lower barometric pressure (i.e. for every cubic meter of air at high altitude there are actually fewer oxygen molecules, than there are in a cubic meter of air at sea level).
      2. It can also refer to decreased oxygen available, or present, in the body's tissues.
      3. Of the factors mentioned, hypoxia exerts the greatest amount of stress on human physiological systems, especially the heart, lungs, and brain.
   C. People who reside at higher elevations, especially newcomers, exhibit a number of manifestations of their hypoxic environment.
      1. Reproduction is affected through increased rates of infant mortality, miscarriage, and prematurity.
      2. Low birth weight is more common, probably because of decreased fetal growth due to impaired maternal-fetal oxygen transport.
   D. Adult acclimatization to high altitude occurs when people, born at lower elevations, acclimatize to the higher elevation.
      1. These are usually short -term modifications.
      2. Adult acclimatization to high altitude includes:
         a. increase in respiration rate,
         b. increase in heart rate, and
         c. increased production of red blood cells.
   E. Developmental acclimatization to high altitude occurs in people born in high altitudes in which they acquire their adaptations during their growth and development.
      1. Developmental acclimatization to high altitude includes:

a. greater lung capacity,

b. larger hearts, and

c. more efficient diffusion of oxygen from blood vessels to body tissues.

2. Developmental acclimatization provides a good example of physiological plasticity by illustrating how, within the limits of genetic factors, development can be influenced by environment.

F. There is evidence that populations can adapt to high attitudes.

1. Highland Tibetan populations appear to have evolved accommodations to hypoxia (over the last 25,000 years) and do not have reproductive problems.

2. Both highland Tibetans and highland Quechua (from the Peruvian Andes) appear to utilize glucose in a way that permits more efficient use of oxygen.

a. This implies the presence of genetic mutations in the mtDNA.

b. This also implies that natural selection has acted to conserve advantageous mutations affecting glucose metabolism in these groups.

IX INFECTIOUS DISEASE

A. Infectious disease refers to those diseases caused by invading organisms such as bacteria, viruses, or fungi.

1. Throughout the course of human evolution, infectious disease has exerted enormous selective pressure on human populations.

2. Infectious disease influences the frequency of certain alleles that affect the immune response.

B. The effects of human infectious disease are due to cultural and biological factors.

1. Until the advent of agriculture and sedentary living sites, infectious disease was not a major problem to human populations.

a. Eventually human settlements became large, crowded, unsanitary cities where the opportunity for disease was great.

b. Humans also domesticated animals that carried diseases that affected humans.

C. Malaria is the disease that more humans suffer from today than any other.

1. There are between 300-500 million people worldwide suffering from malaria.

2. Recently some of the malarial parasites have become drug resistant.

D. AIDS (acquired immune deficiency syndrome) is a viral infection that was first reported in 1981.

1. The virus that causes AIDS is HIV (human immunodeficiency virus).

2. Viruses consist of single strands of DNA or RNA enclosed by a protein jacket.

a. Once a virus invades a host's body it enters target cells.

b. Viral DNA is inserted into the target cell's DNA.

c. The end result is that the viral DNA directs the cell to produce virus particles which go on to infect other cells.

3. HIV is transmitted through the exchange of body fluids and cannot spread through casual contact.

4. HIV can attack a variety of cell types, but its predilection is for T4 helper cells, one of the cell types that initiates an immune response.

a. When a person's T cell count drops below minimum levels, "opportunistic" infections, pathogens present but not HIV, are able to mount an attack on the body.

b. A receptor site is on the plasma membrane of some immune cells, including T4 cells.

c. Pathogens, including HIV, attach to these receptors and invade the cells.
5. Some individuals test positive for HIV, but show few if any symptoms, even after 15 years.
   a. This suggests that some individuals may possess natural immunity or resistance to HIV.
6. Some individuals possess a mutant allele that results in a malfunctioning receptor site to which HIV is unable to bind.
   a. Homozygotes for this allele may be completely resistant to HIV.
   b. In heterozygotes, infection may still occur, but the progress of the disease is much slower.
   c. The mutant allele occurs mainly in people of European descent where the allele frequency is around 0.10.
   d. The allele is not present in Japanese and West Africa samples; however, it does occur at a frequency of around 0.02 in African Americans, perhaps due to gene flow from Euro-Americans.
   e. The allele may have resulted from selection for an earlier disease that occurred in Europe.
   f. This selection was not against HIV, but another pathogen that required the same receptor site.
   g. This earlier selective agent provided some resistance against the later HIV.
   h. In 1999 a group of researchers reported that a virus related to the one that causes smallpox can use the same receptor site as HIV and suggested that this may be the mysterious agent of selection.
E. Smallpox
   1. During the 18th century this disease was estimated to have been responsible for 10-15% of all deaths in parts of Europe.
   2. By 1977, modern medical technology totally eradicated this killer disease.
   3. Individuals who were blood type A or AB were more susceptible to smallpox than blood type O.
   4. This was explained by similarities between the A antigen and one on the smallpox virus.
   5. Therefore, the immune systems of blood type A and AB individuals did not recognize the smallpox virus as foreign and did not mount adequate defenses.

X THE CONTINUING IMPACT OF INFECTIOUS DISEASE
A. Humans and pathogens exert selective pressures on each other.
   1. Disease exerts selective pressures on host populations to adapt to that particular organism.
   2. Microbes also evolve (very quickly) and adapt to the various pressures exerted upon them by their hosts.
      a. From an evolutionary perspective, it is to the advantage of any pathogen to keep its host alive until it can reproduce and infect other hosts.
      b. Selection frequently acts to produce resistance in host populations (a benefit to the host) and to reduce the virulence of the disease (also a benefit to the host, but this also benefits the disease organisms because it enables them to reproduce more efficiently).
   3. Of the known disease-causing organisms, HIV provides the best example of how pathogens evolve and adapt.

B. Before the 20th century, infectious disease was the number one limiting factor to the growth of human populations.
1. Human cultural practices are currently speeding up microbe evolution.
2. Increases in the prevalence of infectious disease may be due to overuse of antibiotics.
    a. Antibiotics have exerted selective pressures on bacteria and some species have developed drug-resistant strains.
3. Another factor associated with today's rapid spread of disease is the widespread mixing of peoples everyday; this includes the crossing of borders and penetration into remote areas.
C. Some diseases are making "comebacks."
1. Tuberculosis is now the world's leading killer of adults and this disease, once controlled by antibiotics, has developed drug-resistant strains.
2. Cholera has also developed antibiotic-resistant strains.
    a. Recent cholera outbreaks have been partly attributed to rising ocean temperatures, lack of sanitation, and overcrowding.
D. Fundamental to the spread of disease is the increasingly large human population size.
1. Overcrowding leads to unsanitary conditions and the spread of communicable disease.

KEY TERMS

acclimatization: short-term physiological response by an individual to changes in the environment. The capacity for acclimatization may also typify the entire population or species. This capacity is under genetic influence and is subject to evolutionary factors such as natural selection.

AIDS: acquired immune deficiency syndrome. A condition caused by suppression of the immune system due to the human immunodeficiency virus (HIV). The syndrome includes any number of "opportunistic" infections which are able to attack the body due to an inefficient immune response.

biological determinism: the concept that phenomena, including various aspects of behavior, are governed by genetic factors.

brachycephalic: having a broad head in which the width measures more than 80 percent of the length.

coevolution: evolution of two or more species in which they are exerting reciprocal selective pressures on one another.

dolichocephalic: having a long, narrow head in which the width measures less than 75 percent of the length.

endemic: in regards to disease, a population in which there is always some individuals that are infected.

ethnocentrism: viewing other cultures from one's own cultural perspective. This often leads to thinking of other cultures as odd and inferior.

eugenics: a former scientific discipline, now largely discredited, that promoted the improvement of the human species through controlled breeding and sterilizations of "undesirables."

homeostasis: a state of equilibrium in which the body's internal environment remains within a stable range. Homeostasis is maintain through a series of negative feedback loops which act to bring the internal environment back into its stable range.

homeothermy: characteristic of mammals and birds. These animals are able to regulate their body temperatures independent of outside (ambient) temperature fluctuations.

hypoxia: a lack of oxygen, either in the body's tissues or in the atmosphere (at higher altitudes).

intelligence: mental capacity: the ability to learn, reason, or comprehend and interpret information, facts, relationships, meanings, etc.

monogenism: a theory that all living humans are descended from one original pair of humans (Adam and Eve) and that all subsequent human biological variation is due to environment.

pandemic: an extensive outbreak of disease affecting large numbers of people over a wide area; potentially, a world-wide phenomenon.

pathogen: any organism or substance that causes disease.

plasticity: physiological change in response to the environment.

polygenism: the theory that living humans are descended from many different pairs of humans (other Adams and Eves) that has led to different human races.

polytypic: referring to species composed of populations that differ with regard to the expression of one or more traits.

races: populations of a species that differ from one another in some aspect of the visible phenotype. Biological (i.e. geographic) races are taxonomically expressed as subspecies.

stress: in a physiological context, any factor that acts to disrupt homeostasis. In this respect, stress can be microbes or environment extremes such as climate or altitude, as well as psychological factors.

vasoconstriction: narrowing of blood vessels by decreasing their diameter permitting reduced blood flow to the skin. Vasoconstriction is an involuntary response to cold and reduces heat loss at the skin's surface.

vasodilation: an involuntary expansion of blood vessels by increasing their diameter, permitting increased blood flow to the skin. Vasodilation permits warming of the skin and also facilitates radiation of warmth as a means of cooling.

vector: an agent that serves to transmit disease from one carrier to another.

INTERNET EXERCISES AND *INFOTRAC COLLEGE EDITION* EXERCISES

Take a look at Syracuse University's "All of Us Are Related, Each of Us is Unique" cyber-exhibition "exploring the concept of race." (http://allrelated.syr.edu/) After reading the descriptive blurb on the first page, click on the "View the Exhibition" button towards the bottom right. That will take you to a page that displays thumbnails of all 18 panels of the exhibition. Before cycling through them, open up another browser window and click on "Full Text Panels 1-18". This will allow you to view the panels in one window while switching back-and-forth with the other so you can read the full text associated with each panel. How do the perspectives in this exhibition jibe with your text?

In *InfoTrac*, do a keyword search on "scientific racism Blakey" to read an article by Howard University physical anthropologist Michael L. Blakey titled "Scientific Racism and the Biological Concept of Race" published in the journal *Literature and Psychology* in 1999. This very thorough treatment of the subject takes you from attempts to define race, through its historical development to manifestations of scientific racism today.

CONCEPT APPLICATION

Arrange the 16 figures (labeled A-P below) into two groups of 8. Record the criteria that guided your decisions to group the figures the way that you did. Compare your groupings to those of a classmate. Do they differ? If so, why? If they don't, is there an equally logical way to group them again so that your groupings differ from your classmate's? What does this exercise have to say about attempts to classify humans into races?

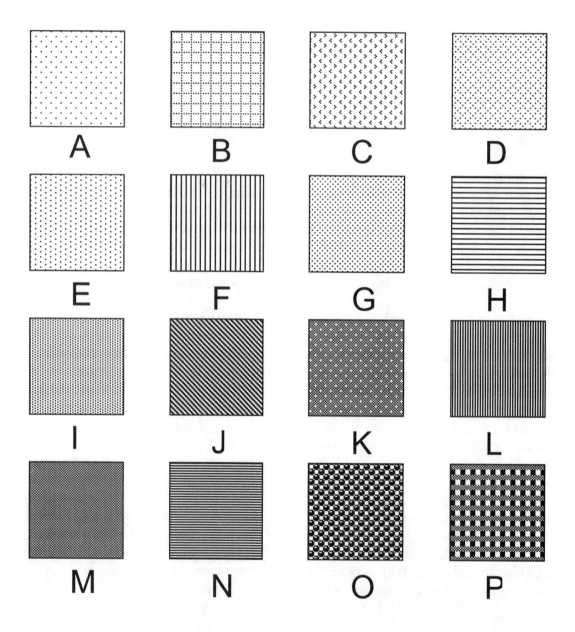

Now answer the True/False, Multiple Choice and Short Answer sample test questions. Following completion of the tests correct them with the answers and textbook page references at the end of this Study Guide chapter. Note the areas in which you are strong and weak to guide you in your studying. Finally, answer the sample Essay Questions.

TRUE/FALSE QUESTIONS

1. An historical idea that stated that human races were not all descended from Adam and Eve was known as monogenism.
    TRUE   FALSE

2. All contemporary humans are members of the same polytypic species, *Homo sapiens*.
    TRUE   FALSE

3. Today, most physical anthropologists view race as the central explanatory concept to apply to human variation.
    TRUE   FALSE

4. Lewontin's 1972 study showed that only 6.3% of genetic variation could be explained by differences between major continental groupings of people (i.e. "races").
    TRUE   FALSE

5. The most detrimental outcome of biological determinism is racism.
    TRUE   FALSE

6. Comparing populations on the basis of IQ scores is a valid use of testing procedures and provides convincing evidence that populations vary with respect to cognitive ability.
    TRUE   FALSE

7. Dark-skinned human populations in the tropics are protected by their melanin from the adverse affects of intense ultra-violet radiation.
    TRUE   FALSE

8. Allen's rule states that body size tends to be greater in populations that live in colder climates.
    TRUE   FALSE

9. The most important stress at high altitude is hypoxia.
    TRUE   FALSE

10. HIV can be transmitted from person-to-person by casual contact.
    TRUE   FALSE

1. The polygenist explanation for human races
    A. stated that all races did not originate from the single original pair.
    B. emphasized the wide gap in physical, mental and moral attributes between Europeans and other races.
    C. rejected the modifying influences of climate and environment in producing racial variation.
    D. All of the above

2. In 1842, Anders Retzius developed the _____ index to describe various _____ shapes.
    A. caudal; tail
    B. Bergmann; body
    C. cephalic; head
    D. brachial; leg

3. A local sheriff believes that the people in his district, who have high arrest and conviction rates, are born thieves because of their genetic constitution. Which of the following exemplifies the sheriff's attitude?
    A. relativism.
    B. homophobia.
    C. biological determinism.
    D. post-modernism.

4. The philosophy that provided "scientific justification" for purging Nazi Germany of its "unfit" was
    A. anthropometry.
    B. eugenics.
    C. genetics.
    D. monogenism.

5. Within *Ammodramus maritimus* , the seaside sparrow, there are four distinct populations that differ from one another in at least one trait. This sparrow is an example of a
    A. monotypic species.
    B. polytypic species.
    C. chronospecies.
    D. syngamic species.

6. The consensus criterion for identifying a biological race is
    A. At least 50% of the members of one population of a species must be physically distinguishable from those from another population.
    B. Two populations of the same species are located in two different geographical areas.
    C. Two populations have different vocalizations or, in humans, languages.
    D. There are no established criteria for identifying races of plants and animals (including humans) today.

7. An objection to the use of racial taxonomies is that they are
   A. typological in nature.
   B. based on polygenic traits.
   C. based on continuous traits.
   D. evolutionary in nature.

8. A gradual change in allele frequencies in populations dispersed over geographic space is called a
   A. race.
   B. phenotypic grade.
   C. cline.
   D. Hardy-Weinberg equilibrium.

9. Multivariate studies of population genetics seek to
   A. prove races exist.
   B. understand one genetic trait at a time.
   C. describe the pattern of several traits at one time.
   D. find non-adaptive traits that can be used to describe groups.

10. In Lewontin's multivariate computer study of race, he concluded that
    A. there is more genetic variation between races than is found within any one specific race.
    B. the seven "geographic" races cluster independently, indicating that they are true races.
    C. there is more genetic variation within any one race than there is between races.
    D. the idea of race is valid.

11. Modern studies of human variation emphasize
    A. the adaptive significance of variation.
    B. differences between large geographically separated populations.
    C. description of geographically separated populations.
    D. polygenic traits such as skin color.

12. Which of the following statements is true?
    A. Many anthropologists consider groups such as the Japanese to be a race.
    B. Forensic anthropologists can identify the ethnicity of a skeleton 100% accurately.
    C. Many physical anthropologists see human race as a meaningless concept.
    D. The five races of Blumenbach are still the standard in modern physical anthropology.

13. Which of the following statements is true?
    A. Individual abilities are due only to an individual's genetic inheritance.
    B. IQ can change within an individual's lifetime.
    C. IQ scores are essentially the same thing as innate intelligence.
    D. IQ scores reflect innate cognitive differences between populations.

14. Black children adopted by advantaged white families score better on IQ tests. This suggests that
    A. IQ is correlated with race.
    B. genetics has absolutely nothing to do with IQ scores.
    C. the social environment plays a dominant role in determining the average IQ level of children.
    D. All of the above

15. If an Illinoian leaves the 300 foot elevation of Urbana-Champaign and flies to Quito, Ecuador, elevation 8,000 feet, this person's body will begin to produce more red blood cells to compensate for lower oxygen levels. This type of short-term physiological change is called
    A. habituation.
    B. homeothermy.
    C. acclimatization.
    D. remodeling.

16. The pigment that absorbs ultraviolet radiation, thereby protecting the skin against its harmful effects, is
    A. carotene.
    B. melanin.
    C. lactose.
    D. hemoglobin.

17. When insufficient ultraviolet radiation is absorbed during childhood the condition resulting from a Vitamin D deficiency is
    A. rickets.
    B. gastroenteritis.
    C. cancer.
    D. trisomy 21.

18. Which of the following is **not** associated with human adaptation to heat?
    A. Vitamin D synthesis
    B. sweating
    C. vasodilation
    D. the evolutionary loss of our "fur coat"

19. Alaskan Inuits are short and stocky, while many east Africans are long and linear. This is explained by
    A. Bergmann's rule
    B. Thompson's rule
    C. Gloger's rule
    D. Kleiber's rule

20. The long arms and legs of the East African Masai, and the short arms and legs of the Inuit conform to
    A. Bergmann's rule
    B. Allen's rule
    C. Gloger's rule
    D. Cope's rule

21. Which of the following processes is most associated with human acclimatization to cold?
    A. sweating.
    B. vasodilation.
    C. vasoconstriction.
    D. evaporative cooling.

22. Which of the following is **not** a short-term response to cold?
    A. increased metabolic rate.
    B. shivering.
    C. increased food consumption.
    D. vasodilation.

23. The people with the highest metabolic rates in the world are the
    A. inland Inuit of the Arctic.
    B. Ainu of Japan.
    C. Australian Aboriginals.
    D. Choctaw of Oklahoma.

24. Which of the following is **not** a way that the Inuit adapt to the cold?
    A. clothing
    B. high fat diet
    C. dark skin
    D. a short, stocky body build

25. A problem associated with high altitude stress is
    A. kidney failure.
    B. low birth weights.
    C. high red blood cell counts.
    D. high white blood cell counts.

26. There is some evidence that highland Tibetans
    A. do not need to breathe oxygen.
    B. have made genetic adaptations to hypoxia.
    C. have evolved more efficient kidneys.
    D. need to go down to lower elevations in order to reproduce.

27. A disease that currently infects 300-500 million people worldwide, and has had a great effect on recent human evolution, is
    A. rickets.
    B. malaria.
    C. bubonic plague.
    D. Ebola virus.

28. Serious concern(s) of medical workers is/are that
    A. disease causing microbes are evolving resistance against antibiotics.
    B. insect vectors have developed resistance against pesticides.
    C. infectious diseases are on the rise again.
    D. All of the above.

29. Which of the following statements is true?
    A. HIV can be transmitted through casual contact.
    B. HIV can be carried by an insect vector.
    C. HIV is transmitted through exchange of body fluids.
    D. HIV is the immediate cause of death for a victim.

30. Which of the following fundamentally affects infectious disease patterns in today's world?
    A. soaring human populations sizes
    B. weather disturbances in the southern Pacific Ocean
    C. increasing aridity in north Africa
    D. clear-cutting primary forests in Amazonia

SHORT ANSWER QUESTIONS (& PAGE REFERENCES)

1. How does monogenism differ from polygenism? (pp. 392-393)

2. What was the importance of Lewontin's 1972 genetic study? (pp. 397-398)

3. What effect does ultra-violet radiation have on human skin? (pp. 402-403)

4. Why do you vasodilate when you're hot and vasoconstrict when you're cold? (pp. 404-406)

5. How do high-altitude natives acclimatize during their growth and development? (pp. 407-408)

ESSAY QUESTIONS (& PAGE REFERENCES)

1. Review the development of the race concept in Western thought from its origins in the 16th century through its catastrophic effects during the 20th century. (pp. 392-394)

2. How do physical anthropologists regard the concept of race today? Discuss the variety of viewpoints present in the field on this topic. (pp. 395-397)

3. How do biological determinism and racism enter into the debate over IQ, intelligence and claimed cognitive differences between populations? (pp. 394, 399-400)

4. How does HIV and AIDS illustrate the dynamic nature of the relationships between host, pathogen and human culture? (pp. 409-412)

ANSWERS, *CORRECTED STATEMENT* IF FALSE & REFERENCES TO TRUE/FALSE QUESTIONS

1. FALSE, pp. 392-393, An historical idea that stated that human races were not all descended from Adam and Eve was known as *polygenism*.

2. TRUE, p. 395

3. FALSE, p. 396, Today, most physical anthropologists view race as *meaningless in explaining* human variation.

4. TRUE, p. 397

5. TRUE, p. 399

6. FALSE, p. 400, Comparing populations on the basis of IQ scores is a *misuse* of testing procedures and provides *no* evidence *whatsoever* that populations vary with respect to cognitive ability.

7. TRUE, p. 402

8. FALSE, p. 405, *Bergmann's* rule states that body size tends to be greater in populations that live in colder climates.

9. TRUE, p. 407

10. FALSE, p. 409, HIV can be transmitted from person-to-person *only through the exchange of bodily fluids*.

ANSWERS AND REFERENCES TO MULTIPLE CHOICE QUESTIONS

1. D, pp. 392-393
2. C, p. 393
3. C, p. 394
4. B, p. 394
5. B, p. 395
6. D, p. 395
7. A, p. 396
8. C, p. 397
9. C, p. 397
10. C, pp. 397-398
11. A, p. 395
12. C, p. 396
13. B, p. 400
14. C, p. 400
15. C, p. 407

16. B, p. 402
17. A, p. 403
18. A, p. 404
19. A, p. 405
20. B, p. 405
21. C, p. 406
22. D, p. 406
23. A, p. 406
24. C, p. 406
25. B, p. 407
26. B, p. 408
27. B, p. 409
28. D, pp. 412-413
29. C, p. 409
30. A, p. 413

CONCEPT APPLICATION SOLUTION

There is no "right answer" for this exercise. One possible division of these figures would be the first two ("lighter") rows (Figs. A-H) versus the 3rd and 4th ("darker") rows (Figs. I-P). Alternatively, a division of "dots" (Figs. A,C,E,G,I,K,M,O) versus "lines" (Figs. B,D,F,H,J,L,N,P) is equally defensible. This concept application is meant to illustrate the arbitrariness of human racial typologies (pp. 395-397).

CHAPTER 16
LEGACIES OF HUMAN EVOLUTIONARY HISTORY

LEARNING OBJECTIVES
After reading this chapter you should be able to:
- discuss examples of the interaction of biology and culture in human growth and development (pp. 419-423).
- understand nutrition's impact on human growth (pp. 423-424).
- understand how and why we age (pp. 425-426).
- explain the benefits of examining human behavior from a behavioral ecological framework (pp. 426-431).
- discuss explanations of sexuality, aggression and reproduction from the perspective of behavioral ecology (pp. 426-431).
- place humans within the context of other life on the planet (pp. 431-432).
- understand the exponential increase of human population and the effects of our species' overpopulation on us, and the planet's biodiversity (pp. 432-435).
- explain how we hasten the evolution of other species and how that is not necessarily a good thing (pp. 436-437).
- answer the question: "Are We Still Evolving?" (p. 437).

CHAPTER OUTLINE
Introduction.

As we have noted throughout the text, modern humans are the result of evolution in which there was a strong interaction between biology and culture. In this final chapter we explore the impact that human biocultural evolution has left on three levels of organization: the individual, society and our planet.

I   BIOCULTURAL EVOLUTION AND THE INDIVIDUAL
   A. To gain a better understanding of biocultural evolution and its effects on individuals, the growth and development of humans should be examined.
   B. There is a lot of variation in how certain characters will be manifested in adult individuals.
      1. For example, some traits (like albinism) will be expressed no matter what cultural milieu was present during growth and development.
      2. Other features, like intelligence and adult height, reflect a greater interaction between an individual's environment and genetic makeup.
   C. Life history theory is utilized by many physical anthropologists and primatologists.
      1. These scientists study primate and human growth from an evolutionary perspective, focusing on how natural selection has affected the life cycle, from conception to death.
      2. Significant questions, such as "Why do humans have longer periods of infancy and childhood when compared to other primates?" are addressed by this theoretical approach.

a. Humans are distinctive because our "life stages" (e.g. infancy, childhood, adult…) are relatively extended compared to other mammals.

b. We have also added stages (e.g. juvenile, subadult, post-reproductive) compared to other mammalian groups.

c. Most of these life cycle stages are well-marked by biological transitions.

d. However, in humans these transitions are complicated by culture.

e. Collective societal attitudes toward these transitions (e.g. puberty, menopause) affect individual growth and development.

D. Growth in infancy and childhood

1. Humans are characterized by delayed brain growth compared to other primates

a. Human infants are born with only 25% of their adult brain-weight, compared to 50% for most other mammals, including non-human primates.

b. This results in very helpless human infants, but the major benefit is that much of our brain growth occurs in the much more stimulating "outside world" instead of in the womb.

c. Delayed brain growth may also be very important for language acquisition.

d. There is evidence that this pattern of brain growth was established by early *Homo erectus* times.

2. Nursing in infancy typically occurs for four years in humans.

a. This may seem surprising given that in Western societies nursing rarely lasts more than a year.

3. Humans have unusually long childhoods during which a great deal of learning takes place.

II   NUTRITIONAL EFFECTS ON GROWTH AND DEVELOPMENT

A. Nutrition has an impact on human growth and development at every stage of the life cycle.

1. There are five basic nutrients needed for growth and development:

a. proteins,

b. carbohydrates,

c. lipids (fats),

d. vitamins, and

e. minerals.

B. However, today's Western diets are often not compatible with the nutritional requirements that our species has evolved over the past five million years.

1. The pre-agricultural diet was high in protein, but low in fat.

a. The diet was high in complex carbohydrates, including fiber.

b. The diet was low in salt and high in calcium.

2. Many of our biological and behavioral characteristics contributed to our ancestors' adaptation, but may be maladaptive in our modern industrialized societies. An example of this is our ability to store fat.

a. This was an advantage in the past when food availability alternated between abundance and scarcity.

b. Today, however, there is a relative overabundance of foods in western nations. The formerly positive ability to store extra fat has now turned into a liability which leads to degenerative diseases.

3. Perhaps the best example of a disorder that reflects how our former hunting and gathering lifestyles conflict with our modern diets is Type II diabetes (adult-onset).

      a. In 1900, this disease ranked 27th among the leading causes of death in the U.S., today it the 7th leading killer.

      b. It is projected to increase significantly around the world over the next ten years as well.

    4. Overpopulation in today's world also leads to malnutrition, undernutrition and starvation in many developing nations.

C. Human longevity

    1. Compared to most mammals human have a relatively long life span.

      a. Maximum life span in humans is around 120 years.

      b. While life span is unlikely to increase, human life expectancy at birth (the average length of life) has increased significantly in the last 100 years.

      c. One of the major reasons that people are living longer today is because they are much less frequently dying from childhood infectious diseases.

    2. Aging is a synonym of senescence, the physiological decline that occurs at the end of the life course.

      a. Recall from Chapter 2 that natural selection favors traits that increase reproductive success.

        i. Most causes of death that have their effects after reproduction are not subjected to selection.

      b. Many of the genes that enhance reproductive success in younger years may be detrimental in later years and lead to debilitating disease such as hypertension and cancers.

        i. These are pleiotropic genes and have multiple effects at different times in the life span or under different conditions.

      c. Free radicals are also believed to contribute to senescence.

        i. Free radicals are byproducts of cellular metabolism that can damage cells.

        ii. Vitamins and some enzymes provide some protection against free radicals.

      d. There is also evidence that programmed cell death is also a part of normal senescence.

      e. The "telomere hypothesis" suggests that the DNA sequence at the end of each chromosome (the telomere) shortens each time a cell divides.

        i. During a lifetime of cell divisions, the telomeres eventually get so short that the cells no longer divide and thus the cells undergo degenerative changes.

    3. Far more important than genes in influencing how we age are lifestyle choices, such as smoking, diet and physical exercise.

    4. Life expectancy varies from country to country, between socioeconomic classes, and from sex to sex.

      a. For example, a girl born in Japan in 2001 can expect to live 84 years, and a girl born in the same year in the U.S. would have a life expectancy of 80 years.

      b. However, a girl in Mali born in 2001 has a life expectancy of only 48 years, and today in Zimbabwe (primarily as a result of the AIDS epidemic) life expectancy is only 39.

III   EVOLUTION AND SOCIETY: BEHAVIORAL ECOLOGY

A. Behavioral ecology is the examination of human behavior within an evolutionary framework.

    1. Behavioral ecologists suggest that humans, like all other animals, behave in ways that increase their reproductive success (fitness).

2. Suggesting that evolutionary processes influence human behavior raises some thorny issues.

B. For example, evolutionary psychology employs the tenets of behavioral ecology to try to explain hot-button issues as human sexuality, aggression and violence.
  1. Many people are uncomfortable the idea that there may be evolutionary constraints on our behavior that may be difficult, or impossible, to overcome.
  2. However, this is not to say that there are "genes for" who we mate with, how aggressive we are and how violent we might be.
  3. Human behavior is an extremely complex phenomenon whose expression, in all of its forms, is the result of innumerable interactions between our environment, our genes and our individual experiences.

C. Despite its attendant controversies and limitations, behavioral ecology can generate predictions about human behavior that can be tested through field studies and other methods.
  1. For example, a logical prediction about our evolutionary past would be that young hominid females would have been selected to have as many babies as possible as early as they were physiologically able.
    a. This pattern is suggested because throughout most of our evolutionary history, life expectancy was low and infant mortality was high.
  2. However, today the opposite situation occurs (long life spans with low infant mortality) yet nevertheless there remain remarkably high rates of adolescent pregnancy in many societies around the world.
    a. Although this pattern of early pregnancy may have been adaptive in our past, today it often is not.
      i. For example, higher infant mortality rates are associated with lower mother's age at first birth.
    b. Women who delay their reproduction until they are also emotionally, socially and economically mature are likely to have more surviving offspring in contemporary society.
      i. However, if young mothers have help from extended families, social and/or government agencies, their reproductive fitness may not be compromised.
    c. The path to reproductive success is clearly more complex than behavioral ecology models can predict, but hypotheses must be somewhat simplistic in order to remain testable.

D. Another question addressed by behavioral ecology concerns the quantity and quality of human offspring.
  1. Like most other anthropoids (monkeys and apes), humans typically produce one offspring per birth.
    a. Twins (and triplets…) are rare and the survival rates for these multiple births are much lower than for singletons.
    b. The quality of parental care is compromised when there are too many dependent offspring.
  2. Although primate infanticide has been explained by behavioral ecologists (see Chapter 6), how can these researchers explain a human mother killing her own child?
    a. This apparently maladaptive behavior has been documented in many human societies.

b. Behavioral ecologists have provided an evolutionary explanation for mothers that abandon their newborns.
    i. If the mother does not have adequate resources to care for the child so that its very survival is in doubt, it pays (from an evolutionary not a moral perspective) to not invest in a doomed child but to delay further reproduction until the situation improves.
3. This illustrates that for most indications of reproductive fitness, the quality of produced offspring is more important than number.

E. At the other end of the human life course, another peculiarity of human life history has been addressed by behavioral ecology: menopause.
    1. Unlike all other mammals (including non-human primates), human females live a significant portion of their lives post-reproductively, in a state we refer to as menopause.
        a. Around the world, this usually occurs around the age of 50.
    2. Various theories have been proposed to account for this additional phase in female human lives.
    3. The first suggests the role of parenting is important.
        a. Since humans generally need 12-15 years to raise a child to self-sufficiency, this extra time was necessary to make sure that the last child survived to adulthood.
        b. This suggests that the maximum human life span (before agriculture) was around 65 years (50 years to menopause + 15 years to raise the last child), a number that accords well with current estimates.
    4. Another explanation states that menopause is not selected for at all, but is simply an artifact of the relatively longer human life span.
        a. All of the ova are present at birth in human females and there is evidence that these eggs have a maximum cell-life of only 50 years.
    5. Finally a third theory has been called the "grandmother hypothesis."
        a. This suggests that an older woman could increase her lifetime fitness by aiding her daughter in raising her grandchildren (who of course share 25% of grandma's genes).
        b. Researchers have garnered support for this idea by studying the Hadza, a foraging group from Tanzania, whose grandmothers' gathering typically contribute more to the family pot than mothers or unmarried girls.

IV HUMAN IMPACT ON THE PLANET AND OTHER LIFE FORMS
    A. Most of us humans have a pretty high opinion of our species that borders on arrogance: we often think of humanity as the most successful and dominant species on the planet.
        1. But it may be informative to put us in perspective within the context of other life on Earth.
            a. For example, there are more bacteria on this planet than any other life form; by that measure, bacteria are life's biggest success story.
            b. We are one of 200 primate species, and primates are a minor order of mammals that includes upwards of 4000 species.
            c. In comparison, 750,000 species of insects have been identified and it is estimated that over 30 million exist!
        2. We are also a relatively young species, having been around for perhaps 400,000 years.

       a. In comparison, *H. erectus* lasted for 1.5 million years and some sharks have remained virtually unchanged for 400 million years!

V   OVERPOPULATION

    A. Now that we have been put "in our place," it is still important to acknowledge that we six billion humans have an extraordinary impact on our planet.

    B. Our burgeoning global population is perhaps the biggest challenge that we, and the rest of this planet's life, face in the near and long-term.

    C. Human population size has grown (and unfortunately continues to grow) exponentially, an explosive rate that can best be appreciated historically by looking at doubling time (the amount of time it takes to double the world-wide population).

       1. Estimates of population size 10,000 years ago center around 5 million people.

       2. By the year 1650, the world population had grown to about 500 million.

          a. Therefore, in the intervening 9650 years, human population size doubled seven and a half times.

          b. On average over that time period, the doubling time was 1287 years.

       3. In the next 150 years however, from 1650-1800, the population doubled again to 1 billion.

       4. It only took 37 years (between 1950 and 1987) for the most recent doubling, from two to four billion.

       5. Today we are at six billion and at current rates the human population adds another billion people every year.

    D. The United Nations and other international agencies are trying to stem the tide of human population growth, but the fact remains that over half of the world's population is under 15 years old and has yet to reproduce.

       1. Can technological change and innovations feed the planet?

          a. Perhaps in the near-term this can be done.

       2. But what if populations continue their unabated growth?

          a. Catastrophic consequences may be the result not only for humans, but for the rest of the animals and plants with whom we share this planet.

VI   IMPACT ON BIODIVERSITY

    A. Humans may be unique among species on Earth with respect to our ability to so greatly influence other species' survival and extinction.

    B. There have been 15 mass extinctions in geological history over the past 570 million years, two of which altered the planet's ecosystems.

       1. The first, 250 m.y.a., was caused by the amalgamation of the continents into Pangea and its resultant world-wide effects on climate and habitats.

       2. The second, 65 m.y.a., was likely caused by a massive extra-terrestrial impact, such as an asteroid, that doomed the dinosaurs, among others.

    C. We may be living through (and we, our ancestors and our progeny are likely responsible for) the third planetary mass extinction that began 10,000 y.a.

       1. At the end of the Pleistocene, many large mammal species went extinct in North America, Australia and elsewhere.

       2. Although climate change certainly was a factor (the end of the Pleistocene coincided with the final retreat of the glaciers), human hunting has been implicated in many of these extinctions.

       3. And, of course, human hunting continues to take its toll on animal populations around the world today.

D. However, humanity's greatest impact on extinction is our role in habitat destruction, particularly of rain forests, where it is estimated that over half of all plant and animal species reside.
    1. To give you an inkling of our species' destructive power, in 1989 the combined area of the world's rain forests was approximately equivalent to the lower 48 United States.
        a. Each year, an area the size of Florida was being lost due to human activities such as logging.
        b. If the current rate of loss is not reduced, half of the rain forests' total area will be gone in a mere two decades.
    2. Should we care?
        a. Selfishly, the answer should be "yes" because "wonder drugs" derived from rain forest resources continue to be discovered.
        b. Morally and ethically, the answer is emphatically "yes," by what right do we destroy so much other life on this planet?

VII ACCELERATION OF EVOLUTIONARY PROCESSES
A. Humans are also in the unique position to accelerate evolution in other organisms.
B. For example, human use of antibiotics has hastened the evolutionary development of resistance in the pathogens at which these drugs are directed.
    1. Eventually these bacteria no longer respond to our antibiotics, so in effect, we have "created" more virulent germs.
C. Similarly, the misuse and overuse of pesticides and insecticides on crops have had adverse affects over the years.
    1. Plant pests, like bacteria, evolve resistance to these chemicals.
    2. A telling example was the use of DDT, that was extremely effective at killing mosquitoes when it was first employed.
    3. However, these insects developed resistance and the chemical residues of the DDT proved deadly for many birds, including our national symbol, the bald eagle.
D. Therefore, it is critical that we all understand the processes of evolution because we are (oftentimes inadvertently) directing its path in unforeseen (and potentially deadly) pathways.

VIII ARE WE STILL EVOLVING?
A. Culture has allowed us to bypass many of the limitations imposed upon us by biology.
    1. Today, we humans adapt to our challenges primarily through cultural means.
        a. For example, when we are cold we don't grow a fur coat, but instead we wear another animal's covering (e.g. wool, down, fur, or alternatively a synthetic) to keep warm.
    2. Socioeconomic situations determine how most people in the world will be able to ameliorate their biological conditions.
        a. For most of the poverty-stricken developing world, there is not a substantial cultural buffer that would allow them to bypass biology.
        b. These people often do not have much control over whether or not they are killed at war, have adequate access to medical care or if they can get enough to eat.
        c. Surviving under these extremely challenging conditions is often not possible for many.
            i. For example, 4.3 million children die annually from respiratory infections in the developing world.

d. However, untold other millions survive these conditions and their ability to do so must be in part the responsibility of their genes.

e. Therefore, allele frequencies relevant to genetic resistance to infection are indeed changing generation by generation (in other words microevolution is continually occurring).

B. What about macroevolutionary changes?

1. Will we speciate, evolve bigger brains, lose our little toes, go extinct?

a. These are questions for futurists and science fiction writers, not physical anthropologists.

b. Although we can tell you where we've been, we're not equipped to let you know where we're going.

2. It has been estimated that over 99.9% of all species that ever existed are now extinct, so it is unlikely that humanity will be able to avoid that eventual fate.

3. Nevertheless, until we get there -- you and I, and the rest of the individuals who comprise the species *Homo sapiens*, should strive to make this evolutionary journey as meaningful as we possibly can.

KEY TERMS

behavioral ecology: the study of the evolution of behavior, emphasizing the role of ecological factors as agents of natural selection

development: differentiation of cells into different types of tissues and their maturation.

essential amino acids: the eight (nine in infants) amino acids that must be obtained by humans from the diet.

evolutionary psychology: the study of how natural selection has influenced how humans and other primates think.

fertility: production of offspring; distinguished from fecundity, which is the ability to produce children.

growth: increase in the mass or number of cells.

Holocene: the most recent epoch of the Cenozoic, beginning around 10,000 y.a. and continuing to the present

life history theory: viewing growth and development from an evolutionary perspective, with an interest in how natural selection has operated on the life cycle, from conception to death.

malnutrition: a diet insufficient in quality (i.e., lacking some essential component) to support normal health.

menarche: the onset of the first menstruation in girls.

menopause: the end of menstruation in human women.

pleiotropic genes: genes that have multiple effects and can have different effects at different times during the life cycle

senescence: the process of physiological decline in body function that occurs with aging.

telomere: the DNA sequence at the end of each chromosome that shortens after each cell division.

Type II diabetes: a disorder increasingly frequent in today's Westernized societies of sugar and fat-laden diets; adult-onset, non-insulin dependent form of the disease.

undernutrition: a diet insufficient in quantity (calories) to support normal health.

INTERNET EXERCISES AND *INFOTRAC COLLEGE EDITION* EXERCISES

In your text, you read that the United Nations set a goal to contain the world's population to about 7.3 billion by 2015 and to prevent future growth (p. 433). On the internet you can go right to the source and see what the UN is doing to reach these goals. The United Nations Population Fund has published a comprehensive report on "The State of World Population 2001" (http://www.unfpa.org/swp/swpmain.htm). Make sure to read the most anthropologically-relevant Chapters 3 ("Development Levels and Environmental Impact") and 4 ("Women and the Environment").

To discover more about evolutionary psychology, check out the University of California at Santa Barbara's "Center for Evolutionary Psychology" hosted and maintained by two of the leading figures in the field: Dr. Leda Cosmides (Department of Psychology) and Dr. John Tooby (Department of Anthropology) http://www.psych.ucsb.edu/research/cep/. Click on their "Evolutionary Psychology Primer" to learn more about the field. Navigate through their home page to read about recent research findings, ongoing projects and critiques of their discipline.

In *InfoTrac* do a keyword search on "human longevity Olshansky" and read the fascinating article titled "Confronting the Boundaries of Human Longevity" by Olshansky, Carnes and Grahn that was published in *American Scientist* in 1998. What information did you glean from this paper (and was unavailable from your text) that helped you better understand the evolution of extended human life spans?

Now answer the True/False, Multiple Choice and Short Answer sample test questions. Following completion of the tests correct them with the answers and textbook page references at the end of this Study Guide chapter. Note the areas in which you are strong and weak to guide you in your studying. Finally, answer the sample Essay Questions.

TRUE/FALSE QUESTIONS

1. Life history theorists view growth and development from an evolutionary perspective.
   TRUE   FALSE

2. Like all other primates, human infants are born with 75% of their adult brain weight.
   TRUE   FALSE

3. The incidence of Type II diabetes has been on the decline since 1900, dropping from the 5th leading cause of death then to the 25th leading cause of death today.
   TRUE   FALSE

4. The process of physiological decline in all systems of the body that occurs towards the end of the life course is known as senescence.
   TRUE   FALSE

5. Evolutionary psychologists study how natural selection has influenced how humans and other primates think.
   TRUE   FALSE

6. In our evolutionary past, it would have benefited hominid females to delay reproduction because life spans were long and infant mortality was low.
   TRUE   FALSE

7. Like apes and monkeys, human females have a significant, post-reproductive stage of life called menopause.
   TRUE   FALSE

8. Humans are the most numerous organisms on the planet.
   TRUE   FALSE

9. The greatest single challenge facing humanity is our population growth.
   TRUE   FALSE

10. It is estimated that over half of all plant and animal species live in rain forests.
    TRUE   FALSE

MULTIPLE CHOICE QUESTIONS

1. An example of a cultural factor that has a strong influence on growth is
   A. an individual's skill as an artisan.
   B. marriage status.
   C. socioeconomic status.
   D. religious beliefs that require an individual to eat a particular species of animal.

2. If a culture values thinness in women, what could we expect to be a behavior among young girls?
   A. Instigation of vomiting to purge food that the girl has just eaten.
   B. Constant dieting, sometimes to the point that it adversely affects health.
   C. Eating as much food as a girl can manage without getting sick.
   D. Both A and B are behaviors that we might expect.

3. Humans, compared to other animals, have _____ life cycle stages.
   A. more
   B. fewer
   C. the same number of
   D. fewer than some, more than others

4. At birth the human brain is only _____ percent of its adult size.
   A. 25
   B. 50
   C. 90
   D. 95

5. Delayed brain growth may be particularly important for a species that is reliant upon
   A. carnivory.
   B. language.
   C. instinct.
   D. All of the above

6. Great apes and women from foraging societies typically nurse their children for
   A. 4-5 years.
   B. 1 year.
   C. 6-8 months.
   D. 7-8 years.

7. Which of the following are nutrients needed for growth, development and body maintenance?
   A. carbohydrates
   B. proteins
   C. vitamins
   D. All of the above

8. Why are some amino acids labeled "essential?"
   A. Because they are the only ones that the human body produces.
   B. Because they must be produced only when we are infants.
   C. Because they must be obtained from the diet.
   D. Because they can not be absorbed in the gut.

9. Which of the following does **not** characterize the preagricultural human diet?
   A. It was high in protein.
   B. It was high in complex carbohydrates.
   C. It was high in saturated fats.
   D. It was high in fiber.

10. The life cycle phase that ends with birth is
    A. gestation.
    B. infancy.
    C. weaning.
    D. childhood.

11. The language centers of the brain
    A. are difficult to find on the human brain.
    B. are well developed at birth.
    C. develop in the first three years of life.
    D. do not develop until puberty.

12. The ability to store fat in our evolutionary past was
    A. maladaptive because fat is always unhealthy.
    B. adaptive because the fat could be used as a backup source of energy during lean times.
    C. irrelevant to the early hominid lifestyle.
    D. variable, with tropical populations storing much more fat than Arctic peoples.

13. Which of the following has **not** been offered as an explanation for senescence?
    A. the effects of pleiotropic genes
    B. the effects of antioxidants
    C. the effects of free radicals
    D. lifestyle factors

14. Which of the following has increased significantly over the last 100 years?
    A. maximum human life span
    B. average human brain size
    C. length of the teen-age years
    D. average life expectancy at birth

15. Behavioral ecologists suggest that humans, like other animals, behave in ways that increase their
    A. fitness.
    B. fat intake.
    C. IQ.
    D. biodiversity.

16. Human behavior is extremely complex and its expression depends on
    A. genes.
    B. environment.
    C. individual experience.
    D. All of the above

17. A clear sign of puberty in girls is
    A. menarche.
    B. pregnancy.
    C. menopause.
    D. senescence.

18. For menarche to occur normally and for ovulation to be maintained,
    A. females must have high levels of circulating calcium.
    B. high levels of vitamin D must be stored in the liver.
    C. there must be a minimal amount of body fat.
    D. there must be high protein stores available.

19. Which of the following has **not** been proposed to account for menopause?
    A. Women needed to live 12-15 years after their last birth so that they could raise the last child to self-sufficiency.
    B. Natural selection caused women to live longer so that they can help men on big-game hunts after they stopped having children.
    C. Menopause is not the result of natural selection but is simply an artifact of the increase in human life span.
    D. Post-menopausal grandmothers increased their fitness by helping to feed and provide care for their grandchildren.

20. If we define biological "success" as the species that has produced the most individuals on the planet, the "winners" are
    A. bacteria.
    B. humans.
    C. fish.
    D. rats.

21. Evolutionary "success" can also be gauged by species
    A. average body size.
    B. dental formula.
    C. average cognitive capacity.
    D. longevity.

22. Which of the following has/have contributed to the current crisis of overpopulation that humanity now faces?
    A. Our ability to produce food surpluses.
    B. Medical advances that have allowed many to survive formally fatal diseases.
    C. Reduced infant mortality and longer average life spans.
    D. All of the above.

23. Which of the following in **not** true?
    A. Approximately half of all of the people living in the world are under 15 years of age.
    B. One billion people are added to the world's population every 11 years.
    C. In 1650, the global human population was already 2 billion.
    D. In the 37 years between 1950 and 1987, human population size doubled.

24. If current human population growth rates remain unchecked, the global population will swell to 10 billion by the year
    A. 2009.
    B. 2050.
    C. 2100.
    D. 2125.

25. The current mass extinction event has been caused by
    A. continental drift.
    B. climate change.
    C. an extra-terrestrial impact.
    D. humans.

26. In what habitat do more than half of the world's plant and animal species live?
    A. deserts
    B. mountains
    C. rain forests
    D. grasslands

27. The great geneticist Theodosius Dobzhansky said "Nothing in biology makes sense except in the light of _____."
    A. genes
    B. evolution
    C. culture
    D. humanity

28. Which of the following is **not** true?
    A. Human cultural activities have very little influence on human biological evolution.
    B. The appearance of new pathogens, or old ones that have become resistant to our medicines, will have an effect on human evolution.
    C. There is a disconnect between our biology and our 21ˢᵗ century cultural environment.
    D. The human species continues to evolve.

SHORT ANSWER QUESTIONS (& PAGE REFERENCES)

1. What are the life cycle stages that humans progress through? (pp. 420-421)

2. How did the preagricultural diet differ from those in today's Western cultures? (p. 423)

3. What is the "telomere hypothesis" of senescence? (pp. 402-403)

4. Why did many large mammals go extinct at the end of the Pleistocene? (p. 434)

5. How are humans accelerating the evolution of bacterial virulence? (p. 436)

ESSAY QUESTIONS (& PAGE REFERENCES)

1. How and why does human brain growth differ from other primates? (pp. 421-422)

2. Compare and contrast the various explanations that have been put forth regarding the unique human characteristic of menopause. (pp. 430-431)

3. Why is human overpopulation often characterized as the single greatest challenge facing humanity and the rest of world's life forms? (pp. 432-435)

4. Are we still evolving? (p. 437)

ANSWERS, *CORRECTED STATEMENT* IF FALSE & REFERENCES TO TRUE/FALSE QUESTIONS

1. TRUE, p. 421

2. FALSE, p. 422, *Unlike* all other primates, human infants are born with *only 25%* of their adult brain weight.

3. FALSE, pp. 423-424, The incidence of Type II diabetes has been on the *increase* since 1900, *rising* from the *27th* leading cause of death then to the *7th* leading cause of death today.

4. TRUE, p. 425

5. TRUE, p. 426

6. FALSE, pp. 428-429, In our evolutionary past, it would have benefited hominid females to *hasten* reproduction because life spans were *short* and infant mortality was *high*.

7. FALSE, p. 430, *Unlike* apes and monkeys, human females have a significant, post-reproductive stage of life called menopause.

8. FALSE, p. 431, *Bacteria* are the most numerous organisms on the planet.

9. TRUE, p. 432

10. TRUE, p. 435

ANSWERS AND REFERENCES TO MULTIPLE CHOICE QUESTIONS

1. C, p. 420	15. A, p. 426
2. D, p. 420	16. D, p. 427
3. A, p. 421	17. A, p. 428
4. A, p. 422	18. C, p. 428
5. B, p. 422	19. B, pp. 430-431
6. A, p. 423	20. A, p. 431
7. D, p. 423	21. D, p. 432
8. C, p. 423	22. D, p. 432
9. C, p. 423	23. C, pp. 431-432
10. A, p. 421	24. B, p. 433
11. C, p. 422	25. D, p. 434
12. B, p. 423	26. C, p. 435
13. B, p. 425	27. B, p. 437
14. D, p. 425	28. A, pp. 436-437